BUTLER ON WHEELS

BUTLER ON
WHEELS

Paul Wheeler

The Book Guild Ltd

First published in Great Britain in 2019 by
The Book Guild Ltd
9 Priory Business Park
Wistow Road, Kibworth
Leicestershire, LE8 0RX
Freephone: 0800 999 2982
www.bookguild.co.uk
Email: info@bookguild.co.uk
Twitter: @bookguild

Typeset in 11pt Adobe Garamond Pro

Printed and bound in the UK by TJ International, Padstow, Cornwall

ISBN 978 1912881 758

British Library Cataloguing in Publication Data.
A catalogue record for this book is available from the British Library.

Contents

Preface

A job is something you tolerate, but a career, now that's something you choose. When I first came to London, I had a friend who was a taxi driver. His cabin was his office, and I remember frowning at the thought of being cooped up all day in a car. Then I thought, lots of people sit in an office all day peering into a computer. I didn't have the knees to be a footballer or the vocal cords to audition for *The X Factor*, although I had been a chef, working in the hotel industry at the highest level. I had also been a butler, so I thought it prudent to use the skills I had developed and remain in hospitality. And I like cars, and driving. That's why I became a chauffeur and joined a top-class agency to get work.

The role of a chauffeur is an intimate one. I drive the clients' cars, never my own, under their insurance, which they subscribe to. A chauffeur is likely to spend more time with the client than they would with their own spouse or even family. A conventional day would consist of the school run, taking the husband to work, then back to take his wife shopping or attend to her errands. Maybe a little maintenance in and around the estate and back to the office to drive him to meetings, lunch, a brothel or a bar mitzvah.

A chauffeur could spend anything from a single day to several years with a client, but as most high-powered businessmen (and they are mostly men) have a short attention span and many of them suffer from paranoia, a few months is more usual.

Finding a client you get on with should be paramount, but it isn't. Clients at this level conduct themselves differently. You're likely to be sharing space with a career-driven social climber. They may become fickle and paranoid. The higher your client climbs, the more rarefied the atmosphere, which makes them insular, distrusting and aloof.

Each day is different, and some of them are exciting, as the chauffeur never knows how the client will spice up the day's activities. It could be all smiles and champagne and then on the way home, you could take a wrong turning or get stuck in traffic and send the client's temperature and blood pressure soaring. He may even get out of the car and walk off, leaving you without a job. If you're really unlucky, he might even physically assault you, leaving you with a two-toned shirt and a headache.

But don't let that put you off. There are aspects of the job that compel an unemployed chauffeur to go straight off to find another psychotic employer and risk the same treatment all over again. The right job can be addictive. The cars are often mind-blowing, and they can get you hooked. The hardest part is holding to your own ethical parameters, and remembering to be on the alert at all times. Because life really does come down to a few critical moments. The key is appreciating when you're lucky enough to have been given a coveted position and making the most of it.

So here's one chauffeur's frank account of a world which will be unfamiliar to most. The job can be exciting, even captivating, although at times it makes you feel empty and unnecessary. It's never dull for long.

Paul Wheeler
December 2018

Chapter 1

Punctures and punctuality

Music playing. Adele, *Chasing Pavements*.

Patience might be a virtue, but so is getting to work on time. It's 06:17. I can't believe I'm late. One thing chauffeurs cannot be is late!

It's a Friday morning in the latter part of August. I'm racing along the A421, otherwise known as the Bedford Bypass, heading for the M1 south. Why did I not react to the first alarm? My phone is usually at the bottom of my bed, so I'm actively compelled to go on a hunting exercise first thing, but today for some reason it's on my pillow. But excuses are a waste of time, because the person you work for will not be interested. No compassion.

This is why I always aim to arrive an hour early in case of eventualities. An accident. A puncture, which would mean ditching the car at a service station and catching the train. Actually, that would only work if you had run-flat tyres, which let you drive up to 40mph for the same number of miles. Yes, those tyres are expensive, but they are jolly dependable. They just make sense. In a world where most of us live a whirlwind life, time is of the essence. You simply cannot stop because of a puncture. Imagine it, late for work because of a puncture – no boss is going to be remotely interested. I've no idea why more people don't have them. You don't need special wheels. The latest wheels have some sort of device that monitors air pressure reduction, which sends a signal to the LCD display and informs the driver. I have an old car and I've bought second-hand tyres which look brand new and are half the price of a new set. So I need never sit by the roadside again.

Until you try them yourself, you'll never know. Oh, make sure they have a B wet rating. Great in the wet. Not as good as A, but A tyres are soft and will wear out a lot quicker – they're mainly for the winter, which is great if you can afford to keep changing for the seasons. Actually, criminals love them – if they hit a police stinger they can still keep going. All the wheels will puncture, but you can still do up to fifty. No stopping for anyone, no moving everything in the boot, no more feeling vulnerable in the middle of nowhere. So, mothers on the school run, go in peace.

I had a client who was taking his wife and daughter to the theatre from Henley on Thames to Covent Garden when the front tyre went. No drama, on the dash it simply highlighted the tyre symbol in red, indicating a puncture. I could still drive and steer – it felt a bit heavier, but I could travel nonetheless. I was beginning to panic though, as this was a special night out for the family. So I pulled over on the M40 outside High Wycombe, traffic whizzing by. I got out to check the wheel and could see it was deflated, but the metal run-flat ring around the outside of the tyre was preventing it from immobilising the car. I calculated the time it would take to Covent Garden, and knew we wouldn't make the start of the show. Great! What do I do? Furthermore, what do I tell them?

As I walked back to the driver's door, I saw worried faces. All had been calm a few minutes before, but I knew they were a fiery couple – especially him, he had a very short fuse. He was an OCD type and everything in his house was regimented, like he had just left the army. I took a deep breath, remembering my training to keep calm and keep a step ahead when these situations arise. He was a stockbroker, and always working. His wife had finally got him to finish early one Friday and somehow persuaded him to take her and the child to see *The Lion King*. Since then he had huffed and puffed about it until the day arrived. His mood swings were as volatile as the markets he traded in, irrespective of the fact that every night when he got home, his bath was waiting and his evening clothes were prepared and waiting at the end of the bed. Dinner was always ready and timed to his arrival without fail. Plain English food, no frills, as he hated sauces and French cuisine. Whenever I dropped him home, she was always cheerful and ready to serve him – she should have been paid. She would always launch into the day's proceedings about the kids, family and friends, but he would want to just come in and be himself.

I would drop off his things in the kitchen and prepare the car for the morning. Once, he began to ascend the stairs and she was right behind him, and then she mentioned the Lion King. He about-turned, put his palm up in front of her face and shouted, 'Honey, please shut that mouth of yours, will you? PLEASE! For one bloody minute!'

She continued, 'But I just need to know you're on board…'

'Enough! I would like to go to the toilet and make an omelette in peace! That OK?'

He continued up the staircase mumbling, 'When will she understand? Bloody hell, I'm a man. Food. Sex. Silence. That's all we want. Feed me, beat me and shut the hell up! It's not that difficult, is it? She does this on purpose, gets me in this state.' He continued to mumble, while she sought to find a way to justify his outburst. I would often feel for her, but she gave as good as she got. As time went by I think I found what gave her the confidence to react in that way – her name was on the mortgage. With the majority of couples I have met, the wife's name isn't even on the council tax, let alone the Land Registry. Sometimes when they've traded insults during an altercation, I hear her shout, 'It's my bloody house, you know!'

I climbed back into my seat with all eyes on me. His wife, in a calm voice, asked, 'Paul, what's wrong?'

'We have a slight problem,' I replied. 'Somehow we have a puncture. But here's what I propose…'

Before I could tell them, she snapped back, 'A puncture? A bloody PUNCTURE?'

'Hang on, let's see what Paul has to say,' he said. No pressure then…

I drove away and levelled off at 40mph. Horrible feeling, cars racing past. I felt helpless. At this speed, we would be lucky to make half the show, I told them. Now that did not go down well at all. They kicked off.

'Look,' he said, 'maybe it's a sign, we're just not meant to go. You've been sitting in the lounge like Lady Muck with your Dior sunglasses in your hand and there ain't no sunshine. Come on, I know you'd rather be off out with the girls.'

I started to adjust the rear-view mirror, which I usually point towards the roof. When I drive Arab women, they don't really like eye contact, so it's easier to adjust the mirror upwards – that way I don't see her face and she doesn't see mine. Today of all days, it was wise to leave it as it was, because I felt her face stiffen.

'Oh, so you found an excuse then?' she snapped back. 'I knew it, back at the house you were looking for an excuse. Pacing up and down the stairs, in and out the flipping kitchen like a mouse on crack!'

An altercation began to fill the cabin. I noticed the child adjusting the volume on her headphones, a default setting of hers, I would presume, as she would deploy this tactic when a situation arose. I adjusted the volume on the radio slightly to find something to change the atmosphere. On came Fleetwood Mac. Flipping hell, not that song. I turned the radio down for fear of someone saying, 'You trying to tell us something Paul?'

I'm a Christian, so I began to pray. I needed something to defuse the situation. Try a different station on the radio – Magic FM. Adele, *Turning Tables*.

Then I recognised the blue motorway exit markers: 3, 2, 1. Something was telling me to exit. High Wycombe. I began thinking why, then on the slip road a van drove past me and on the back was the slogan 'Restoration for Road And Rail'. *Good golly*, I thought. *Get the blinking train!*

At the traffic lights I interrupted them and said, 'There's a train to London every twenty minutes from here, straight into Marylebone. Then take the Underground the rest of the way. You will be there on time.'

It worked. I raced to the station and, as luck would have it, a train was on the platform. I limped back to Henley, swapped cars, then raced into London in time to pick them up at the end of the show.

This morning it's a mad twenty-minute dash to the motorway, with this particular part of the county fortunately free of speed cameras. Why I have no idea, maybe the council ran out of cash. Anyway, we drivers are grateful. Problem today is, if you're not on the motorway by 6 am, forget it. But I don't like going by train. A return ticket costs more than the petrol I'd use for the same journey and furthermore, there's this privacy thing in your own car. Just about every car I see has one lone 'egg in a box'. What happened to car share? People are so protective of their privacy.

OK, three miles to go and cars are beginning to concertina. This doesn't look good. It's just dawned on me why I am late. I remember I woke up at 4 am in a mad panic. Now chauffeurs and drivers in London have one massive impediment – traffic wardens. If you're sitting, say, just off Oxford Street waiting for clients who are shopping, or even a side street off Park Lane where many of us catch half an hour's shuteye, invariably at some point you'll hear a tap on the window, and very rarely is it someone wanting directions. More often than not, it's another driver with a less desirable car than yours who wants to exercise his gums to someone because he's lonely and can't stop his nose from bleeding, because excavating it whilst looking at himself in the mirror was all he had left to do. In fact his clients have taken a taxi back to their apartment because they'd had enough of his driving or his bad breath. Rich people are seriously fickle and somewhat blunt, believe it. I was working in tandem with another driver who was a vegan, and the woman got out of the car with her housekeeper. As she walked past she said about the driver, 'His breath was that bad, I'd happily look forward to his farts.'

The obvious contender for the tap on the window is of course Mr (or Mrs) Traffic Warden. They come in all shapes, sizes and colours. I know, someone's got to do the job, but they do have an adverse effect on me. This is what my dream was about. I was apparently on a rare day off. I had arranged to meet my friend Victoria, who was on her way, and rang to inform her I was in a Caffè Nero. As I was on the phone to her chatting away, I must have forgotten I was on a day off. I turned to face the door and to my horror a traffic warden was photographing my black Mercedes. Blind panic – I pushed back on my seat and knocked over my hot chocolate! The warden stared at me, stating it was too late. 'Your car, I presume?' he grunted. I reached into my pockets to search for my car keys and began to panic – what on earth… And then it dawned on me – I came by blinking train. The black Benz was someone else's. 'No problem,' I replied, and turned on my heel. It was about there that I woke up. Walking back into the shop would not be a pleasant experience. I know, I have done that a couple of time when I was awake!

Half a mile to go. 2,500 feet, 800 metres. Remember an A road only provides half a mile notice, while a motorway gives a mile because you're travelling at higher speeds. To a chauffeur, the most valuable commodity is information.

I'm starting this job on a Friday. When a client has as much cash as this one, and he doesn't work, he comes and goes as he pleases. Not very often though. Just two weeks this time. He's an African king, with a wife and two concubines. He pops back to the UK intermittently, just to indulge himself in our fabulous healthcare services. He heads to Harley street for a medical diagnosis (the bad news), then on to the NHS (the good news) for an operation. Then he will fly back home in his private jet to convalesce. So they are here for just two weeks at a time.

I've looked after the family for three years now. The work comes from the agency in south London which I have worked with for a long time. I created space so I could do this job. It's great, all they do is shop. The King has a number of properties in the Harley Street area, looked after by one of his thirty children, who actually possesses a law degree. The only drawback is he goes on about God all the time (I'll explain later). I now have to drive to the back of Harley Street for 10 am. His flight gets in at 9:37 and he'll be greeted by a host of Virgin Atlantic lackeys and whisked through to the VIP lounge. I just drive him back. I hate Heathrow, it's more emotional than a hospital. I just drop off and say goodbye. Besides, I'm missing an episode of *Coming to America*. When they walk through the terminal, followed by a load of baggage porters pushing all their Louis Vuitton cases, it's hilarious.

The M1 wasn't at its kindest that day, but I forced my way through to arrive at Harley street for 09:45. Once the traffic began to move, it flowed. The cameras force it to stay at 70mph all the way, and it often drops to 50, then goes back up to 60. Some people have to travel this way day in and day out. It's no joke.

When you're tired of London, you're tired of life. It's like flying over water for hours with nothing but sea to look at, then, your destination suddenly comes into view. After driving on the motorway for ages, you arrive in the city and everything just comes alive, including you. You have to, otherwise you could lose your driving licence and be broke before you get there. Roads switch from 30 mph to 20 in a blink of an eye. You get points for infringing the bicycle boxes at traffic lights. A hundred quid for yellow boxes, bus stands, bus lane violations. Oh, don't forget the motorbikes always squeezing to the front of your car, and the cyclists who actually own the roads, or you'd think so with the verbal abuse they give you. Look, I do cycle when I get a chance. I appreciate momentum. It takes a lot to get going again. A lot of cyclists don't even stop at red traffic lights. So yes, you really do wake up when you arrive in the city with no pity!

Like a lot of people, I love London. I think only the birds have a problem with it. When I leave the country in the early morning, the birds sing, loudly. When I enter the Marylebone zone, they don't sing any more – they cough.

I quickly park up on Wigmore Street, run into the office and get the keys. On my way out, I am holding the keys and reading instructions for the day. First words: 'Morning Paul, the Roller battery might be dead and the girl who rents the other half of the garage is parked in front of it. You'll need to run round to Queen Anne Street to pick up her keys. Oh, and I think she will need a wash. Be with you by half ten.'

Marvellous. OK, I need to call the girl whose car is in the way and… I look up at my own car and remember the Congestion blinking Charge. It's £12, but it goes up to £80 if not paid by the next day… WHAT? Stop! I'm here! A traffic warden is getting intimate with my car, leaning over the windscreen looking for a clean spot to place the ticket. 'Oh you're so lucky,' he says. 'Now move it.' Yep, that's how they speak to you. I might have received a softer tone if he had managed to write the ticket. So nasty. I just drive off.

I arrive at the back of Devonshire Place, the beautiful mews where the King's Roller is kept. The lady's car is on the other side of the garage – good, I haven't got to call her. I walk to the back of the garage, where the gleaming black Phantom awaits attention. I press the key to engage this beautiful beluga-coloured long-wheelbase Phantom. Nothing – it's just a lump of cold metal. She's been sitting here for months with no one to play with her.

Across the mews are a couple of Eastern Europeans who own a wrapping company. Don't ask. They wrap lights and interfere with the aesthetics of the car. I open the door and there's a white E class Mercedes AMG in front of me, gleaming, what on earth could you do to tart that up? I borrow their snap-on booster pack, which thankfully is fully charged.

The Phantom has two massive batteries, of which one is auxiliary. The other will take the charge and provide power to the auxiliary whilst running. I won't be able to switch this engine off for a while. Why not just buy a trickle charger and leave it on? To be honest, the family hate spending money on things they deem unnecessary. They hate spending money, full stop. This car takes £120 worth of petrol, and whenever I fill up I ring up at least two members of the family to get payment. I used to pay it myself, but then I would struggle to get the cash back. They'd question my expenses and toss it around from family to accountant then back again.

Actually, looking at them, I can't remember which battery. Right, I'll go through the bonnet and locate the positive metal terminal, then connect the negative to the bonnet hinge. Lovely. As soon as the negative touches the hinge, all the lights in the cabin come on. I love this car.

I stand for a second to admire the engine bay, assaulted by German magnificence. The bay is so big you could fit two V12s in there. It resembles the bow of a cruise liner, huge and stunning. I run round to the driver's door, remembering they open the opposite way. Depress the start button and she fires into life. The engine is *sooo* quiet and graceful. Bonnet down, don't slam. OK, enough drooling, I need to squeeze this thing through the garage doors and declare to the world I am a carbon creator…

Daylight reveals how dirty she is, and the nearest car wash is half a mile away. She wafts along the Mews. Three hundred K to purchase this beautiful car and unceremoniously, dump it on the street. London's filled with prestige cars dumped all over the place. Not forgetting the eight per cent insurance premium – you could buy a nice sports car or SUV and still have change left over.

No, I never think about scratching it. You can't, that would simply bring an attack of anxiety at every boy racer who whizzes close by and every garbage truck reversing. I feel seriously loved by these beluga armchairs. There was definitely no barbed wire in the field this animal perambulated in day after day. No, this cow died of natural causes.

The seats support my 238 pounds without prejudice or complaint. It's a long wheelbase, only five of these in the country. There's a huge hole behind me, and the back seats are a mile away. I only ever think about the king in the back, cause he and his wives do not wear seatbelts. That's his prerogative – I simply have to pay more than the usual attention to the roads.

Although sometimes, things don't go to plan. His daughter was at university in Leeds. On our return we were cruising at 70 on the M1, in the middle lane as there was a contraflow, not to mention nosey activity around the cruise ship. Cars were racing alongside, looking at the Rolls and trying to peer inside. I had cruise control on with radar (a device which is an option on most luxury cars, as it prevents the car colliding with absolutely anything) to monitor my surroundings. Some young kids dived in front of the Roller and the radar activated the brakes before I could, just a trifle too abruptly. The King and one of his wives were watching *Sky News* on their TV monitors. I was mortified – they both just continued to travel at seventy until they concertinaed up against my chair, him with his face squashed up against the

TV screen. Seriously, the noise was horrendous. They had all their African regalia on, hats, and outfits. I had to pull over. When I got out, cars began to hoot and people were laughing, thinking the Roller had broken down. I opened the door and inside was a mess. They were on the floor trying to hoist themselves up. I thought no, I refuse to lift her up without mechanical assistance, I'm like a toy next to her. And no, they never put on the seatbelts thereafter. Never! At least, with the average speed around London roughly 12mph, hopefully that little problem isn't likely to strike twice.

I am now rushing down the Westway towards the Hilton Metropole. Round the back is a twenty-four-hour car wash. Turning left on the Marylebone Road, I encounter heavy traffic. This car will point blank refuse to venture along the back roads. She is way too long and expensive to play those games.

The phone rings. 'Paul, don't forget petrol!'

What? I thought. *He didn't fill it up?* I look at the petrol reserve. Under a quarter of a tank. Great!

'Sorry Paul, I just didn't have time. Besides, I don't have the patience for that.'

'Ok, so I will need £150. Shall I run to the office?'

'A hundred and fifty?' he shouted. 'Does it take that much?'

Now he knows damn well how much it costs to fill the Phantom – he just wants me to pay for it, then argue the point when I ask for it in my expenses. See, this is how the rich become rich. He's tighter than a duck's backside.

'Look,' I said. 'With a quarter tank, I won't get far and I'll probably have to push this thing to the gas station. I'll need twenty for the King's peripheral things, papers, etc.'

'Ok, sorry I didn't get a chance to fill it up.'

'So shall I run to the office?'

'Er, no. Actually there should be a couple of hundred in the glove compartment.'

I open the glove box and there's the cash. See what I mean? Tight!

The Phantom has many expensive habits – tyres, oil, petrol, it devours everything. It weighs three tonnes and is the size of two small cars. Gas stations in London are quite small, so when filling up, it takes up two pumps and holds others up. The looks of admiration soon turn to disdain. No one has time to wait any more.

A friend of mine bought a Bentley Mulliner. He visits the gas station so often they have a cup of tea waiting for him.

So here I am wafting along steering with my hands positioned at twenty past eight, minding my own business, when in my offside wing mirror I notice a man on a bike wandering along at his own pace. I ignore him. The bike then pulls up alongside and begins banging on the boot (this is London, expect anything at any time). This guy begins shouting. I'm surrounded by cars, and it's busy. So what drugs is he on – or supposed to be on? I get out of the car, turn to this guy and ask him to identify himself and tell me what he wants. I meet a torrent of vitriolic abuse. He rambles about how our streets are getting smaller while I'm driving around in this monstrosity. 'Look at it, why in God's name would you drive round in this?'

It transpires that he's a campaigner for the poor. I tell him, 'Hey, I am poor too. This is not my flipping car. Now do you mind?'

He wanders off up the main road. If there are any dents in the car, I haven't got the idiot's details, so how am I going to make him pay? Great!

Rich or not, we are all out here pounding these streets for cash. London is a jungle and the majority of people are not humble. I'm guessing it is not easy for anyone but will him shouting the odds help the situation? I doubt it.

I love Marylebone, the High Street one side and Regent's Park to the north. You simply couldn't fake it around here, or fly in from Eastern Europe having set up a company for pensions, accumulate a shedload of cash, then run over here to seek asylum. I remember a Czech businessman did that a few years ago, robbed the mature citizens of his country of their pensions and hard-earned cash and flew over here to spend it. He was out to lunch at Le Gavroche, I believe, and blew forty grand on lunch with two friends. He even ordered a bottle of Petrus 1961, and summoned the maître d', complaining that the wine was somewhat 'immature'. 'Let the staff have it,' he said in a dismissive tone. He bought a Grade 1 listed property in the area and the following day, he brought in a skip as he was knocking down the walls. His lease was revoked and he lost his purchase investment. He must subsequently have realised that a few million is nothing in London if you're going to be frivolous. Back in the 1980s a million meant something.

A heavyweight boxer, who was an absolute hero to the underprivileged, once boasted of blowing two hundred million in his short career. Anything less than that, you could blow on a good summer holiday on a drug or gambling habit. Well you know what they say about a fool and his money. They were lucky enough to get together in the first place.

Around here, the money is as old as the dinosaurs. You just couldn't get rid of it. Arabs have been investing since long before my existence. Having experienced their vast wealth, you couldn't imagine them simply shutting up shop and relocating. One Emirate country that comes here year in and year out employs a colossal army of workers. A hundred drivers, security personnel and an abundance of household staff. Their own police force conventionally utilises the path of least interference at local airfields, with enough take-off and landing asphalt available for the private jets they so fortunately are allowed to use. The Royal Family arrive with pockets so deep that they could not only eradicate most countries' deficits but would make most of those around the world who claim to be rich look like charity cases. Amazing.

13

Every time we fill up at the petrol pumps, we're inadvertently topping up every aircraft they own whilst suffocating ourselves with their fumes as they empty their tanks for landing in an attempt to diminish the fireball if an accident happened. They like the UK – who doesn't? – they just don't love it. Unlike the Chinese, who love how we roll and muck in with designer clothes, opera, musicals, cars and postcode homes. The only thing we share with the Arabs is the petrol pumps and the roads. It's a safe second home for them and their families are safe, as long as they don't stray from selected postcodes – Mayfair, W1, W2, Knightsbridge, Kensington. God forbid if the driver ends up in unfamiliar territory. I drove for them for many years, and when I started I ended up in a not-so-nice part of Battersea. My phone rang, so I pulled over to answer it, as it was from the office. I was asked why I was in that part of the capital. Then I realised that the two women in the back had texted their handler or contact and snitched on me for going off the scheduled route into a rough neighbourhood! But the West End is intoxicating in the summer when the sun shines and everyone's enjoying themselves.

I am heading north up Upper Wimpole Street to greet the weight of metal on Marylebone Road, thinking of my carbon footprint. I will have to leave this 6.7 litre beast running most of the day. Not good. It's twenty-six degrees outside and by 1,500 hrs I should be able to fry eggs and chips on the bonnet. I'm sitting dazzled by a sea of red lights in front of me for a good quarter of a mile.

My phone rings. Probably the King or his son seeking my whereabouts and checking that I haven't taken the Phantom for a private gallop. I have six to eight regular clients who call on the off chance in an emergency to ask me to help out.

OK, it's Mr Lover Man from Monaco. Had this client for around three years. Mr Lover Man? Simply because he just loves young girls. Yet he's about to (if registered here) pick up his pension book. Is it a problem, I ask? Does anyone really care? When you have serious amounts of cash to burn, in London, if you're new, you'll find what you're looking for, even if you don't know what it is. If you're cold, you can find the sun whenever you want to. If you're alone, you'll find a female for whatever occasion, situation or reason you need her for. Welcome to London, where only if you're broke will the negatives that do exist in this city become more apparent. You're not likely to bump into a stray woman with millions because she left her husband or even ran away for the night. Nope, Monaco is like buying a pair of Christian Louboutin shoes, it's an achievement, and no woman after working so hard to get there is about to relinquish her shoes or her coveted position through stupidity. It's a kingdom where most residents are equal – lots of cash. It's two million pounds for a small studio flat overlooking the harbour, with a trophy wife and surrounded by an abundance of his personal possessions. Nothing more to look at. For me I love the drive, nine tolls costing roughly 120 euros. It's 945 miles through some of the finest countryside anywhere. From Calais down through Reims, Dijon, Lyon, Avignon, Marseille, Nice and then paradise... well, almost. Châlons-en-Champagne, an hour south of Reims. The whole Champagne region needs time to be explored and dissected, though for me it's just been a multicoloured blur. It's just the roads are so long, no matter what your speed. You could make a cup of tea and make breakfast before you reach a bend or a corner. The horizon is invariably in view, but you incessantly try in vain to reach it.

Past Nice, the atmosphere changes to debonair. It could lift the melancholic and probably clinically depressed soul. I conventionally drive through the night, as I don't want to miss daylight on the Côte d'Azur.

I drive all sorts of cars, but the most consistent, refined and eloquent performer is the S Class Benz. I refill it twice, whereas an Audi A8 I drove was ragged at high speed, of huge significance in refinement, and developed a drink dependency problem, requiring three and a half fill ups. Seriously, at the car's terminal velocity, you could empty the tank in forty-six minutes. It's a tough drive. You just have to focus and get it done, only stopping for petrol.

The American car wash is at the Hilton Metropole intersection. Approaching this part of town, it's advisable to cover your mouth if you're cycling. The air is black round here, as are the buildings, the road and railings, and you can see the pollution in the air. I press the air recycle button. All unwanted air stops in the engine bay. It's goo, just one car in front of me.

The phone rings. It's the King's son informing me that all baggage and personnel are heading to the cars waiting in the VIP section of Heathrow. Good. I am not involved in that chaos. Let them get on with it. The King at some point will remember something he will simply want to look at, say a magazine. Just about everyone will be involved in searching the baggage for it. Why? You see, rich people are fickle. All could be nice and calm, then someone will decide they need some attention, so they will ask for something irrelevant or orchestrate an argument. See.

'Hi Paul,' says the King's son. 'Dad says can you get the seven-seater out of the garage, as everyone needs to go shopping?' Great. The battery will be so dead on the Mercedes Viano, it won't even allow me to open the door. The last time, it just shouted at me, 'Get lost!' I could not get into it for love nor money. The deadlocks were definitely working. It reminded me of that old series, Kit the car in *Knightrider*. Michael thinks the car is acting strange, so he gets out and goes to a phone box to call Devon, his boss, but K.I.T.T.'s listening to the conversation. Michael runs back to the car, grabs the door handle and shouts, 'Come on Kit, let's get the bad guys.' The door won't open. 'Kit, you OK buddy?'

Kit replies, 'Go away Michael, not today, I've got a headache.'

I'm on my way back and the phone has now rung three times. 'Have you sorted it yet? Is the Viano OK to drive?' Oh my good granny! Next they will be asking me to run one of his cold baths for him. Oh yes, he loves them. Apparently it helps with sharpening his reflexes. But he can hardly walk, what about arthritis? Oh, we'll go shopping later and the car will HAVE to be right outside the shop door. Probably Peter Jones, Sloane Square. No matter if there is a single yellow line, a double, a zig zag, or even a traffic warden. 'Just let the warden take the ticket,' he'll exclaim. 'But not the car! My legs!' he'll groan. I and a couple of the wives will assist. Seriously, his legs buckled once and two of us had to dig deep into reserves to elevate him back up till his knees locked into place. The strange thing is, once the credit card comes out, I won't see him for three hours. Like the pain just disappears! I'd be summoned to relieve him of his accumulated baggage.

Right. Swap to Radio 3. Need peace before the family get here. I throw back my head against the head rests, feeling the embossed RR through my hair. I should jolly well put my phone on silent, like the King does. He selects a handful of people and allows them free access to his phone, but people of lesser importance or none at all, he blocks. So when I ring his number, it goes straight to answering machine, although he receives a message report that some nonentity of an servant dared to call him today.

I love Radio 3, it's like the B side to all of Classic FM's A sides. Beautiful, *Madam Butterfly* is on. Act Two, Part Two – well, it's the finale actually. So Butterfly is in ominous tone, then there's a pounding of drums depicting a suicide theme. She blindfolds her child and sends him into the other room to play, so he can't witness what she is about to do. Her husband runs in and is assaulted by utter devastation. Then the familiar theme of *Madam Butterfly* rings out. Yes, it's utterly sad but a beautiful production. This particular one is a recording from the night before at the Metropolitan Opera House, New York – would so love to be there.

But I'm not, I am here in this beautiful concrete jungle, ready to put in a day's shift.

Phone rings. 'Hi Paul, we are on our way, and Dad said to forget the Viano, the other family members will use one of the Addison Lee cabs.' See what I mean? They just love the sound of their own voices.

Right, I am back now, sitting on Harley Street, where some kind of drama always happens. Hospital Street. Funny, as the sick who come here don't say, 'I am really struggling, can I have a wheelchair?' Nope, they will step unassumingly out of their Bentley 4x4s, refusing any assistance (in public), and slide straight on in through the front door to whichever department they require.

Halfway down the street is a walk-in doctor I have used for a prescription drug, because I have acid build up, which probably stems from anxiety. Yes, this job at times can push you to the limit, but you just can't display your symptoms or emotions, however strong. You simple manage it. When I become stressed, my insides close up, so when I eat, the food stays on my chest; it just will not descend. What little food makes it through to my stomach soon makes its way back to the surface. Not nice. Lansoprazole simply opens up my insides and clears a way for my food to pass easier. Now no appointment is required. Run in and see the doctor, he asks a few questions, I throw him £80 in cash for the initial appointment. Other walk-in doctors around the country may start around £30. Just you get what you want. Blood test the next day. Most of us need a doctor now. Mine is ninty miles away and it would take two weeks to see her. This way I get sorted, fast.

The sun is effulgent, but the air is dirty. The cyclists are wearing masks. The odd person is sitting on a wall outside whichever department they've attended, probably waiting for results. See, money cannot be the root of all evil, because those who have an abundance can attend a clinic, go outside and lick an ice cream and by the time you've finished comfort eating, hey presto, you've got your results! No hanging around for weeks, as the impoverished do. I mean, imagine waiting weeks for an oncology test result, an AIDS test or even the sort of test you might need if you had an adventure with the wrong kind of lady last night? That's just cruel.

They should be here soon. Right, well, I am not people watching, the political correctness these days will have me locked up for that, so I switch on the TV. As I'm flicking through the channels as we men do, there's a tap on the window. Oh no, fingerprints! I turn my head with a smile. A lady on crutches with Tippex teeth is summoning my attention. I know this woman. I open the door, because lowering the window leaves water streaks. 'Oh it's you!' I say in delighted tones. She's one of many Rolls Royce admirers who feel fortunate to pass the car. Even rich people stop to admire, and the odd one even has the temerity to open the doors and try to step into the back. Because he can afford one, he thinks that gives him the right to try mine out.

Now I cannot for the life of me remember this woman's name, but I have been speaking to her for the past two years. 'Hi, how's things? Where's your lovely scary-looking husky-type dog, and what's with the crutches?'

'Oh dear,' she says. 'How long have you got?'

I look at the clock and said, 'About ten minutes, give or take. They're all on their way from Heathrow.'

'Well, I don't know where to start,' she huffs. 'It wasn't long after you left last year, I was taking the dog for its afternoon walk up Harley street, over Marylebone Road and into Regents Park, but I had forgotten his poo bag. So I rang my husband and asked him if he could meet me at the park with a poo bag. Do you know what, he declined! Said he was busy on the laptop and had some calls to make. I was fuming!

'Well that developed into an altercation on the phone. I thought the road was clear, because the lights were on red. I stepped out onto the road and from the corner of my eye in slow motion I caught the glimpse of something moving rapidly towards me. I heard a muffled noise, like someone shouting, and as I turned my head, wallop, a motorcycle courier smashed into me, and I mean *smashed*. It was the worst moment of my life. The impact lifted me up above him but I felt my right leg get caught in his handlebars. It's like I somersaulted and hit the ground, hard! I had no idea where the bike was.

'I was knocked unconscious and there was a weird silence – I remember it as if it was an hour ago. I remember hearing muffled noises, then all of a sudden, my life came back to me. I rolled over, tried to sit up. I could see parked cars fifty to seventy feet away, all parked neatly in a line, then I looked down at my leg. It was, as God as my witness, hanging by a thread high up my thigh. I remember screaming and screaming for help. From across the road a woman came running over towards me, stopped, stared straight at me, bent down and shouted, "WILL YOU SHUT YOUR EFFING FACE!" And she ran off.'

'She just ran off?' I asked her.

'Yes, just ran off and left me in the middle of the flipping road. Blood like I have never seen in my life around me and I'm on my own in the middle of this damn road!'

'Then what happened?' I asked, reluctantly.

'Well, I carried on screaming in hope for some help, a passer-by, a motorist, even the flipping private hospital, which was right there. Nothing, no one. Then it dawned on me my dog wasn't around me, I couldn't see it. So then I started to shout for him. Where the hell was he? And then out of all the commotion I heard, "Look what you've done to my bike, LOOK AT IT!" It was the motorcyclist screaming at me and holding his shoulder. I was incredulous. Here I am in this state and the motorcyclist is bending down shouting at me!

'Next thing I knew, someone grabbed the motorcyclist, shouted at him to back off, sit down on the kerb and wait for an ambulance. He turned around to me, I remember his face, horror was written all over it. He bent down and lowered his tone, but spoke affirmatively. "Look, you're in shock, I've summoned an ambulance for you both." He was holding a jumper in one hand. He laid me back and put it under my head. I shouted, "But my dog, my dog has run off! Have you seen him? He's a husky and he must be terrified."

'He told me to calm down, and said he would go and look for my dog. I watched him jump onto the pavement and through the main doors of the private hospital. Whilst he was talking to someone I saw a nurse look out onto the road. It felt like forever, but a minute later he came back. "Where's the nurse?" I shouted. "OK, OK, calm down," he said. "They said that as a private hospital, they are not insured to attend to a road traffic accident or any other incident outside the premises." I tell you, I have never felt so alone in all my life. Finally the ambulance came. My husband arrived. I lost the dog, nearly lost my leg, and guess what, I ended up having to pay the motorcyclist a few thousand for a new bike. Yep, I did step out in the road. However, I just say thank God that for saving me.'

Now what gets me is – why thank God? Why? What for? Why would he save her and not millions of kids in Africa who haven't seen food or felt a drop of rain for years? Hundreds dying a week and yet God saves her? What makes her so special? There's no element of logic to that at all. I'm delighted she lived to see another day though. Whatever happened, good luck to her.

When she left, I must say I felt quite queasy. You're left with this gruesome picture in your head and it goes round and round. OK, need to unravel. Oh no, *Wives with Knives* is still on. What she went through was just as gruesome.

Right, King's presence is imminent. Will go and talk to taxi guy. His car's rammed to the roof with luggage, and there must be another four more taxis like that. The whole street comes to a standstill when they arrive. The whole scene is extraordinary. The King exits the taxi, in his own time. He steps out, looks around, like for some kind of adulation. He gets none. They are all waiting to get through the door, as only he has the only front door key, which he takes from his son who has been looking after the place.

It doesn't matter what you are in your country, over here you're just someone with cash. I remember last year we went to a high street bank and the King walked right to the front of the queue. Now, by convention, over here in the United Kingdom we form an orderly queue, which the teller politely informed him when he walked straight to the front. I recall his face quite well – 'slapped bottom' springs to mind.

I've double-parked the Phantom to create two parking spaces, which I stand in until they pull in. Once the cars are all stationary, my attention towards the King is undivided. As a chauffeur, your allegiance is conventionally directed to the one who sanctions your wages, unless instructed otherwise. Different job, but the same ethics still apply. Butlers on wheels is what we are, with the willingness to go that extra mile without diminishing our skills of etiquette and diplomacy. These are small moments in the life we create where we feel a little importance and simply enjoy it, for the little time that it lasts.

'Welcome back, King,' I say in a jovial tone. 'Delighted you all brought the sunshine!'

'Paul, how are you?' he replies. 'You look younger than last year.'

'Terribly kind of you, King,' I reply.

'How have you been keeping yourself?'

Well, apparently in a deep freeze, King. Thank you.

'Now!' says the King. He is standing before me, slightly bent from the flight and the taxi journey. In the background, the road has come to a standstill. The five cars with their drivers are waiting to dispense with their loads, and the three wives are waiting to plant bright red lipstick on any space they can find on my face. He continues, 'Paul, we will probably have some breakfast, make a few phone calls and I need to meet some people from the church foundation later. I'm confident of an early finish, as I will most certainly need to rest tonight. Oh, by the way – Sloane Street first stop. So, See you shortly.'

I offer my arm for leverage as he ascends the few stairs to the front door. As he opens the door, I turn to find the Three Degrees waiting to greet me – his wives. One by one they plant indelible lipstick over my face. Lovely! The King affirms that I should deal with the cars and luggage and allow the street to breathe again. I direct the drivers where to place the endless suitcases and carry cases into the corridor. The guys are quick. They get paid by the job, so no hanging around.

I answer my phone, as it's been buzzing in my hand incessantly.

Chapter 2

Collateral damage

It's my colleague Colin on the phone, sounding distressed. He works in Essex for a guy who's rich but not wealthy, a CEO who is still climbing the ladder, which isn't all in all a good thing. One-to-one chauffeurs like to stay clear, as their bosses are conventionally stressed, angry and resentful and possess no natural affection for anything. Well, maybe a dominatrix. Hard on the outside, cold on the inside.

'What's up Colin, how's life in the stockbroker belt?' I ask. He tells me it is not all good. My dear friend is married to an alcoholic who either doesn't know it or refuses to accept it. At times she displays a side that could render her a prime candidate for *Wives with Knives*. Colin's been in his new job for about six months and is struggling with the behaviour of his clients, a couple who live in Essex and run a mid-size company in the city. Girlfriend and boyfriend apparently, been together twenty-odd years. Apparently it's true love, but they have separate everything. Cars, cheque books, toys, holidays… OK, if it works for them. They hate the thought of marriage. Hate children. Not just the thought of them, they hate them, full stop. Their bilateral consensus from the inception of their relationship was not to litter their career path with sprogs. They have two dogs in place of kids and that's the way they love it. Colin was driving them one afternoon when a news report came on saying that a baby girl had been born with her heart on the outside of her chest and had had a successful operation to place the heart back in its rightful place. Now any human with a heart would simply applaud the science behind this operation, the cardiac team and the individual who came up with the thought in the first place, but not these. Oh no, this guy, a CEO, responsible for many staff, his company, oh and two dogs, blurts out, 'Why couldn't they just leave the kid alone? It's not as if the world needs any more effing kids, is it?'

I warned Colin at the outset that this pair would be trouble, interfering, whingeing like a squeaky wheel incessantly demanding all the attention. Look, company bosses fight day in day out for cash from clients, customers, ninety-day accounts, staff wages, purchasing accounts, the taxman, paying back tax avoidance schemes that initially brought joy, inducing the emotion that involves two fingers. Couriers, lunches and being seen in the right restaurants. Wives and their shopping and their hairdos and their shoes and lunches and holidays. Money consumes them. They cannot sleep.

I had one client who called me at one o'clock in the morning. 'Paul?' he whispered down the phone.

'Yes, what's up?'

'I need to go out. Are you asleep?'

'Well, I'm not now. What's up?'

'Come and get me, I need to go out. Call outside and I'll throw the Range Rover keys out to you. I'm at the town house in Hay Hill.'

'Right,' I said.

Do you know, I drove him down to Swindon, all the way down the M4 and straight back, just so he could sleep! The Range Rover rocked him off, and when we got back he was still asleep and snoring with a vengeance. It got louder and louder. I looked over at him once and said, 'You're doing that on purpose! How does the missus put up with that?' I thought of a couple of women friends who were pregnant, wondering if the next time he can't sleep he can call them and they would provide him with some hot fresh milk before bed!

The love of money leads to the root of all INJURIOUS things. Those who lust after it will stab themselves with many pains. – 1 Timothy 6:10. 2 Timothy 3:5

It transpires I was right. I also told him to test the Neat Garden Rule. I practise it every time. I arrive at a huge house, long driveway, neatly manicured trees and grass, nothing out of place. Beautiful big gates, an Englishman's castle. But as soon as the gates start to open, another long driveway, more manicured grass and trees… yes it's nice, but quite often I see there are no flowers – not so much as a daffodil. Easy maintenance, maybe? No woman on the premises, maybe? Or maybe the owner of the house has no feelings. I know the owner of the property is going to be unequivocally nasty. Or simply cannot help themselves displaying emotions that are deeply unattractive.

'Talk to me, Colin. What's up, my friend?'

'Paul, you know me. I'm a tolerant man. Just things getting on top. Sorry, I just need to give vent to my feelings once in a while.'

'Colin, I know you. It's not a problem, you know I'm here. But I'm broke.'

'Me too,' says Colin.

'No. Seriously Colin, I am wounded, I'm so broke that if someone robbed me right now, they'd just be practising.'

'Do you remember running around after five or six clients?'

I flipping do, I thought. Having just one client would sort things, extra time with family, space, more cash.

'So what's happened?' I asked.

'I had an early Stansted this morning, picking up at three-fifty am. So I began to warm up the car, and the lady friend pops out in night clothes. Last thing I wanted was to be racing up the M11. My alarm went off on time and woke me, but I just didn't seem to recover. Without a fuss, I went back to sleep. An hour or so later, my alarm went off. So I picked my boss up on time, but I missed the turning for Stansted and the next exit was nearly twenty minutes away! Add on the same amount of time to come back, and she nearly missed her flight. Her abuse was vitriolic. About how much money they'd lose, how important the day was. She just went on. To be honest, Paul, if that was the only time, I could cope with it. But it's ongoing. If a car cuts us up she moans loudly: "Ow, we just missed that." Or "What about the bus, the BUS, you're not letting it out, I'm not in a hurry you know!"

'I tell her nothing about my life and she hates that. She has to know so she can gossip. Every day she would talk about their last chauffeur. Good points, bad points. I was four minutes late the other morning. I sent her a text as I thought it would be later. I got to the house and she was standing outside in the blinking rain! What for?'

'Colin,' I said, 'I do not want to say I told you so. But it seems like they intend to highlight your discrepancies by gossiping. Or compound your errors. I'm surprised she doesn't ask you to apologise for every bump in the road. So how much sleep did you get?'

'Don't even go there. My son was reprimanded at school for being in possession of a knife.'

'A knife?'

'Yep. The school has suspended him, pending an investigation. Apparently he was being bullied and we never even knew. In retrospect, he did provide evidence, coming home with one shoe one week, no coat the following week. I had a go at him, trying to remind him how tough things were. At times he'd look at us as if to say, the parents' job is to provide, not ask me questions. I cannot imagine what he was going through. The teacher said he seemed relieved when the knife was found and confiscated. I expressed my feelings to the Head, and added a few stern comments of my own, after they admitted that they had recognised his school work was sliding but had done nothing except monitor the situation. So I expressed disappointment in their lack of support.

'Then there's the wife. I didn't realise anything was wrong till I got home. I called as I do when entering the house and received no reply. I hung up my coat, walked into the living room to find the TV talking to itself. I walked into the kitchen and she was lying face down on the island in middle of the kitchen, next to the shoulder of lamb she had cooked for dinner with her hair lying in the gravy. Next to a half-empty bottle of vodka.'

'Is she alive?' I asked.

'Yeah. It's a regular occurrence, Paul. She blames the boy's attitude on me not being here. How can I be in two places at once? I do my utmost, I try my hardest. After seeing her in the kitchen, I scooped her up, carried her into the lounge and lay her on the couch. I went to bed. I had been driving for seventeen hours, I had nothing left. I set my alarm for 3 am for the Stansted run. I woke up to feel something cold over my face. Realising it was beer, I jumped up and found her staring at me. The mad cow had thrown a glass of Stella all over my face. She was just staring at me.'

'What was wrong, what the hell did she want?' I asked.

'A chat! She was angry I had left her downstairs. She moaned that she had been on her own all day. She said, am I supposed to simply accept the bed I made and lie in it, or go and find a middle-class man who can provide what I need?

'Actually, lately I've noticed her staring at me.'

'Staring at you?'

'Yeah, it's like she's trying to tell me something.'

'Like what?'

'You're asking me?' Colin recoiled. 'How the hell should I know? OK. Hang on. Let me consult the lady with the wide nostrils on the psychic hotline.'

'OK Colin. I can see how wound up you are about this. I am just as shocked as you. To be honest I think she could be fed up, sitting in all day waiting for you. I know the boy doesn't help with his attitude. Allowing him to go to bed when he so desires doesn't help the situation.'

'Yes, she lets him have his own way. All the flipping time. Easy life. As if life is easy. She's turning him against me. I have no idea why. Hang on!' Colin's suddenly remembered my last sentence. 'Fed up? She has the whole day to herself and you think she'd rather be in an office? Coming home and telling me who's got on her nerves? She hates me, doesn't she Paul?' he added in low tones. 'She'd rather be somewhere else instead of sitting here with me. It's like she is praying, dear God, please let something happen to him!'

'Look, I know she's not happy,' I said, 'but that's a trifle extreme. It could be anything. Depression. I mean let's face it, loneliness is the heaviest thing to lift in the world.'

'Well I've had enough and I'm considering moving out, before she kicks me out. I haven't before because of the boy, but there's no love, no affection. Nothing. I'm not living the rest of my life like this. Life is way too short.'

'Colin, you barely have enough for the mortgage next month. Where are you going to get the money for a solicitor? You can't remain separated indefinitely until you get some cash.'

'Well... shall I simply ask her what he wants?'

'That's the worst thing you can do. What if you don't like the answer? Look, let's meet over the weekend. Actually, no, I've just started this job, but I do get Monday off. We'll continue this over a pint. Try and excavate deeper in an attempt to resolve this problem.'

He hangs up, frustrated that we haven't solved the issue. He loves his son but I do feel for him, unequivocally. His problem, as I see it, is that he holds himself reprehensible for simply going along with her from the start. She demanded a drink from him in a Soho bar. Her attire was provocative, the atmosphere in the bar was captivating. It's Soho, you know how it is. So it was she who initiated things. Her outward appearance was good, pretty almost. Chemistry can be overwhelming. Yet the fact is, he had left her before, a few years back. Why? Same old story, her behaviour. She didn't love him then. She trapped him, and then the time arrived when he knew he had had enough. His heart desired a break from her possessiveness. Randomly picking up his phone and reading it, informing him when it was time to laugh and enjoy himself. The house started to resemble a morgue most of the time.

So he left and she let him go, to just walk through the door. No altercation. He said he was leaving and she shrugged. At the front of his mind he knew he couldn't entirely trust her, but he walked out through the front door anyway.

A mile down the road he sat in his company Jaguar in a petrol station, trying his utmost to dispense with his inner conflict. You think you miss someone, but it's just the familiarity. After an hour sitting there, looking at his phone, he called her. He said he had to. He felt he simply had to explain that a break might do them both some good.

'What was her response?' I ask.

'She stopped me mid-sentence and told me to go. And then she said, "Go sort your head out whilst I bring up our baby on my own." "Baby?" I shouted. "What baby?"

'She replied, "Your five-month old fetus, honey!"

'My baby?' he asked her again. There was no reply. He shouted down the phone line, 'Well answer me then? Are you still there?

He began talking to himself saying, 'What a joker! She's lying, I know it. She must be lying.' Silence at the other end. He disconnected the phone from the car, forced it to his ear and began to listen. Now you know the scenario – the quieter one person speaks, the harder the eavesdropper listens. Colin did not like what he heard next…

'Has the fool gone? Did you tell him?' said a man's voice.

'What fool?' he shouted at his wife. 'Told me what, and who's that?'

He rammed in the starter, igniting the mighty V8 into life. He then closed his eyes and allowed his chin to rest on his clenched fist. He forced the gear lever into drive, tossed his iPhone onto the passenger seat, grabbed hold of the steering wheel and with his right foot, lit up the rear Bridgestones.

He felt utterly confused. It was as if he felt unqualified to explain or confront his own psychological conflict. How can a woman simply push a button and internally combust the deepest part of a man's soul. In retrospect, whenever a man displays his unattractive side, it's usually money or a woman that induces it.

Colin had walked out on a consensus, or so he thought, so why this, now? Unfortunately something had to give. Something had to take the brunt of his animosity. Half a mile from the house, Colin approached a roundabout at some unstable speed, his mind racing with thoughts, suggestions, revenge and despair, all emotions which, when involving a man with such multitasking requirements, simply collide. He threw the Jag into the roundabout faster than he had anticipated, and in an attempt to rectify his mistake he tried for a straight line, skimming the kerb and through the other side, but that didn't happen. His mind had disengaged from the immediate task in hand and now it was too late. Colin inadvertently clipped the kerb and lost all control of the steering, quickly becoming intimate with a lamppost that was quietly minding its own business. The noise was horrendous, the impact embarrassing. The impact caved in the driver's side front wing and ripped off the wing mirror and the car ended up with the lamp post rammed right up into its rib cage. By this point Colin had long given up on regaining control and braced himself for impact. His face was already covered by his arm, anticipating the worse.

The noise stopped, except that he could hear the hazard lights ticking and the sound of water cascading all over the car. Removing his arm from his face, he decided to inspect the damage. He turned his head and saw the lamppost wedged up against the door. With his thumb he depressed the start button, not remotely knowing what was going to happen next. The engine fired into life. He had to exercise full lock to prise the Jag away from the post without dragging the whole thing with him. He pulled away amid a loud screeching noise. Once he was free he tried to look in his mirror, but it had gone. 'Someone bloody help me please!' he shouted.

Back on the road, he stopped and tried to switch on the hazard lights, but they were already on. He left the engine running and opened the door. The water had stopped – it was a sprinkler providing refreshment for the daffodils. The lamppost had seen better days and the grass would require resurfacing.

He then turned to look at the car. 'Look at the state of that,' he murmured to himself. At that moment a car with some people in it slowed down to work its way around the debris. Colin was preparing to say thanks for stopping, but then the rear window of the car descended and a couple in the back began taking pictures with their iPhones! Gobsmacked, Colin turned his attention back to the car. A huge dented lamppost lay before him. He looked at the crumbled remains of the front wing, and picked up the smashed wing mirror, getting a faceful of water from the sprinkler.

Then he remembered what he had been doing and what had happened. The missus! He climbed back into the car and limped back to the house in a state of deep melancholy.

They discussed the situation and Colin decided he was trapped. He had no choice but to shut up and stay. Abortion wasn't an option. It turned out that the chap he had overheard on the phone was just a concerned neighbour. Oh, and the office demanded to know how come there was so much damage to the Jaguar and no other car was involved.

Why do people today have so little natural affection? Spouses, employers, politicians, workers – everyone. So many people are angry and ready to lash out at any time. You wonder where it's all going. People don't have a decent role model to follow. So what was Christ? Is his memory on earth so distant that he's not applicable any more?

When talking about religion, everyone has different viewpoints. Surely they can't all be right? What about his father, 'The Almighty'? Most people feel that God, if he exists, has abandoned the planet and has gone and sworn allegiance to other alien life. Does that make any sense? After all, Genesis chapter 6 verse 6 states that God was saddened as the inclination of the human heart back then of all humans on earth were BAD and he regretted making man… but weren't they all Israelites?

I am staring through the windscreen reflecting on Colin's plight. We all do what we can to survive. He drives between 300 and 500 miles a day, and that's just not sustainable long term.

I hear a knock on my window and turn my head to see one of the King's wives peering at me through the double glazing. I open the door and she's standing there with a glass of water. I thank her for this undeserved kindness. Believe me, when a gesture is made like that, you remember, because it seldom happens.

'Paul,' she says in a gruff voice, 'we'll be leaving in ten minutes and we'll go to Boots just off Bond Street and then go directly to Peter Jones in Sloane Square.'

At that moment, a member of the local church calls her name, and she turns and walks over to greet him with open arms. I walk round the car on to the road and tip the water into the drain. Yes I know, ungrateful, even indelicate, but I have a feeling about tap water. We give so much to cancer research and yet it's so aggressive. One in three people! Could the additives in tap water have something to do with it? I'm not taking that risk. I know anything could trigger it. So I've been making adjustments in my life. Sitting in front of this steering wheel all day, every day is injurious to one's health. No coffee or tea, or salt although it's a preservative, way too many suffer with high blood pressure, and salt apparently is to blame. And I've been cutting my meat intake down for a while. I struggled with crispy bacon and sweet New Zealand lamb on a Sunday, but today is my last day. Doesn't feel normal not eating meat. Once I drop off the King, I'll go to the Builders Arms in Chelsea, a fantastic pub with a great atmosphere, to try one last time. My body isn't feeling it any more. It rejects meat, making me feel nauseous. No such problems with fish though.

Eating in the day is invariably a no no. A driver can't be running to the facilities every couple of hours. But as I'm hungry, I will try their cottage pie. Absolutely no pop though. Well, I was partial to a glass of lemonade at dinner, but with eight or so teaspoons of sugar in each tin, no thanks! I drink Evian all day, but when I use my kettle or iron, I use Volvic. With tap water your kettle soon needs descaling. Same with the iron, but Volvic leaves them both as clean as a whistle. My cup of peppermint tea is accompanied by a large teaspoon of honey, taste clean and free from any undesirable agents – just don't go to Tesco's looking for it.

Finally, all the family and friends begin to trickle out on to the street. Within minutes roughly thirty people have congregated around the Phantom, for salutations and cheques probably. I recognise one of the guests as one of priests of the Presbyterian church on Marylebone Road opposite York Gate, which is the last road turning right or heading north until the A5 Edgware Road incidentally and annoying. Funny, whenever there is a gathering, the Phantom seldom feels left out. Someone invariably refers to her or displays some affection towards her. Some touch and stroke her. Some hold on to her keys after a party and hold alcohol reprehensible for their selective kleptomania! Some actually park their derrières on the bonnet of all places, and some stand in front admiring her for too long when the engine is running. The Phantom welcomes disciplined, mature individuals. She simply would like you to reciprocate your kindness in the way she welcomes you with her warmth and grace.

Oh lovely. Here are some children. Now kids and Rolls Royces don't mix. I turn to get out of the car when one of the children decides to make his acquaintance with ten fingers spread right across my side window. Great, oh and it looks like his mother has just creamed his hand. Don't want to get those little hands of yours dry, do we? I bet he thought, yes, I can make sure everyone sees my prints on the window now…

He and his brother peer through the window. They're engrossed in a confab. What are they talking about, I wonder? Then I realise. They are verbally wrestling for the superior position of the front seat, only in a Phantom, the superior position is in the back. Kids! Think they know it all.

'Hi Paul!' the boy shouts in a loud voice.

I reciprocate with a clenched fist, the form of African greeting he is familiar with.

'Oh, cool,' he replies. 'Oh, and you've polished the car, Mr Paul.' He drags a packet of Monster Munch from inside his jacket, like he's hiding some kind of family heirloom. Flipping pickled onion flavoured Monster Munch too!

'So,' I ask, 'is the car clean enough for you?'

'Oh yes,' young master replies, 'and I am sitting in front with you?' He moves away from the window and begins looking at the door.

So I ask, 'What on earth are you doing?'

He replies, 'Well am looking at how clean you did this and it's strange when I can see my own face in the black paint.'

OK, I thought. *I will refrain from indulging.* 'Well I am delighted you like how clean it is, I did it so you can throw your Monster Munch all over the inside,' I tell him.

'Why would I want to do that?'

'Oh, it's just a game, I thought you'd like it.' Bless him.

So leaving the King's fan club was an intimate affair. I appreciate they haven't seen him for a few months, but everyone bows down to him. One lady was quite a size, and she lost her balance and grabbed on to the Phantom driver's door – I wouldn't bet it would have stayed on its hinges.

Now four adults entered the cabin and began to play musical chairs in the back. A couple of teenagers sat on the floor (the long wheelbase version is huge) and I had the young boy up front. The first-class cabin suddenly became very loud.

Classic FM is on, so I adjust the volume. Music in background – Barbara Hendricks, *No Balm in Gilead.* I adore this soprano. But I can see in my rear-view mirror that the King is looking a trifle disturbed. I don't honestly believe he can handle noisy kids. The kids locate their favourite radio station, Capital UK, and start singing. Lovely. Hip Hop. Fifty Cent. Window Shopper. I think I am the only one window shopping. The King looks uncomfortable squashed in the back seats he paid 300k for. 'What is this station, Paul?' he asks. I thought, *You're asking me.*

A driver must be careful playing the blame game, because you could quite simply lose your job. The driver who is exposed as a snitch seldom recovers. The kids will psychologically abuse you. The wife will deploy her Miss Marple detective tactics, rendering you radioactive, and the husband, well, he'll just punch your face in. There's no loyalty with new money, they really are fickle. You're a nonentity and you must never forget it.

Complacency leads to mistakes, and will one day acquaint you with emotions you had probably forgotten about. There's nothing as soul-destroying as your boss giving you a P45. *Put the Phantom back in the garage and the bus stop is outside, but please use the one down the street, don't stand outside the house.*

Once when I was working with a Russian family, the wife was showing me how to put chemicals into the swimming pool. She was beautiful, but I didn't allow that to distract me. She stumbled as we were on the edge of the pool, lost her balance, grabbed on to my arm and we both fell in. Not funny. She didn't have much on to start with. I helped her out and then climbed to safety myself. I turned to see if she was OK, and she was, but what clothes she had on were soaked. And who was standing over her in his £3,000 Brioni suit? A stern-faced hubby who didn't even offer an arm to help her up, let alone me! You're right, I didn't stay in that job long. Nothing to do with complacency on this occasion, just that the position became untenable. They don't trust anyone other than their own, which is why I couldn't go to the Middle East or Russia to work. For one, I wouldn't want to be more than a few hundred miles from our NHS. Anything goes wrong, you're on your own.

We all make mistakes, that's why they put rubber on the ends of pencils, but these people are unforgiving. When I started there were no satnavs, and the pressure they put the drivers under is immense. They shout at you from behind, because their English isn't great, and quite often words become entangled, which leads to complications. When he's stressed the wife displays similar symptoms, but either of them could wake up with a headache and if you're in the vicinity at the time, you'll get it, verbal or physical. However the boss decides to ridicule you and your incompetence, you simply have to take it or walk. Someone like this guy arrives in the UK with a shedload of cash, enough to settle a small nation's deficit and applies for asylum. He gets it, on the proviso that his intentions are to feed the UK and not to bleed it. The first-year profits of his company were 1.1 billion. It's like they're on cocaine. The only thing that humbles them is when it's brought to their attention that there are others with even more cash than them.

Even the wife assumes an erect stance, ears pricked, and manages to display a smile not seen by her husband before.

Just to illustrate how ruthless new money can be, a Russian family was one of my first clients way back when. I remember approaching the gates on a street called Bishops Avenue, East Finchley side, as the other end of the road is Hampstead. I waited a minute or so to enter the property – it was a sprawling mansion, the type even footballers can only dream about. I was greeted by the maid, who welcomed me in but told me my shoes must be left outside. It was winter, and bitterly cold. The first thing I remember was pure opulence, something I had never had the privilege of experiencing as I had not long started chauffeuring. Walking on this neutral coloured marbled floor, I noticed this gentle heat rising up through my feet. I was a trifle confused as the house wasn't on fire and I didn't smell any smoke, so I thought this must be normal in their world. Then I saw a man descending a marbled spiral staircase. It was him. He walked up to me and handed me the car keys. He then walked me outside and pointed to the car on the other side of the drive. It was a brand-new Mercedes 600.

'Switch on car and warm for kids,' he grunted in a deep voice.

Now I wasn't fazed, but it was definitely an intimidating situation. Him. The house, as quiet as a morgue. But I was excited at being given the keys to play with. I had only ever read out them in car magazines. I pointed the key at the car and heard, 'STOP!', so I turned round and he was standing at the door, signalling with one hand for me to give him the keys. So I walked back, wondering why he had interrupted my buzz. He took the keys and looked at me. Confused, I didn't know what to expect.

'You start car like this,' he said. He pushed the button on the key fob, and twenty yards away the Merc's engine roared into life. It must have been specially adapted because I know for certain, in all the car magazines I read, I had never seen anything like this. 'Now go and switch on the seat heaters and cabin heat, make very hot,' he ordered. Mesmerised by the Mercedes, I went about my work merrily.

It was probably a week later that I was speaking to my boss at the agency and he was asking how the job was going. He listened and then told me he had some information. As he hadn't long left the police force and set up this company, it became apparent that he was still privy to information via his own sources. It transpired that a month prior to my starting, this guy I was working for had lost his last chauffeur while he was working for him in Paris. The driver had been waiting for him outside his apartment. As the boss waited for the lift, he looked out of the ninth floor window, maybe looking for his car. Or maybe because he heard a noise. As he looked out, his Mercedes somersaulted into the air in a ball of flames. Flames ripped through it with no regard for the chauffeur, whose head was apparently removed, while the car was blown to smithereens. It was at that point that I remembered being told to stand back and start the car from a distance. I did so every time after that. Did he have an attack of conscience, or did he simply not need to bring trouble to his door with another dead chauffeur? To this day, I still don't know.

Anyway, the King and family all disembark and head off to Boots whilst I take five. The King has a huge reluctance to walk most places, but today he seems to be on the Lucozade or wanting to run from the kids. Spending his cash seems to have that effect.

Time to give the cabin a once over. Opening the rear doors, a pile of monster munch crumbs on the carpet greets me. The sheepskin rugs are askew and I'm just in time to watch the beluga leather seats slowly inflating, in order to regain their original shape. Some chauffeurs who are fortunate enough to have a better than average credit rating purchase one of these seats and pimp it out. Now for me, you have to be emotionally detached to grow skin thick enough to ignore clients passing wind all over your armchairs when they cost as much as a two-bed flat near Heathrow. I simply couldn't do it.

Music playing: *Rinaldo,* by Bach, performed by Arleen Auger, who actually performed at two of the Windsors' weddings in Westminster Abbey.

By now all the components in the 6.75 litre V12 must be red hot and working hard to satisfy the children's comfort, yet it's so quiet that from behind the double-glazed glass you have to check the reserve gauge to indicate the engine is still alive. By the time I've spruced up the cabin, the heat from outside is beginning to consume me. Like when a small cloud wafts in front of the sun and immediately diminishes its awesome power, I flick a couple of expensive switches, sit back and feel the power of the Phantom's climate control, telling the heat to scurry back from whence it came. My head is thrown over the headrests as I listen to my favourite piece of music. Remember the Harrods Boxing Day sale advert? Well the beautiful piece of music attached to it is that, by Arleen Auger.

Chapter 3

Prayers and polygamy

An hour or so passes before I see the King and his entourage again. I'm watching them in the rear-view mirror, wobbling up Oxford Street. One of the wives is holding a Happy Meal in her hand, but there are no kids with them, so it must be for her. As she once told me, 'Paul, I don't have a weight problem, I just can't wait to eat!' She's making a weak attempt to make it appear that the Happy Meal is for the kids, but she can't wait in traffic for five minutes without wanting to exercise her jawbone. I knew the kids were getting on his nerves. He soon dispensed with them – after all, shopping is supposed to be therapy.

Thing is, it doesn't take much to get VIPs like him agitated. Everyone annoys him. He shouts at his accountant. Maybe he's a 'stick to the letter' type. In this climate, anyone applying for whatever role must be able to multitask. Even a nanny must be able to display domestic skills and educational ability and be able to speak another language before she begins to babysit. When we all submit our invoices, what response will we get from our employer? A genuine smile of appreciation, or the vacant stare straight through you? Only one individual will your boss tolerate, and that's the bank manager, because he can give him what no one else can.

Most of the time, the person you're driving is late. That's because everyone else is of lesser importance than himself, even those who are even richer. You'll find the bank manager is seldom late for a meeting with him.

So, we're off to Sloane Square. I guess we won't be stopping at any shops on Bond Street as we have no kids. I watch for the assistants in each shop and they're watching to see if I pull up. When a car like this pulls alongside, they think yes, I could meet the manager's targets for the whole day in one go. It's lovely when couples finish in a shop and the lady comes out grinning from ear to ear. She'll say, 'Oh, they were so nice to me honey!' The man will put things in perspective. 'But darling, I just spent thirteen grand on three items, how else would you expect them to be towards us? To be honest, they didn't suck up enough, if you ask me!'

The King isn't flattered by designer labels. He would rather don his African regalia. He's just old school. In his kitchen, he still uses bleach to wash his tea-stained teaspoons, but he wouldn't carry the bleach into the loo as he still uses a toilet brush. Like most of us he won't have clicked on to the fact that what bleach does for stains on the teaspoon it will do for the toilet. In fact, apply a couple of squirts of bleach and in two minutes they'll be radioactive.

As you waft down New Bond Street, you come to Grosvenor Street lights. You'd think you were sitting on a mini earthquake there, but it's actually just the Central Line tube running underneath you. Continue down to Old Bond Street, which demands your undivided attention. You cannot simply glide past on your magic carpet. Even people-watching is amazing. So lovely to watch people moving, walking, shoppers' lips talking, although from behind my double-glazed windows, I can't hear a single thing. It's like watching your TV at home with the volume off. It's funny, because a street like this highlights which one of a couple has the cash. The one who walks in front invariably possesses the lion's share. Occasionally it's the woman. On the other hand, if they're holding hands, it probably implies they haven't negotiated the prenuptials yet or simply decided a piece of paper isn't worth the 'sanctity' label. So, if it isn't broke…

I had a recent client who was so loved up his fiancée took immediate advantage. His family could see he had on his rose-tinted glasses and found it prudent to interject. Without being indelicate, they simply reminded him of prenuptial advantages. When you're so loved up it's so difficult to identify one another's flaws. Because she was funny and he was besotted. Once she realised he was under her influence, he just rolled on like a lamb to the slaughter and she went for his jugular. His derisory prenup offer, by declaring the existence of a lawful impediment, she subsequently threw back at him, sending him back to his office like a boy, to rethink and devise an offer she could establish some common ground with. It's a sight to behold, a grown man under total control of a female. I've seen men disintegrate. Disempowered, humiliated by women who empty the fool's pockets from a safe ten miles away. Company bosses are relieved of their power, their companies, their homes and even their liberty. Slapped round the cakehole by that indestructible piece of apparatus, a majority of men, when a window of opportunity presents itself, are helpless to defend themselves. It's not too dissimilar to being on anti-depressants. It appears like you're at the wheel, but someone else is driving.

Even stranger, she never kissed him. She was cold. He'd race home to see her and she would offer a cheek. I heard him talking to his mother, asking whether it was him that made her that way, but it's like a smoker will read on every cigarette packet: 'the contents in this box will unequivocally kill you and cause distress to your loved ones and you probably won't see your grandchildren', and you just carry on. You can almost visualise the end. The court scene. The husband is optimistic that the judge is capable of the odd moment of common sense. The morning leading up to the court case, the wife and a select few friends congregate at Starbucks. They implore her with their experience and insight, 'Now darling, remember you do matter, yes you do count! You're doing this for the kids. No judge in their right mind will allow him to just run off into the sunset. Now, let's be strong, let's get through this and look forward to your divorce holiday and party.'

The wife is so grateful for the support. I mean if she wins, there's absolutely nothing the girls would require for their assistance and fortification. 'How do I look? I've just been to a new hairdresser. Am I ready for my close up?'

'Oh yes, you're ready, my darling, you resemble a woman who looks like she already got used to the billionaire lifestyle.'

'Jolly good!' the wife replies. 'Delighted you like my hair. It's all been *soooo* worth it!'

Back in the courtroom, the husband gets prescribed the customary prize, some Court Required Quality Time with the kids, whilst the wife's lawyer presses on with the boxing match, demanding half his (as I remember) 1.1 billion, although he couldn't lose a billion and stand up. In his defence, the husband concludes, 'OK, yes your honour, I will honour the child maintenance. No problem. But as she testified, I spoilt her and she became familiar, and she got used to this and accustomed to that. I have one question, your honour. I got accustomed to sex twice a week and I was sincerely grateful, so can that also still continue? I swear that's all I ask.'

So I have been wondering how the King would fare in a similar situation with three women. I'm aware that there were plenty more. Did he pay them off?

I remember a disagreement over some property he had with a business associate and it hit some sort of brick wall. His business partner offered a court appearance to settle matters. The King declined, quoting a scripture to mitigate absence on the day. 1 Corinthians 6 verse 1: 'Why take another to court, are you not competent at dealing with trivial matters between you?' Or his other scripture was Proverbs 25 verse 8: 'Plead your case with your neighbour and do not rush in to a legal dispute.' Now, I've seen the wives and they appear like they'd give as good as they get. Especially when they are hungry.

We arrive at Peter Jones in Sloane Square. 'Oh Paul.' The King summons my attention. 'Right by the door please.'

I jump out to provide my arm for assisting with his 'rigor mortis', as he calls it.

'Paul, we'll be a while. Go eat, relax, do what you need to do and I'll call you in a couple of hours. 'Thanks King. Lunch, round here? I'll be in the car when you need me.'

He stops on the spot and digs into his pocket, then withdraws his wallet, pulls out a wad of cash, then carefully peels off a fifty-pound note. I was just about to say that I have some cash for minor expenses, but he just hands me this fifty. 'Take this and go have something nice to eat.'

I nearly keel over. Clients just don't give tips any more. I'm confident that people don't give because they are rich, they give because they are happy. He must be happy today. So I run along, delighted.

Food. It's midday and I'm hungry, so I'm heading west down Kings Road, to a free house called the Builders Arms on Britten Street. I've taken a peep at the menu online and fancy the cottage pie. The menu even provides a picture to show the difference between cottage and shepherd's pie. Now apparently cottage pie made its first appearance in 1791 and its principal ingredient was beef, topped with sliced, overlapping potatoes to resemble the tiles on a cottage roof. Shepherd's pie is an 1877 dish made with lamb (never beef) and topped with creamy mashed potato to resemble the fleece of a sheep.

Irrespective, I feel today is my last day for eating meat. Like smoking. You cut gradually down and keep on till you lose the urge. I've been experiencing discomfort with meat – not digesting it properly, then feeling sick when I eat it, like my body is rejecting it. My conflict is that it doesn't feel normal to remove meat from my palate, like I am losing something my body needs. I'm wondering what will happen to my internals without protein. Well, I am about to find out.

The pub is busy, filled with liquid lunchers. The sun is out, effulgent at twenty-six degrees, just hot enough to provide a feeling of being pampered, like a gentle warm massage on your back. London is glorious when it's like this.

So I order the cottage pie and I'm waiting. I order a vegetable fried rice too, with extra green pepper and extra egg but scrambled, just in case. As I'm hungry, I can't wait another twenty minutes. Breakfast these days is cashew nuts with no salt and or an olive-filled bread roll. I used to have porridge with blueberries, but my abdomen distends terribly with milk, dairy, salt and blinking sugar and now I'm about to reject meat. I panic, thinking what's left to eat? Hey ho.

Whilst I wait, I'm watching people outside, holding drinks and engaging in conflabs with people they like. The sun really elevates people's self-esteem. You can see why winter induces deeply unattractive emotions in people. I believe it's fine, not for the rich but for the wealthy, they can find the sun wherever it may be hiding, whenever the mood takes them. They just down tools and go in search of it. It must be a fantastic feeling to be able to find the sun when you want to. I had a client who for his wife's birthday called a private helicopter company, had them wrap an Agusta Grand (it's a helicopter) up in birthday paper finished off with a bow, just for his wife's birthday. Wasn't even a special day. Straight into Paris, Rolls Royce straight to the Georges Cinq Hotel, money no hindrance. Yes I witnessed it, just it isn't my game to play. I've had a few clients that can afford to decide on waking up, let's get the hell out of here and head off to Monaco or Nice. Call their personal assistant and have her call the driver, then the helicopter pilot and the fixed-wing pilot. Oh, and not forgetting the captain of the yacht. The helicopter picks them up in their back garden, then flies to an airfield like Farnborough or Biggin Hill, a small airfield with enough asphalt to allow a small jet to land and take off. The chopper descends a few metres from the waiting jet. A short walk across the concourse, with your stunning, beautiful arm candy. An umbrella, waiting in the hands of a humble servant whether it's sunshine or rain, to accompany you in that short walk. Your chauffeur to transfer your luggage and dispense with the car as he pleases, as the boss really doesn't care. Oh yes, the PA, especially if she's gorgeous. Immigration comes to you on the jet to check your passports!

Settle in with your air hostess, summoned for the day to attend to yours and your wife's needs or requirements. Unless you left the wife at home with a new gold card and her own chauffeur, that is, then the hostess's attention becomes your own undivided pampering time.

You've got to be seriously wealthy to play this game. I know rich people who have to settle for first class on a jumbo and be forced to share their privacy with others of lesser importance, even in first class! Not everyone in first class has money. Ministers or diplomats, company executives, corporate courtesans… you could be sitting right next to one and didn't even know it. So to be able to avoid first class and live life like you're really living it, not existing, either marry a billionaire, become a PA or simply ask a courtesan for intimate details before selling your soul for a temporary moment of pleasure. If you can find one!

Living life the liberated way of a billionaire seems fantastic. Someone who is merely rich simply couldn't play these games. I heard one billionaire dismiss a well-known and successful celebrity as a 'welfare case'.

In reality you can see why most people couldn't live God's way. Too restrictive, interfering. No one wants to be told what to do. There's a saying though, that life is not a matter of just holding good cards but playing a poor hand well. No one except Adam and Eve has been dealt a perfect set of circumstances. Often the secret to obtaining self-control is learning both to accept those circumstances and to work within the limitations they impose.

The Bible promises a time when all people will be able to have a satisfying measure of control over their lives. Apparently they will be able to live to their full potential, uninhibited by frustrating circumstances. But it's so difficult to believe in something you cannot immediately see. According to the Apostle Paul's second letter to the Thessalonians 3 verse 2, faith is not the possession of all people, although Hebrews 11 verse 3 states, 'By faith, we perceive that the system of things was put in order by God, so that what is seen has come into existence from the things that are not visible. We cannot see the wind, but we know it's there. If we summoned the devil via practices he approves off, he will come running to you.' In the book of James, 2 verse 19 states, 'So you believe there is one God, do you? Then you're doing quite well, and yet the demons believe and shudder!'

I can feel and hear a buzzing sound. I begin to wonder why someone won't realise it's their phone. Then I feel in my pocket and realise it's mine, I left it on silent.

It's Mr Lover Man from Monaco. 'Paul,' he says in a soft but firm tone, 'I need you Monday, I'll arrive Terminal Five at 05:38.'

Nooo! Monday is my day off. I recently had to extend my weekends, because they just were not long enough. Workers get between a month to two months' holiday and I take two Mondays a month. The regularity will help one's mind, it's an incentive to look forward. I'm confident your doctor would prescribe it. Monday mornings have become wearisome, even painful at times.

OK, it's only one day, presumably.

'So when's your return flight?' I ask.

'23:05,' he says.

Great, and then the King on Tuesday morning! But these clients are few and far between. No loyalty. If you don't serve them, they will bring it abruptly to your attention that there's an abundance of others who will fill the breach.

I'm thinking. Meanwhile, beeping noises in my earpiece interrupt the phone call. Great, it's the King. 'Paul, where are you? We're ready. Oh, and I need to attend a small gathering of friends enjoying afternoon tea at the Dorchester in a while.'

'I thought you were going to text,' I say.

You know, my memory decides to desert me sometimes at its own convenience. OK, we are having a drink in the cafeteria, text when you are downstairs, oh and could you pay a visit to collections first and pick up some presents that we purchased. I agreed and switched back to Mr Monaco. 'Yes,' I confirmed. 'See you Monday.'

Racing back down the Kings Road, I was hoping for a short day, but now that seems unlikely. Halfway down, I pull over at a Pret à Manger, as I need stock for later, couple of bananas and a gluten free sort of cereal bar and some cashew nuts. I pull up alongside on Walpole Street and rush out. I am then greeted by a street sleeper and a dog that looks like it has seen better days, poor thing. Now I seldom pass by a homeless individual without looking to help, although I am somewhat more inclined to purchase food of their choice than give them cash. That way at least I know they eat something. Sometimes I haven't got it, so I can't give it. I remember a pop star I was driving. We pulled up at a cashpoint on Haymarket, in the middle of theatre town, and he jumped out and withdrew a thousand pounds from the cash point (it can be done if you have the funds, just ask the cashier at your bank to increase your withdrawal limit). A beggar politely asked him to assist and he appeared genuine, and this well-known pop star looked at him, folded his cash in half and shoved it in his inside pocket. He said to the beggar, 'Working and surviving in the UK is as hard as you like and I've no intention of giving you my hard-earned cash.' I know working in the UK is hard, but I will never forget the words that pop star uttered to the beggar. It's definitely true, people give because they are happy, not because they are rich.

You know, quite often at moments like this, you feel more like purchasing a nice piece of KFC for the dog and stuff the bloke for putting it in this situation in the first place.

'All right mate?' he said. Now I wasn't indelicate, even though I was in a genuine hurry. I stopped to see at least that he was OK.

He said, 'Looks like you're in a mad dash, but I won't keep you.'

'Yes,' I replied. 'What is it? Sorry but I've only got a credit card.'

He continued, 'Are you aware that when you are late, it invokes the devil? You may not think about him, let alone worship him, but you could end up providing him with some comedy relief. Don't be late. Lateness could get you into problems you'll be unable to rectify.'

'What?' I shouted.

'It's cool,' he said. 'Allow me to provide you with some insight.'

'No thanks,' I said. 'Take care of yourself though.'

But he carried on. 'See, the problem is, when you're late, it induces emotions you don't need. Anger, frustration, anxiety and aggressiveness. That's like a cauldron of toxic emotions that inevitably collide, deep inside your soul. When they do, it ain't nice. Everyone else will think your driving behaviour is not to dissimilar to that of a terrorist. That leads to panic, which is the root to all sorts of injurious things. Even the Bible says somewhere in Proverbs 29: "A man prone to anger stirs up strife. Anyone disposed to rage will commit many transgressions. Don't be late. If you're unfortunate and annoy someone, stand firm, don't reciprocate in a like-minded manner. Fire meeting fire is apocalyptic. Oh and remember, conduct yourself in a manner consistent with whom you represent, family or work. Don't ruin your day. Remember, learn by other people's mistakes, not your own. Most drivers don't make it to work without some kind of episode. Actually, you know what? A lot don't even make it to their destination at all. Now look, I don't require a credit card, but a sandwich and a Coke would be knock out. Oh, a packet of crisps to accompany the sandwich would be sound. Thanks ever so much.'

I walked into Pret trying to process what I had just heard. 'Did I just hear that?' I was focusing on which emotion to induce to either assault him or display empathy.

I purchased my items and bought him a Coke, plain Walkers crisps and a coronation chicken salad with dill. I thought, *maybe a snack will bring him to his senses.*

Outside, the sun was merciless. I wondered if I should buy him some deodorant, but one never knows these days, a compliment could be taken as a hostile act with a lot of people. I got thirty feet from him and he said, 'Er, what's that?'

'I got coronation chicken gourmet style, you'll love it,' I said.

'No I bloody won't! I'm a vegetarian mate, I can't eat meat! Especially out of a bag with the devil's star on it!'

'What star?'

'On the bag, the star in the middle of the bag, man, it's a star from the zodiac!' Look mate, its Pret's way of taking the Michael out of its customers, whilst you pay for their pleasure. Thanks but no thanks, you know what I mean geezer!'

This geezer was a teaser, I concluded. What the hell was I going to do with the chicken? I thought about going back to the shop, but had to run. What a waste. I don't drink fizzy drinks or eat crisps. So I placed the bag in the passenger side footwell and drove on.

I get to Peter Jones' collection department and there's a boot full of stuff. Anyone would think it was Christmas. He had even got them to wrap a few things. Now the Phantom's boot is huge, but even that can't hold everything. The King enquires, 'How come they didn't fit in the boot?'

Because you act like you've never been shopping before! No, I didn't say that.

By time I've got the King and his wife in the car, I realise I have an audience, mostly women. Women love shopping, and a group of shoppers are obviously amused. The Roller simply seduces people. She really does.

'Paul!' The King summons my attention. 'Let's drop my wife back and offload a few of the presents. It will take an hour for me to get changed, then we'll go to the Dorchester. I need the car on the front, so people from my meeting know I am there. So please sort it with the door concierge.'

Now I'm thinking, *Doesn't he know it takes hard cash to occupy a spot right outside the door of number 53 Park Lane?* Well, this will be interesting. He hates tipping, or as he calls it, giving money for no apparent reason.

The wife, I think it's his number one wife, has just finished a meal. The family have this strange method of flossing. Instead of using a toothpick they spend the immediate half hour after eating sucking in between their teeth in an attempt to dislodge stubborn pieces of food that have chosen to cling on for dear life to their veneers. When it's five or six people doing this, it's like birds in a tree first thing in the morning. It really is quite comical.

To give him his due, he is not averse to the odd conflab. You see, billionaires who do not work are somewhat more amiable than those on the ladder. As chauffeurs we speak when spoken to, one rule we try never to compromise. The wives are happy to exchange a few pleasantries as they spend most of their lives inside. Back home they don't walk anywhere – I suppose they're at risk from terrorist groups or the like. There's always the chance that the old man might think, 'Oh well, I still have two left,' and leave the lost one to reflect on his early warnings about 'straying or wandering aimlessly'.

'So Paul. Let me know when we are five minutes from the house, so I can ring ahead for someone to put the kettle on. How is life, and how's your lady?'

'Life is good, King, thank you for asking. As for the lady situation, I think I have enough bad habits. A lady is not one of them.'

'Oh, I'm sorry. Relationships are difficult these days. Really difficult.'

Changing the subject quickly, I state that things are not so problematic for himself with three women. 'Don't you believe it!' the King retorts. 'Where I come from, you bet on a sure thing, and if that is precarious, then choose three. Seldom does an old man like me place all his eggs in one basket. It's imperative to fortify the emotional side to your body.'

Now, he just gave us that information in front of his wife – and she just allows him control? He is religious. I'm wondering what his God makes of his self-centred view. I thought all Christians praised one God, yet each professed Christian holds a different view of him, their own self-made opinion. So I ask him a question I've always wondered about.

'Please tell me this. Now I know you love religion and all the pomp and ceremony. So tell me, are you a follower of Christ?'

'Of course I am!' he responds in amazement.

I quote Ephesians 5:29–30: "For no man ever hated his own body but he feeds and cherishes it, just as the Christ does the congregation, as we are members of his body. For this reason a man will leave his father and his mother and he will stick to his wife and the two will become one flesh." King, are you familiar with that verse, or did you skip past that page?'

'Ah, now, let me explain,' sayeth the King. 'What I am is born again. Which simply means my transgressions are forgiven.'

So it's a get out of jail card relating to transgressions. To clarify: 'born again' denotes a person who has converted to a personal faith in Christ. For example evangelicalism, being born again, is a popular phrase referring to spiritual rebirth or a regeneration of the human spirit from the Holy Spirit. Now I don't recall a chapter or verse anywhere stating that God or Jesus endorsed or gave approbation to the notion that a man can transgress as often as he likes with impunity. In God's eyes it's a sin when impropriety is practised. A few scriptures from the Bible have helped me to obtain a more accurate understanding. My conclusion is that the opportunity to have a relationship with God and gain salvation is open to all. Apparently God chooses those who will be born again or anointed with holy spirit, it's not about an individual's desire or his efforts. You must not get confused with an emotional connection to a spiritual one. So the expression 'born again' can also be rendered 'born from above' or simply from God.

The King's reply is resolute – he and God have an open channel and his connection is watertight. He states that God doesn't mind how many women you have as long as you have enough cash to support them. He then reminds me of Solomon's 800 wives. 'And he was the wisest man on earth,' he says. 'God gave him everything, so if it's all right for him.

I'm confused, because all the way back to Genesis 2:24 it says the two will become one flesh. Not a ménage à trois. Oh, and why did God allow Solomon free rein? What happened to the law?

Trying to understand all of this, allowance is not the same as approbation. God allowed Solomon to make his own decision to obey, as it's obvious, he doesn't force us or he didn't make us robots so we did exactly as he required. That wouldn't be free will, would it? God laid out his law, blessed Solomon with wisdom and expected Solomon to simply comply. Solomon's marital arrangements were in direct violation of God's laws, according to the scriptures. Solomon knew what was right, so how come he didn't follow the right path? In Deuteronomy 17:17 God's clear instructions warn him of the consequences of more than one wife. In 1 Kings 3 verse 5 he requests wisdom from God. What happened to that? Evidently, Solomon forgot his own counsel and wisdom. But a wiser Solomon did write in the end: 'God will bring every deed to account.' In Ecclesiastes 12:14 Solomon concluded with 'we should simply fear God and keep his commandments', which is simply the whole obligation of man.

I ask the King about his feelings in regard to Solomon and recite Ecclesiastes 2 verse 8 where Solomon laments his behaviour: 'I accumulated more things than my predecessors before me in Jerusalem. I denied myself nothing. I did not withhold any sort of pleasure, my heart was joyful. I gathered female singers for myself as well as what brings great pleasure to the sons of men – a woman, yes many women…'

The King displays his support for Solomon, telling me to remember that he was dust, an imperfect man.

'Oh,' I say, 'so you recognised he made mistakes?' God spoke about the sanctity of marriage. It must have meant something. He calls it an honourable estate, instituted by himself. He ordained it initially for the procreation of children, of which I know the King has thirty-odd, plus an abundance of grandchildren. Then he also made it as a remedy against sin. It signifies the mystical union between Christ and the church and therefore it wasn't meant to be undertaken lightly or wantonly to satisfy one's lustful appetite but reverently, discreetly, advisedly, soberly and in fear of God, duly considered for the course of which marriage was ordained.

The King replies, 'He wasn't perfect, but God still loved him.'

We agree to differ. Besides, he's paying my wages, so I will allow him to continue skipping pages for now.

He then invites me to his church to obtain some further insight, reminding me that a contribution would be welcomed.

I had wondered when that bit would surface. It reminds me of a movie I watched where a congregation had assembled and the vicar submitted his obligatory tax speech, reminding them that the collapse of the roof was imminent. 'Oh we welcome the cash that jingles, but we would rather the type that falls.'

We arrive back at the house on Harley Street. 'Now Paul,' the King says, 'we'll continue this discussion further at a later point. Give me an hour, then whizz me down to Park Lane.'

'Not a problem,' I reply. 'Just allow me a second to come round and help you.'

It's OK – they have no problem discussing a topic as long as they feel unchallenged. Threaten their intellect and fisticuffs will ensue!

I assist him and his wife out of the car, dragging a number of bags at his request. I just hope he has bought some prezzies for the other two. That's just hard work as he would have to keep all the wives happy. It's got to be harder than running a business.

I assume my customary position on the left side of the door, opening the door with my right hand, which then allows me to offer my right arm as an aid (remember it's the Phantom I'm driving, where the doors open differently – in a normal car, I would position myself on the right of the door opening with my left arm as an aid). My arm is there to provide a form of contraception, desisting the unwanted efforts of an assailant or individual with dishonourable intentions. But more importantly, if it's a lady I'm assisting, my position is designed to divert my eyes from becoming seduced by a picture that could have the potential to incessantly repeat itself throughout the day and possibly drive me mad – with pleasure or guilt!

A man's best friend is his dog, but right now mine is my radio. I switch the ignition to position one, so I can listen to it without switching on the engine.

Music playing: Delibes' *Lakme, Flower Duet.* That's the soundtrack for the current British Airways advert. Beautiful.

I allow the soundproof cabin to provide me with some solace. I know driving around in a Phantom appears luxurious, and don't get me wrong, it can elevates one soul, although I do like to drop clients off as quick as possibly to allow for time and headspace for myself. Some days I could be with the client for sixteen hours a day, attending to their needs. The odd half hour here and there should be spent wisely.

My ears are still reverberating from the shock of what I witnessed back on the Kings Road outside Pret. I am still incredulous at that man's temerity. I even looked for a nice meal for him and still got it wrong. Is it any wonder people just walk by street sleepers?

The King is quite calm today, although he likes to keep moving. If I was running low on petrol, no matter where we were he wouldn't wait in the car. He hates waiting for anything. In traffic jams, he will lean forward, as he doesn't wear a seatbelt, and say, 'Paul, use the bus lane.' He'd rather pay for the violation than give me a tip. One-way streets he wouldn't care about, if they give us an advantage, use it! Many clients who care nothing for their hired help will push him to the parameters of what's legal. When you push back because you realise your employer doesn't give a monkey's regarding what you don't like, the threats will begin to fly and you'll often get reminded that there are others who won't require much persuasion. No affinity, no loyalty, just get rid.

A chauffeur is usually kept on his toes. I've never known one to say he is safe. You never know what's going to happen next. A CEO's mood swings are simply amazing to witness up close. The funniest thing is that his mood may not even be your fault. A lot of the time, a wife doesn't realise how fortunate she is. On the way home he's vented his anger on the driver, often picking a fight which helps to ignite an altercation, so by the time he's got home, he's vented the worst of his feelings. You could be sent to get food or a present and the order is not quite right. A bad lunch, either the client or the food. Almost anything can alter their emotional state. But money and women, for some reason, alter their character. A cloud descends and they simply change. I've had clients that approach the car window and say, 'Jump in the passenger seat, I'll drive.' I look at them and think, great, I'd rather not. You know it's not because they want to caress the car and bestow praise upon it.

One client had a gorgeous Bentley Mulsanne, long wheelbase, only three hundred ever made, for a couple of weeks. He was outside on the phone, finished his call and held the phone between his teeth, then turned on his heels and looked as if he was going to kick the Mulsanne in the ribs. He looked straight at me. He then grabbed the door handle of this £200,000 car and snapped, 'OK, I'll drive!' Now I'm thinking, shall I grab my rucksack from the boot, while I have time? I was once left on the street with no coat, money or belongings and they'd expect to see you later at their destination and would simply not mention it, like it never happened. So he shouts, 'Right, come on, COME ON, OUT OUT OUT!' I wander round to the passenger side hoping for a lift. As I open the door I notice him looking down into the centre console. He then begins to gesticulate. I think oh, he's looking for the transmission. I leave him scratching his head, as it gives me time to grab hold of the seatbelt. Then I see it click – the gear stick is on the wheel. He looks a trifle embarrassed and switches his body language back to nonchalant mode. He peers at the rev counter to check if the needle is on idle. It's hovering above 700 rpm. This will be fun. He takes hold of the gear level and pulls it down, then pushes down hard on the accelerator, revving the engine, but nothing happen except the windscreen wipers go into monsoon mode. Eventually he finds the gear and it's straight off the pavement like a rocket. No, it wasn't a pleasant drive back to the office, but he didn't do that again.

A chauffeur's personal life has to harmonise with a job like this. If your home life is turbulent, it simply won't work. For one, you'll be less tolerant of your employer's behaviour, which could be disastrous. Look, I'm not saying all CEOs possess a split personality – just most of them.

I think I'll stretch my legs. As I detach myself from the comfort of the Phantom, the heat and dirty air hit me. I forgot how hot it was. I could even drive the Phantom with a jacket and tie on, it's that chilled inside.

I suddenly hear a buzzing noise, so I return to get my phone. Nope – not ringing. So where's that noise coming from? Oh look, a big fat bumble bee is sunbathing on my hot roof! I'm serious, it's on its back. Probably a queen, it's so fat. It's just rolling around buzzing. For some reason, I blow it across the roof, trying in vain to push it over to the other side. It stops buzzing, and spooks. 'Get lost!' it says.

I look at the bumble bee and ask, 'Who, me?'

'Well, can you see anyone else around here with bad breath?' utters the bee.

'You cheeky fat git, I was only trying to help, or even trying to establish what was wrong with you! I thought you were sunbathing, but because of your cheek, I'm assuming you've stung your last sting on someone and the life that's left in you is almost out.'

'Are you as deficient as all humans?' the bumblebee asks. 'I'm a bee, you idiot, wasps are the invertebrates that have more than one sting.'

'OK, I knew that, was just teasing. So, shall I call a vet? Or do you fancy being doused with Volvic? Or better still, I can get some sunflower oil, pour some over you and deep fat fry you on my red-hot roof?' Never had bumblebee before. Must check my Chinese take away menu for crispy bumblebee.

Next thing, the blinking bumblebee flips over on to its feet looking in disgust at me. It then begins to run across the roof, trying to obtain air speed because it needs so much air under its wings in order to take off. As it reaches the edge, I expect it to fly like a brick, but off it goes. 'Go find someone else's roof to chill out on next time,' I politely remind the bee as it tries in vain to gain altitude.

I am weary of insects. A couple of years ago I was on location in Harrow working for a lovely family. I had taken the mother and her eldest daughter out shopping. On our return I helped the mother, who was disabled, into the house as usual. I then returned to the car to unload the shopping. Now health and safety would invariably advise that one hand can be full but the other should be empty, ready to hold on to anything should you stumble and fall, especially descending a staircase. So here I was jogging to the kitchen across the lawn with both hands full with shopping. Next thing I knew I could see this flying object heading straight for my face. Like a road traffic accident, you always get a minute to reflect before impact. I remember watching this blinking insect on final approach, but because my hands were full, I simply couldn't react quickly enough and it flew straight into my cakehole. I knew it wasn't a wasp or a bee, so I wasn't terribly worried, until this insect began digging a hole in my tongue. I dropped the bags and tried to spit it out, but the damn thing clung on and I could feel it injecting nastiness into my tongue. I grabbed it out of my mouth and it fell to the floor like it had died. It was a weird stick insect type thing. I didn't stamp on it, just laughed at its temerity.

I picked up the shopping and jogged round the back into the kitchen. Inside the kitchen were the cook, the housekeeper and the daughter. Standing there I suddenly felt my tongue tingling, in a very unpleasant way. It began to swell and within four minutes my whole mouth began to blow up and I could feel the poison working its way down my throat. My client's daughter watched me forcing kitchen roll in to my mouth – I stupidly thought it would prevent saliva going down my throat. 'Paul, what on earth are you doing?' she asked. I mumbled a sentence and began to panic. I looked at the daughter and pointed to my throat. She got the message and grabbed me and took me to the car. She was panicking too as she knew something was wrong, she just didn't know what it was. Eleven minutes later we were in the emergency department at Northwick Park Hospital. The emergency department was full of people moaning and groaning, I hate the place, always try to avoid it and here I was, a casualty, not remotely sure if I was going to become a fatality. See how life can change in an instant?

I looked around for my driver to provide assistance but she had disappeared, maybe parking the car. 'Yes, what is it?' the receptionist asked impatiently. I still had the paper towel in my mouth and didn't dare to remove it. 'What is the PROBLEM?' said the receptionist, raising her voice. I pointed to my throat and shook my head. She looked closer at my throat and recognised it was swollen. 'Wait there,' she snapped.

I backed up a little and sat down. I felt dizzy. My head was telling me this was a mayday situation. I know people arrive at a moment in their lives when they 'unravel' and think about unfinished things. Family. Stuff on the laptop you wouldn't want anyone to see. Loved ones. My eyes became blurred and the dizziness became a deep worry. *Not like this*, I whispered in my mind, *killed by a blinking fly*. We're in the UK, not Africa or Australia. There's no dangerous animals here outside London Zoo.

I heard the daughter call my name and she came up and looked at me. I could see her lips moving but couldn't make out what she was saying. Then I remember some people in white coats hoisting me up and on to a bed. What a sight I must have been. I couldn't watch that back on CCTV. All I remember was something large being rammed down my throat and my head being yanked backwards. There were two people administering needles in my arms. A woman hovering over my head nearly finished me off by suffocating me with her boobs as she leaned over me. There were electrodes on my chest and I suddenly became tachycardial, when your heart races. That was a horrible feeling. My heart was pounding, it was talking to me. Oh my granny! This felt bad. I was waiting for the out-of-body experience, but I didn't get one. How come it only works in the movies? Apparently I blanked out. The doctors didn't panic though and waited to see if the drugs they had pumped into me would work. They did, hence why I am here to describe it all.

When I came round, a doctor was right in my face. 'How are you feeling?' he said.

I tried to speak. 'I feel like a bag of fish and chips,' I said. Three hospital personnel and the daughter all laughed. 'Oh,' I continued, 'don't forget some dandelion and burdock to wash it down please!' We discussed what the insect was, but to be honest, I only remember its final approach. It's strange reliving it. But now I appreciate the importance of keeping your mouth shut when you're not eating.

I can hear a rumbling, roaring noise coming down Harley Street and look up. A bright yellow Lamborghini Aventador announces its arrival and parks opposite me. It sits humming on idle with its four exhausts burbling. It's gorgeous. What a noise! I lower the passenger side window to hear the engine. I know the driver is a Premier League footballer, but I can't think of his name. He catches me spying and nods. I reciprocate and nod to try to encourage his right foot. He catches on and attempts to bring the nearby buildings down by creating an earthquake. What a noise! In true Lamborghini style – wow! It's not remotely as arresting as some other supercars, aesthetically, or even as beautiful as a Bugatti Veyron, as pornographic as an Aston Martin or as pretty as a Ferrari, but I wouldn't say no.

Hang on – talking about aesthetics, he's got a fruit tree with him. The car doors fly upwards and he runs round to the passenger side to hoist her out. Jolly good job, with that skirt on. That's not a skirt, more like a belt! Judging by his over-attentiveness towards her, that is not his wife. Now the cloak and dagger charades begin. He's helping her out of the Lambo but looking around all the time. Who's he looking for? And it's mid-afternoon on Friday, shouldn't he be training for tomorrow's game?

He comes over to me and I thank him for the engine tunes. 'Lovely motor,' he says. 'Bet it takes forever to get up to speed though, look how big it is!'

'Ignore the size,' I say. 'Only takes four seconds to sixty, almost as fast as your spaceship.'

We have a laugh as he peruses the Phantom. We are eventually joined by a young lady who is somewhat edible. As usual these days, there are a couple of extra bits added – burlesque rear end, lips and chest. Burlesque, meaning an absurd or comically-exaggerated imitation – although his chest is noticeably more voluptuous than hers. How does that work? She looks edgy, and he can't stand still for a second. She's smiling incessantly with her Tippex teeth.

'We've got to go. Got an appointment at a dentist somewhere near here,' says the footballer.

'No problem, I'll probably be here when you come out,' I reply. He walks off all cool and she wiggles off beside him. He's a North London footballer – well he was, recently transferred to a Yorkshire club. I suppose less money, but he'll still have to keep the cash coming in. You can see those who are in it for the cash, they're first to play a couple of games for a new club and they always play top drawer, maybe even bag a goal or two. Next thing they go missing. Why do they stop playing with the intensity they started with? Afraid of an injury? Apathy? Can't be that, surely a footballer can't get fed up of football… can he? Nowadays, with the tax man robbing them for every legal penny they can get, you'd think they would work harder, or even wiser.

There's a certain player receiving a quarter of a million a week. He can make even more with goals and appearances. Now he runs round the pitch like he's just going through the motions. Week in, week out, he short-changes the fans with a perfunctory performance. Does he care? He knows soon he'll be driving home in his Porsche and he'll probably pull over somewhere to play a game on his PlayStation. His belly now precedes his chest, and he doesn't run as fast as he used to. When the crowd shout at him to run for the ball, he appears like he'd rather sit down and enjoy a beer and a Happy Meal. He looks so fed up. Isn't this shift in his attitude the club's fault? They've simply removed the incentive for him to get off his water bed in the mornings. Who would, on a quarter of a million a week?

He rolls over, and standing there at the French windows leading out onto his huge veranda is his mother-in-law doing her utmost to display her gratitude that he chose her daughter to spend his life with. She's standing there with a silver tray with his breakfast on it. A lovely fry-up with a pack of his favourite sweeties for afters – Smarties or M&Ms? As most rich people like to display what they have, the breakfast veranda is on the front of the house, so he can eat his fry-up looking over his toys in the driveway. Imagine how difficult it must be descending his spiral staircase. Half way down he's looking out through a beautiful stained-glass window and watching his beautiful wife in the indoor pool, swimming naked. And her two friends decided to pop over for a swim too. Then his phone rings, and it's the Queen's bank manager, calling him to see if he's OK and would he fancy lunch, as his kids keep pestering him to obtain the footballer's signature.

As I remember it, this footballer, at his inception, was the youngest individual to initiate a relationship with this bank, even though he didn't have the minimum amount required to set up an account. Then the bank manager reminds the footballer, as he does every Monday morning, 'Hi, did you have a lovely weekend?

I saw your side lost again. Oh, and one of your strikers had his house robbed while you were all in the middle of the game. Was it you, as you didn't seem to be there for most of the match?' He chuckles, but the footballer doesn't find it remotely funny.

If we spoil someone, why do we expect them to behave the way we want? On the roads, there are lots of drivers but not so many chauffeurs. To carry out the duties of a chauffeur or butler you have to learn discipline, then apply it, learning how to elongate that extra mile without compromising etiquette and diplomacy. You get what you pay for. Is that true? A club can pay a hundred million for a player, but it doesn't mean he will do what's expected of him.

Most companies now prefer to employ ex-army personnel. That's because they know what to expect and what they will get – an individual with a disciplined background, with experience in training individuals to obey rules or adhere to a code of conduct. Maybe that's what the government needs to do with youngsters who constantly commit acts of impropriety. Conscription! Surely if someone is mentally regulated in a subject, they will apply it through their lives. Those who are welcomed into the country who then throw our hospitality back to whence it came should receive a custodial sentence and then returned to their homelands. Give people a chance, not an easy life. If our overtime at work was taxed at half the rate, it would provide individuals with an incentive to work more. People respond better when they have to work for their money. Some, if their working life drags on too long, do become resentful and bitter.

Music playing: *O Mio Babbino Caro,* sung by Renée Fleming. She is so adorable and her voice is angelic. This particular song, when it was first recorded by this artist, was used as an intro by a Radio 1 DJ a few years back. I remember thinking, 'What are you doing?'

I hear a tap on my window. It's Mr Footballer. Without the fruit tree.

'You still here then?' he says.

'Yep. This is my job, waiting around, displaying a patient attitude. Are you off now then?'

'Nah, got to wait for my friend. She's getting her teeth done.'

'Hmm, nice expensive day out for you. Not saying she isn't worth it, mind!'

As I now have confirmation she isn't his wife, I begin to fish, in an attempt to induce him to be a trifle more explicit.

'Nah, she just a friend I've known for a while. It actually gave me a window to come back to London. This was my home and being up north, I kind of miss it really. Know what I mean?' He turns his focus to the Phantom. I can see that something about it has caught his eye. Does he fancy being chauffeured? Not from the conversation. It certainly isn't faster than his.

Then he comes out with it. 'So what's its value then?' he asks.

As I haven't the remotest idea, I look it up, then answer, 'It's a hundred grand more than your futuristic-looking vehicle. Hang on though, this has got seats. Yours can barely accommodate you, can it?' Oh, and a few bottles of water, to sprinkle on your fruit tree.

'Yeah, I thought so,' he says with a grin. I knew it was money. You could see his face. His mind is on the money whilst the money is on his mind. I had realised that his recent club move has hit his wallet by sixty thousand a week. That must have hurt. Not a subject he cares to discuss either. Footballers are like accountants, talk to an accountant about money and figures just sprout in his head, talk about anything else, they switch off. At least a footballer can discuss what clubs to go to and how many Valentine's cards they are buying next year.

He looks at his phone. 'How do I wiggle through to Regent's Park?' he asks.

'Come on, I'll show you. At the third set of lights you go left and first right into the park...'

I fancy a roll round the block, So I tell him to follow me. I wait till he gets into the Lambo and lower my passenger side window, just wanting to hear that V12 once more. Waiting... waiting... The old Lamborghinis were like starting a fighter jet up, but now they are owned by Audi, they're a lot easier to simply jump in and go. Yep. There it is. Oh beautiful. What a noise! Like the old Formula One cars. Initially you hear a couple of electronic noises, then ignition. Then the explosion. The automatic choke holds the revs high for a few seconds whilst the oil navigates its way from the heart of the engine, up through the arteries and into the veins, eventually reaching the valve stem guides at the top. Ignorant drivers race off too quickly taking the revs too high before the engine has warmed up. Quickest way to an engine fatality.

OK, we have an audience. Suddenly it looks like the start line at Silverstone. The lights are roughly a hundred metres ahead and they're on red, so I wait. The Lambo pulls out behind me, with the pilot revving it. The street shakes and the audience is captivated. The lights turn green and I floor the accelerator. Although the Phantom gets to sixty in just under five seconds, it does not like to be launched. Now you've got to imagine a tidal wave on wheels. No noise, just the wind it creates, rocking cars and people as we whizz past. Pedestrians stare with their mouths open. They can't believe how fast this magic carpet is.

As I arrive at the next lights and take a right into Devonshire Place, I can hear the Lambo, but dare not take my eyes off the road. No second chances in this, none! I take the right, and the next lights are another hundred-odd metres. I make it and take a glance in my mirror, just catching a glimpse of the Lambo's nose turning right. I take the turning onto Upper Wimpole street – it's clear, though with cars parked either side. I punch the throttle again and the Phantom's huge rear Pirellis begin to excavate the tarmac like pneumatic drills. I take a quick glance at my temperature and pressure gauges to make sure all is OK, and I can see the petrol needle moving. Like a plane dumping fuel when landing to render the aircraft lighter, the Phantom is actually vomiting petrol all over the tarmac behind me. Gauge says 4mpg. I am half-expecting a warning on the display or a woman's voice saying, *'The manner in which you are driving is not consistent with Rolls Royce policy and falls far short of the requisite driving requirements...'* Meanwhile the Lambo gains ground. It sounds like an angry silverback gorilla of a husband, chasing after his cheating wife.

One hundred or so metres from the top and the Lamborghini is screaming up Upper Wimpole Street. The volcanic husband has caught up with his promiscuous wife. The noise is violent and intoxicating and I feel the adrenaline charge. Oh my good granny! I would give my week's wages for an hour in that. The lights at the intersection of Marylebone Road are red. I take the right lane, the footballer takes the left and pulls up alongside. The rear of the Lamborghini is consumed by deep corrosive anger, red hot and ready for a fight. 'You nutter!' he shouts.

I can't stop laughing. 'Not my fault you need driving lessons,' I laugh. 'Hey, take care and don't leave your fruit tree on the street corner, she won't be kept waiting long.'

'Nah, she's like a homing pigeon, I've no worries there,' he shouts.

I point to the direction he needs to take and the Lambo is gone, although not too far. Traffic, I'm afraid. London's average speed limit of twelve miles an hour renders the Lamborghini no faster than a Mini. I sincerely hope he has a TV on board, maybe even a DVD. It can take a couple of hours to get from one side of London to another. Oh, and petrol. I've seen supercars park up on double yellows because they ran out of gas. A full tank only takes them two hundred miles, roughly. The Arabs I worked for, racing around the West End in their supercars, filled up twice a night. That's a grand a week in petrol. Well it's not about money is it, petrol is free for them. Every time we mere mortals have to put petrol in our cars, we put money in their pockets so they can race past us on our way home from work. Who said life was fair?

I can't help thinking about that last stretch of road. The Aventador was awesome, utterly unhinged, but just remember, if you're fortunate enough to be presented with a clear stretch of road in London, don't risk it. You can almost guarantee that the police will be waiting with a camera gun. You know how the establishment is trying to get cars off of the road. The excuse is climate change. Diesel cars, congestion charge. Right now, someone somewhere is drawing up plans to extend the congestion zone. Beware!

Chapter 4

What goes around comes around

As I pull up back at the house, the King is standing there, using the railings to hold himself up. Great, he could have called. He's all dressed up in his cultural regalia. Always getting the hem stuck in the door.

'King, I thought you would have texted,' I say, walking up to him.

'No, I needed some fresh air and I thought you might be sitting outside.'

'Traffic wardens,' I reply sheepishly, 'got to keep circling.'

I help him down the steps and open the rear door. I can feel the heat engulfing the car. Oh no, I can smell the brakes. No wonder it took so long to stop. I try to usher him into the car quickly, hoping he won't notice. Then I feel the contrast of the cold cabin air meeting the heat from the engine. The heat is so intense it pushes the crisp, fresh climate-controlled air back to whence it came.

On shutting the door, I apologise to the Phantom, as she isn't best pleased. I remember an article saying that when a TV car presenter wanted to race a new Phantom with a new Bentley Mulsanne, Rolls Royce declined. I appreciate that, it's definitely not equipped for direct physical abuse.

'OK, the Dorchester please,' says the King.

On the back of the passenger chair is a marbled table which he pulls down and then opens up into a thirteen-inch TV screen. Now he has his own set of controls but is still not conversant with them. I set up *Sky News* to run from the back, so I am not distracted from my position. We roll down Harley Street and right down New Cavendish Street, heading for Baker Street.

'So, Paul,' says the King, 'when are you coming to Nigeria? You can come to the palace and I will have my staff look after you.'

'Umm, wonderful,' I reply.

'You don't sound too keen,' the King replies.

Now, I've had offers to work around the world, but I think humans can get attached to a particular way of living. I know of guys who have ventured to other countries for more cash, or danger money. No thanks! I remember an English football player whose character is larger than life. He had a guy who was head of his security for many years, and this guy decided to follow up a lead in the Middle East for a lot more cash. He had a wife and kids and left them temporarily to make enough cash so they could live in the UK and meet the rising cost of living. He lasted a week and one day before he was due to come home he interfered with the trajectory of a bullet on a mission. So he left a family who had to seek support from others.

A holiday in my own hotel I can just about cope with, but to work, I'm not so sure. Besides, I've no desire to be too far from our NHS. You hear of people getting themselves in all sorts of bother and no official seems to help them. No thanks.

'King, what a lovely thought. How could I possibly decline such an offer,' I say. 'Once I can find a week, I will send confirmation. Is it a lovely country?'

'Oh you won't regret it, it's amazing, I give thanks every day I wake up there,' he exclaims.

I sit thinking. I have friends all over the country inviting me to go and breathe some clean air, but I can't remember when I last left London, let alone the UK. I've been a chauffeur for around eighteen years and I've incorporated in my vocational skills the jobs of butler, chef and private security driver for Russians and Arabs. I am now just a chauffeur. When you get older you try to put some distance between you and the razzmatazz that runs along with it. Security is just as intense as it always, with everyone on edge. Just about every rich house has three or four cameras, plus high electric fences. Security paranoia is palpable. No one knows when, but aggravation at some point is expected.

Park Lane. How come no one wrote a song about London in the way Ella Fitzgerald sang about Manhattan, or Sinatra sang so affectionately about *New York, New York* and *Autumn in New York* and *Vermont?* Although I prefer the Billie Holiday version. London is just as romantic.

I love Park Lane. Actually, I remember owning four hotels on this street! OK, I meant on the Monopoly board. It's like a motorway with a central reservation. Not too long ago there was a gypsy invasion. Romanian beggars had no idea how exclusive the address was, they simply camped out on the central reservation. Gambled there, slept there, peed there, ate there. A coachload of impoverished migrants arrived amid a steady influx. A wonderful picturesque Renoir from within the framed windows of the Grosvenor's £10,000-a-night penthouse, where at first light over breakfast, the fortunate occupants were greeted with this picture…

All the major car companies line this lane. The most expensive hotels own the street. Over on the west side is a view of Hyde Park, lying in wait to offer an escape from the metropolis or even the maddening crowd. I can't imagine possessing enough cash to wake up on a misty Saturday morning here, a mixture of dew on the grass, leaves on the ground and the mist in the middle with the morning sun doing its utmost to burn away the clouds with its early morning strength.

The edge of this park running parallel to the Lane is littered with the fingerprints of different artists. As we roll down in the Phantom I can see the Joy of Life fountain, which replaced the marble boy and dolphin in the rose garden directly opposite Alford Gate North. The fountain is surrounded by 60,000 daffodils planted by a cancer charity.

I roll by Speakers' Corner in my magic carpet, its rear occupant deeply engrossed with *Sky News*. Right next to it is the Reformers' Tree, where people can assemble and debate anything with civility. Initially it was a tree which burned down in the Reform League riots of 1866. The stump became a notice board for political demonstrations. As a driver, I get to see works of art round London whenever I am in the vicinity. If I need a stroll, I go take a nosy. If I'm not working, forget it.

Oh, I know what that is. A nine-metre high sculpture of a man balancing on an elephant. I believe it's named the Dunamis Sculpture. Apparently it was made in Liverpool and symbolises the human struggle to achieve excellence and push boundaries in order to reach our goals.

There's a few more statues further down, and an abundance of them in the middle of the park. My favourite is in the latter half of the Lane near the Intercontinental and sits on a beautiful plinth of red and white marble. The occupant is the Right Honourable Lord Byron, poet and then politician. His hand rests under his chin, holding up his face. It appears he's reading, but he's simply lost in abstract thought. He was a Fellow of the Royal Society, an honour granted to individuals who make a substantial contribution to improvement of 'natural knowledge' – mathematics, engineering and medical science. There have been approximately 8,000 members in total, but only 1,700 still living. The statue is somewhat obscured now, but the original road design meant a panoramic view could be obtained and an even better fly-by view could be achieved from a double-decker bus. The trees are now obscuring it from view, and up close the dirt and grime of the polluted air smother it like a blanket.

We pull up at Dorchester Island amid a madness of people coming and going. There has been a heavy police presence lately, with all the uncertainty. Like buses, you don't see one for a long time then an abundance arrive at once. The increase is only for the rich areas – Knightsbridge, Mayfair, Chelsea. Need to keep the shoppers safe. Oh and those women who need to walk around with a couple of million pounds' worth of jewellery on their arm. And these are not just your conventional bobbies, these are armed to the teeth, with 9mm semi-auto machine weapons of mass destruction. The ammo is stored in a thirty-box magazine, with a 300-yard target engagement and an ambidextrous trigger. The Met were using the SiG MCX, not too dissimilar to the MP5s they use now, except that weapon was faulty and could fire without anyone pulling the trigger. Even in the safety manual it states, 'Failure to follow loading procedure of this firearm has the potential to cause serious bodily harm, or death if pointing at some man's goolies.' So yes, it could render a subject extinct up to 300 metres away with its accuracy. Now apparently the officers holding them work hand in glove with special forces, training with them week in week out. Some top gun shooters in training possess an eighty-seven per cent accuracy rate, but on our streets in a real-life situation, accuracy descends to around fifteen per cent. That why you'll see holes from stray bullets all over the place after an incident. Oh sorry I forgot, the guns were faulty.

I try and circumnavigate the mayhem of this left-hand turn, over a bus lane, round the island and left into a sort of courtyard, a supercar courtyard. All the best cars are trying to get in, only taxis going out. Lined up are roughly ten supercars, courtesy of the door porters. Once your car has lined up by the front door, all the doormen rush to rip the Phantom's door handles off. I always leave the central locking on, until I am ready – any tips to share, well, they're mine! I've been driving the miserable git all day. Invariably though, by the time I get around to hoist him out, the porters have wrenched the doors opened and they're in. One porter actually squashes his nose up to the glass because he can't see inside. 'Wrong side, you trollop!' His colleague gets it right and helps the King out.

'Paul, I need you to hold this spot till I come out, park up on the pavement right outside the door,' he says. Then he walks off. The porter looks at me, turns on his heel and walks back to his post, well, the front door. He opens the door for the King, then turns round. I walk up to him and say, 'I need this spot.'

'Yeah, bring it up closer,' he says, so I do. But I stay in the car and ignored him. Activity is brisk and robust around me, so I decide to settle down. Less than a minute and there's a tap-tap on the window. I reluctantly lower the double glazing.

'All right fella, you staying then?' the door porter asks.

'Well, my boss stipulated I should own this spot.'

'No problem,' says the doorman. 'Just pop out the car and talk to me.'

I really wasn't thinking. A spot outside the Dorchester front door is currency, plain and simple. There were a few cars in front of me, but just not the same. Hence why it was the only spot available. The doorman insisted I needed to be quick, if I got his drift.

'Come on, I said, it's a Roller!' With that he says, 'I tell you what, allow me to show you something.' He placed his arm on my shoulder and adjusted my trajectory – to the entrance. I was genuinely tight-lipped. Four shining, gleaming Phantoms were nudging their way into the small concourse.

'OK, hang on,' I say and scurry inside. The King is still in the reception area talking to his people. He turns and looks at me and instinctively puts his right hand inside his pocket. A batch of new fifty-pound notes emerges with a Costa coffee loyalty card on top. He hands over three of them. You see, with a man like him who is conventionally and invariably tight, there are things in this life which he will regard as important. He will favour the situation with a gesture, usually sufficient to display his gratitude. If he doesn't give you a tip, it's not because you did a crap job, you just didn't make him happy. If you possess the tools to render someone happy, they will reciprocate, it's automatic. The trick is knowing what it is in that moment you need it. A degree probably wouldn't go amiss. I've seen chauffeurs bend over backwards, literally, and still get nothing. You could make your CEO happy all day, you know you're expecting something come evening and then you accidentally scuff the Rolls wheels on the kerb. Some would ignore it, others would just change their minds and forget you were hanging on for a reward. A lot of CEOs would just sack you for that. On the spot and using disparaging vernacular to make entirely sure you received the message loud and clear.

I race back to the doorman, who is busy trying to locate a space for the most sumptuous cars. Strange though, if too many cars all at once becomes problematic, remember not because of cash as all will pay top dollar for their car to be seen, then the doorman looks for the prettiest woman or one he's familiar with in an attempt to establish some common 'teacher's pet' ground.

Our eyes meet and he walks over to me with a frown. 'What you saying, geeze?' I hand him the cash. He doesn't even look at it, but I can see his fingers and thumb seek confirmation. I wait for a response. For a second he looks through me as if to say, 'You sure that's all you've got for me?' I can see him thinking I'm holding back. Yes, I could have done with half of that, but hey ho. Some people have no element of logic to their actions.

He calls to two other porters, shouting, 'This car is not to be moved until I say!' Hmm... I watch him turn around and withdraw his wallet, then immediately shove it back into his back pocket behind his coat. He then forces his right hand into the inside of his long coat and obviously dispenses the cash in his own safe deposit box. His blinking wallet was full. I always wondered why grown men would want to stand up outside the hotel front door, all day in all weathers. Because they make loadsamoney! Why else?

Sitting here outside London's most desirable hotspot means it's inevitable you're going to meet a TV personality. I can sit and watch legally without appearing like some stalker – right by the front door, up close and personal.

Friday night. There are some Arabs about, but it is Ramadan, so most will still be back home in the Emirates. That's why I've noticed that all along Sloane Street, the shops are empty. They say that for each summer, what the Arabs provide is enough to keep the shops open all year, even with each shop paying around a million pounds per annum in rent!

So where is everyone? I've noticed a couple of heads of state and a few Arab royal sons and daughters. They can actually wander around almost liberally, as you really have to work for them, or be a tabloid spotter or a Middle East expert, to immediately identify royals or heads of state. That's why the kids race round all day annoying the police and the Knightsbridge locals by adding to the carbon footprint, because no one knows them. But I suppose it's their home to them, when they are here, usually just for the summer. The amount they spend in this country provides them with a few concessions. Knightsbridge would be like a boarded-up provincial high street if they were to pack up and leave town. I mean one of the UAE countries arrives back in the UK just after April showers in May, as with global warming, the seasons are a trifle behind. The Arabs start to trickle in in early May, so individuals from that particular country's royal family will fly in then. Cousins mainly, then closer family members and by mid-June the immediate family arrive. One of the over-eighteens will have his own jumbo jet, conventionally with four engines. It'll be a 747 kitted out in oak, royal blue seats and gold. If anything could bring a jumbo to its knees, it's gold – tons of it, not gold plated as the ordinary rich would have it. The head of family insists they all travel as safely as conceivably possible, and with four engines you can safely say that after an engine failure, at least one engine will still be functional, if not two or three. Yes, they could take a boat, but obviously there's serious playing time to be had in Knightsbridge, all those indelible tyre marks to leave over our double yellow lines. Remember, if the line colour is broken, the aliens can't stick a ticket on your car. Oh and cafés to drink dry, and bongs to smoke till five in the morning. So no, a boat is not an option.

We are talking of an army of staff to cover an entire summer of attending to the needs of an Arab royal family, from gardeners and swimming pool attendants to cleaners, housemaids and house servants – don't confuse the two, completely different job descriptions. Hairdresser, clothes dressers. Butlers, drivers who pick things up, chauffeurs who pick people up. Security, for the children, for the houses, for the VIP's personal protection. Then they have their own police and their own state secret intelligence service. There's no way they'd allow another country's police force to provide protection for the one man who provides for so many, no way! Oh, and its own agency to recruit this colossal amount of personnel. A man who is simply rich simply couldn't cope with this! Great times working for the Arabs, just with that so many drivers all competing for the lucrative jobs like dogs in a dogs' home, if you don't stand out, you don't eat.

It's so different now – no one tips, except for the Americans, bless them, and seldom do you see a driver getting punched and robbed around the corner any more because someone saw he'd had a windfall. Things have changed.

My phone's ringing. Where is the blinking thing? In the boot. I wonder who has interrupted my people watching. I was looking out for clients I had worked for. They all want to be seen in here.

OK, it's Clive. I started this game a couple of months after he began as a chauffeur. Nine months ago he was appointed to a nice position out in Basingstoke. His employer was also appointed CEO of a Public Limited Company. But I heard this mad CEO punched a colleague and manager a month after he had sacked Clive. Let me ring him back.

'Paul, how's things? Have you been watching the news?'

'Yeah, I have. That nutter punched someone. You know what Paul? He deserves all the nasty things in life coming his way.' Clive is angry. It's an unfortunate situation as Clive did whatever he possibly could to alleviate the stress in that man's life. But he was Scottish, always agitated. I believe Clive lost his job because his boss's wife was plain and simple racist. The CEO told him, after months of hard work, 'Look, I want you to know, I have lots of black friends and I've even got a family member who's of dual race.'

Clive asked him, 'So what's the problem?' The CEO said it was his wife who had the problem and she'd been bugging him with her 'discomfort' for a while. Clive was mortified. He loved the job. I suppose what goes around...

'So your old nutter of a boss punched a colleague,' I said.

'He sure did. I think it was his number three. They were in a bar, there was an altercation and a fight began. Actually, it was a punch without reciprocation. The other guy just went straight to the board and lobbied for his P45. An act of impropriety by the CEO. He pointed it out and the CEO attacked him. The papers' understanding of it was something to do with share price manipulation. Which often means obtaining a pecuniary advantage somehow. Probably buying his son's apartment in the Docklands with company petty cash. According to press reports, he was going to end up with a hundred and fifty million somehow.

Either way, he knew what he was doing. To be honest, I'm not surprised. He's an aggressive so and so. He'll be in the back on the phone, gunning for the blood of one of the line managers, male or female. He'd say, "I am so up for a fight today!" I did what I could for him.'

I interrupted, 'I remember on Friday nights you weren't sure which house you were driving back to. Where were they again?'

'Oh yes. Friday lunchtime, he would call the wife to see what house she was at, their estate in Coventry, the hideaway in Norfolk, the apartment in Mayfair or the family home in Scotland. Imagine at three o'clock on Friday afternoon, a choice of Norfolk or Scotland. Don't forget, I'd have to return, mentally prepared for that drive, first thing Monday morning, listening to the Eagles or Dolly Parton all the flipping way. He had a bad back and I performed physio on his lumbar region to get him going. Then I'd take him to his office, while I ran back and ironed his shirts and trousers. There were errands to run. When they had a dinner party, there was the setting up for the venue. For months, at least twice a week, I'd catch him looking at me. I always wondered why, what the look was for. Disappointment? Hate? Did he want to assault me? Now I know why. The first time I took his wife out, he pulled me aside and warned me that his wife didn't like fast driving, although she had six points on her licence. So naturally, I'm going to heed his advice, right? Well I did. I took her to the Mayfair flat and left. Before I got to the Covent Garden office, he called me on the phone and insisted I came to his office. He was angry that I hadn't listened. He said his wife had said I had gone too fast. I replied, "WHAT? She said WHAT?" He asked me straight out if I was calling his wife a liar. I just stared at him. I didn't know what to say. So I told him, I suppose it could be worse. He asked, how? I said well, she could have told you I put my hand on her leg. Who would you believe then?'

He raised his voice. 'And why would she lie?'

'Precisely,' I replied.

'She never let go from that moment. She kept the kettle boiling, wouldn't even look at me. Pure disdain. He was obviously convinced he was going to leave that company a seriously rich man, but I knew he was mortgaged up to the hilt. He was up to his neck in more nuts than a fruit cake. Who will employ him now? The longer he hung on to me, the angrier she became. Far as I'm concerned, they all got what they deserved. He got two sons, one he adores and the younger one he loathes. Once, instead of giving him a lift around the corner to the station he made him walk. Once when my phone was vibrating on the centre console, he grabbed it because it annoyed him and confiscated it. I'm sure he was unhinged, but he just loved a fight. Apparently, as he's taking the board to court, journalists have been tapping up staff in an attempt to dig dirt up on him.'

I interrupted, 'Leave it. Don't snitch on him, much as you feel he deserves to fall on his sword, just don't you be the one holding it. You did well to maintain your humility.'

'Well, I've been appointed to another position now, over in Buckingham,' says Clive.

'Delighted, Clive. You deserve it. Keep in touch and I'll shout you when I'm out that way.'

Which will probably be never. I never go anywhere unless work takes me.

So I'm still outside the Dorchester and there must be something going on. Think I'll check Google… nothing. Must be a private event. Supercars everywhere. I'll be back here on Monday actually with Mr Monaco. He loves it here. I have seen come past me here at the door three or four Formula 1 personalities. Drivers, a race engineer. Oh, Mr Button in his 599 Ferrari. Yes, it's absolutely gorgeous. His fruit tree is stunning, but I'd rather spend the night with the 599. Once you fill it up it will not complain till it's thirsty again. It won't backchat you, no sarcastic comments, just pure unadulterated fun.

OK, what's this? An Arab-looking lady in a McLaren. Now that's a first. Doorman taking the keys. A stunning woman pulling up in a Maserati Gran Turismo Sport. Sisters are doing it for themselves! She must have money. No one in their right mind would want a second-hand Maserati, they are just a money pit. Looks like an F1 car, sounds like an F1 car, is as expensive as an F1, just the performance is disappointing. Apparently they've even got diesels! Why, in a Maserati? Even worse, they make an off-road version. Like you live on a farm or occasionally you have to take your Chelsea tractor off road, so you purchase a Maserati? OK, each to their own.

A tap on my window makes me jump. I look around and see a chauffeur peering into my window, creating a vapour trail. I can't for the life of me remember him, there's so many people you meet. When he reminds me we worked for the Arabs and we were on the same team at Ascot together, I remember. This bonehead was provided with a special task of driving one of the top men and was given a Bentley 4x4. The rest of us were laughing because he was so enamoured with the vehicle that he kept playing around with it, getting in and out, winding down the windows, winding them up again.

The day's frivolities have drawn to a close and people are wandering back to their cars, whilst the rest of us are on fruit tree watch. Next thing this guy's sheikh comes into view and we all stand by our cars as if ready to assist. I look at the chauffeur and he's standing at the driver's door pulling the handle again and again. He's only gone and locked the blinking keys in the Bentley. Another driver is shouting 'How? HOW?' We work it out. On closing the boot there's two switches, one to shut the boot lid and one to lock the car. In most cars that have a touch button to close the boot, it's just that one button. The Bentley has two and he pressed the other one and locked the car.

Lots of women are either being chauffeurs or seeking valet service. One lady, in a Porsche 911 turbo S no less, tells the valet,

'If there's no parking, just stick it on the road, I don't mind a ticket, just watch the creatures don't lift it up and take it away.' She strolls past me and our eyes meet. She realises I'm a driver, turns and waits for the doorman. Funny thing is, he's on the other side chatting to another lady. The Porsche lady is on the outside waiting. She could use the other door, but no, she might break a fingernail. The other doorman clocks the discrepancy and runs to her aid. 'Ma'am, I do apologise.' He knocks on the window to alert his colleague, who turns and faces the door, pulling it open at the same time. He is full of apology once he has realised he allowed himself to become seduced by forbidden fruit and begins to gibber. 'I am so sorry ma'am. Anything you need, please let me know.'

She replies, 'Yes, there is something. Next time, if you see me coming, open the door!'

The two doormen briefly summarise the topic and returned to their duties. No tip for your skinny backside then.

Now this looks interesting. A black Phantom with distinctive number plates. I used to drive that car. Same chauffeur too, but he used to drive the wife. Same CEO then – real estate. He bought apartment blocks only in five postcodes around London. Santander, the Spanish bank, was his best friend until a Canadian investor offered him a place in their bed. His trajectory was absolute, like the way he rolled. Took no prisoners and had the vision to rise as fast as Rocket Man. After his schooling he worked in sales for Harrods, where his lust for the finer things in life manifested itself. His goals would appear frivolous, like he aspired to be the highest spending shopper at Harrods. Why, I have no idea. Lust, as I say. He just had to climb over everyone else. We all fixate on someone who inspires us, moves us, provides incentive, or plain and simple rivalry.

His first hurdle on the horizon was the word 'BILLION' in cash or on paper, he had to be associated with that word. There was someone else in town he had his eye on, a family that rose through the millions so quick that they annoyed and rattled those who had been digging these streets for gold for years. Strangely enough, the real estate guy decided to make contact one day, just to poke his nose in, to see if they could assist in his rise, or to simply get to retirement quicker than the next man. This family offered him some advice, which the real estate guy took and used to his detriment. He woke up a few days later to find an invoice on his floor for just over a quarter of a million, with a PS at the bottom – 'In the interests of all parties, we seek the remittance within five working days.' The words he later used were not for public consumption before the watershed! The saying goes, there's no honour amongst thieves, and there's certainly none amongst millionaires.

Just looking at his face. He hasn't changed, albeit somewhat fatter. Miserable so and so. It's true, money doesn't make you happier. He has a beautiful wife, absolutely gorgeous, like something you'd put on the fireplace to look at. You know on TV when the commentator says, 'this next footage contains flashing lights' so all those with epilepsy can close their eyes. That's what it's like walking down Bond Street on a Saturday afternoon, diamonds dazzling you every five seconds.

In his attempt to become Harrods' highest-value shopper, this chap would buy some hideously priced items, like chandeliers that couldn't remotely hold a candle to his wife aesthetically. His house was filled with diamond stuff. However, he only ever made number five, the fifth highest spender at Harrods.

His favourite colour was black. All his cars were black and it made his house look like a mafia residence. All who worked for him knew he could and would humiliate you if what he asked you to do was not done to his liking. I remember a man who was a marble tiling specialist. He was finishing off the outside of his house when the real estate guy reminded him he was a day overdue, irrespective of whatever problems he might have encountered and once he was finished, not to bother him with an invoice, because he wasn't getting paid. Oh, he was nasty. I feel the more people fight for a living or even for a divorce, the more resentful they become. He really needed putting out of his misery.

My initial encounter with him was at my interview. Zero eight hundred hours at his office. I spoke to the receptionist and then took my seat in his dark wooden foyer. Twenty minutes into my wait, he came out, spoke to the receptionist and walked back into his office. An hour later, he came out with a couple of staff members. He stood and talked for around three minutes and then walked back into his office. An hour and a half later, he came out and walked down some stairs. His other chauffeur came in and asked me if I'd had my interview yet. I replied no. He said, 'It's OK, this is how he is, if you get the job, you'll get used to it.' So immediately, I was obtaining a picture of my prospective employer which I wasn't sure I liked. As a chauffeur, first and foremost, you try never to aggravate the hand that pays your mortgages, or rent in my case, and you should never aspire to be loved by the boss for what you do. But he who feeds the crocodile should at least expect to be eaten last...

Two hours and fifty minutes after I arrived, I got up and walked outside. What was going on? Was this a test? Was he just ignorant, letting everyone know he was boss? All his cars outside were black. All had personal number plates. His McLaren sat right outside the door. If people did not know he was the boss, then they were blind.

So as I stretched my legs walking round the car park, I looked at an office below ground and there he was at his desk. He looked comfortable, with no intention of moving. I wondered if he had forgotten my interview. Strange kind of office though, just below the car park level. It looked a dark room, with hardly any light. It was like a scene from *CSI* where the CEO of the company is found at his desk, lifeless. No impact wound, no marks on the skin. I know, I watch too much TV. Then right at that moment, he looked up and saw me. I stared back and his eyes retreated. I turned on my heels and returned to the foyer. Two hours and eleven minutes past – well, it's not like I'm not used to waiting. I'm a chauffeur, it comes naturally.

He returned, and as he ascended the stairs, his main driver greeted him. A conversation began which was taken into the main office on ground level, and I think I heard them discussing the McLaren. From what I gathered, the chauffeur hadn't checked the oil level. Loud voices reverberated around the office and the chauffeur stormed out. It was like a lovers' tiff. It really was strange that he raised his voice as loud as his boss, then just walked out, telling him to do it himself. Now I'm thinking, the driver must have something on him to get away with talking to him like that, some kind of currency which provides him with a get out of jail card.

After two hours and twenty minutes, he asked if I would like to come into his office. Well, after all this time, it would have been rude not to.

After the interview he decided that with my CV, I had what it took to get into his office. The question was, did I have what it took to stay? I had to drive him into London, and that clinched it.

I stayed for a year, but it wasn't an easy one. He was certainly a challenging alpha male, in his own world with no one to challenge him or his vision. He lived by his own code of ethics, not answerable to a soul. The job could have been fantastic, but all along you could feel his disdain with regard to his chauffeur. If he wasn't so busy, he'd stick the satnav on and drive himself, and drive over you if he saw you in the street.

So does one make allowances for someone who is so driven? Do the emotions he displays come as standard, living that crazy kind of life?

Two days into the tenure, I began to learn who he really was on the inside. He called his in-house chef and informed her that he had a couple of very important friends coming round, and instructed her to make a gourmet meal. The poor girl had worked incredibly hard all day. When he and the wife and friends got in, he didn't even look to see what she had cooked. At that moment he decided that they were all going out. He told his wife to tell the cook to clean up and go home. Then off they all went to Zuma in Knightsbridge. The wife looked at the cook and wanted to apologise, but she couldn't be seen to be the weakest link in the family, so she didn't.

He was a loner. He seldom invited people round to his home, and whoever came he had invited. Even the wife's parents required an invitation. If he went to a do, he would arrive bang on time, all to his own aggrandisement, just so people could ask who he was. His business associates were kept close and recycled. Trips to St Tropez and Courchevel invariably involved the same party. He simply trusted no one. He got any one he wanted and paid what he felt they deserved. Drivers barely got the steam off his backside. But hey ho.

What is interesting is that he met another businessman down in Surrey, who must have been his twin brother. Same appearance, same size, same colour hair, same round as a pound face and just as ruthless on the inside. He also had nothing but disdain for those who worked for him. His wife was something words could not describe. This guy annoyed his son's private school because he would fly his son in by helicopter. I mean, it was only a Robinson 44, nothing major. See, wealthy people just don't conduct themselves like this. Unfortunately his ruthlessness knew no bounds, and finally his own behaviour held him to account one day. He had some labourers working around the house and they ran over time. He unceremoniously subjected them to a tirade of abuse, so the young guys felt unjustly dumped upon. That night, a window was left open.

Now try and imagine the size of the house. One hundred metre drive, thirteen-foot walls, sitting on sixty acres of land with ten bedrooms. On the house side of the drive were garages with apartments up above. At the end of the garages was a kennel housing two huge guard dogs. So that night, at roughly one o'clock in the morning, four masked men scaled the walls, poisoned the dogs and made it into the house via a small window that had been left unlocked. They squeezed through a small window and dropped four feet on to a white Valentino tiled floor. As darkness enveloped the ground floor, the family slept soundly one level above. As the men ascended the white marbled staircase, they were suddenly cognisant of their surroundings. The smell of opulence was everywhere. Delicate blueish-white stair lights that resembled stars guided their feet. On the landing, the carpet under their feet resembled freshly-fallen snow. The evidence of no expense spared was all around. Yet that wasn't their concern. Currency was – along with getting out alive.

As they were creeping along the landing, someone walked into a cabinet, which infuriated the others. They all turned to assist in the event of something unexpected. It was then decided that he would be the lookout and would remain on the landing. One checked the cabinet with a flashlight and peering through the glass, he saw that it was filled with high-power weapons. They took the weapons and the family were immobilised in under a minute. The raid of the house was absolute and the gang ran away with a quarter of a million in cash. The house was filled with dispensable currency, such was the arrogance of the owner.

The family were fortunate that night. They lived to see another day. But what it displays is that an individual's demise doesn't always come about the way they would expect.

These days, it should be obvious that, just as doctors need nurses, a CEO should value the employees. Especially if they display competence at their job. One CEO exercised a revolving door attitude where staff were concerned, because he didn't trust anybody. He actually felt that keeping staff on their toes made them concentrate more on their jobs. But to go back to the medical analogy, how on earth is a nurse meant to extract blood from a patient's arm or spot a life-threatening illness when the boss is harassing her unnecessarily? With so few jobs available, people will take a vacancy knowing it could be problematic. Look at some football clubs. The managers know it's only for a few games, but they still apply. Life has become like that, like the demand for fast internet. People's consciences have become desensitised. Seldom do many care regarding the welfare of others under their care.

One thing I can't see going down well is a workplace pension for all staff, even if there is only one employee. In hard times, the company has to conduct itself like the poor man and start looking at the bank accounts before they spend. That's when they realise that the only healthy thing about their company is the pension pot! Temptation surrounds us.

When things get tough for a chauffeur, we often look for a toilet to hide in. I was in Claridges the other day and just needed to run out. I was desperate. So after giving a tip to the bell boy, who actually deserved it, I made for the urinals. As I was standing there, a well-dressed man darted into the cubicle. Doggy steak tartare maybe? Next thing, I was engulfed by a rising stink coming from behind me. I began to panic, as I didn't want the scent to cling to my clothes. I walked out quickly and said to the bell boy, 'You so deserve a tip from him in the cubicle for putting up with that.' Was that written on the job description, rich people will make you earn your minimum wage? Look, I don't have many clothes and what I do have are not expensive, but I point blank refuse to go around smelling of fart. Even clients with dogs will invariably smell a human fart over a smelly dog, and they always act like someone passing wind is a criminal offence! 'Oh my goodness, even my dog doesn't smell like that!'

I'm actually feeling a little peckish. Oh, and I haven't paid my congestion charge. It's only eleven pounds fifty, but each day it adds up. Tomorrow, Saturday, I wouldn't have to pay for, but the garage is full and I'm definitely not parking on the road, with street parking in the West End exceeding the minimum wage. So I will have to park in Golders Green, the only borough in London exempt from that phrase 'parking permits only'. Grab a bus to the nearest tube, then take the Northern Line into the madness.

For afternoon tea it's cashew nuts and Volvic water. It's enough. I can't be running to the toilet every five minutes, especially sitting in the next cubicle to Mr Steak Tartare. Some people in those cubicles sound desperately ill. You feel like asking, 'You OK mate, I could call an ambulance for you?' 'No thanks, just making an omelette!' Then you have to find the right toilets, with tiled floor, cleaned regularly, warm, with newspapers and stuff on the wall to look at.

Couples in relationships should really provoke one another straight off. Saves time and effort. Otherwise you spend six months tiptoeing around each other, then one day after spending a whole night you see her in the morning. 'Oh, I didn't know you looked like that!' Or it's, 'Why do you leave toothpaste in your mouth after brushing, why not spit and wash your mouth out? I never knew you did that!' Or, 'Wow, you get through three bottles of wine a night!'

Why do celebrities break up so often? They have everything, adoring fans, dollars, lifestyle… I can't work it out. Recently I read an article on why a couple, who were both actors, broke up. Apparently he said to his wife, 'Look honey, there's a new actress on set and she's a little nervous about the bedroom scenes, so we're gonna book into a quiet hotel up in the hills and practise!' So he's seeking permission from his wife to spend the weekend with a young and beautiful actress in a hotel bedroom, no film crew and no video camera, I'm guessing, so he can provide her with insight on how not to be shy with him, and how not to react to the camera when their naked bodies are entwined. See how distorted life can get, for some? How much of that can a wife really take? I know a British actress who's regularly in bed on screen with different men. She's been married for years, so what – he likes it? Maybe he watches? Or maybe he's just a plain and simple PIMP!

I've just greeted an old client, who was with a business friend, so I couldn't talk with him. I haven't seen him in years. I worked for him for over a year, when he had just received his inheritance, which was enough for him to play along with the big boys. I remember as a newcomer he couldn't get into the right places, so he tagged along. When he was out with his own friends, he'd turn up at top restaurants and night clubs using his friends' membership. But as he wasn't with the member, he'd get blown out of the water when the bill came – a nightclub table for six people would have a minimum spend of roughly six grand for the evening. He'd somehow end up paying double. He really couldn't handle drink, and it began to eat away at his short pockets. I think he believed he had hit the big time because he was associating with big-time people. He purchased his main house off the back of Park Lane and bought a number of apartments in and around the West End. He got married and had two kids, and life was great. But then he began to spend. Nights out, cars. The wife partied like she had a money tree in the basement. I struggled to understand that this guy had been provided with a platform to play on, bypassing years of hard work, ulcers, gallstones and maybe a triple heart bypass, and had then thrown it all away. For all of us, life comes down to a few short moments, and for him, that was surely one of them.

It was unfortunate that the banks foreclosed on his portfolios because he couldn't balance the books. His family were seriously wealthy, but after his frivolous display of ineptitude, they arrived at the conclusion that he wasn't worth saving. I suppose it would have been better if he had not become acquainted with that level of status, rather than getting far and failing.

I did hear he found the appetite to return and he got lucky – he found a liquid divorcee, an old friend of his apparently. No honour amongst business associates then, or even friends for that matter. On becoming a divorcee, she also became a stray, in the eyes of a carnivore. So, without thinking twice, he unceremoniously dumped the wife and kids overboard, with a promise that as soon as he was back on his feet, he would attend to their needs. What is it, ignominy, shame, the realisation that as a poor man in the United Kingdom he would also be labelled a disease? The label meant far more to him than getting a job at an estate agent's and providing for his family. Anyway, he got another chance. I wanted to talk with him, but he gestured to me to phone him.

Someone once asked him if he was Russian, because when he went out, his pocket was filled with fifties. He loved them. Sadly, the only likeness to Russians was that his money was new. Lucky he was provided with another go. This isn't Monopoly, you can't just press the reset button. Meeting that lady was eye through the needle stuff. He had to think on his feet, stay with family, roll his sleeves up and display his fists. Or abdicate the sphere he had cultivated and swear allegiance to a woman who had provided him with solace and a get out of jail card – when you pass go pick up your cash and your new car and start your new life.

I know what he will say, as he is a Catholic: 'God must still love me, I hadn't called on him in a while but he turned up in the end.' Now that's a statement many make and I've always struggled to see how that works. How can God give one person wealth and leave another in abject poverty? How can a musician receive an award and say, God won it for me? In Kensington rich and the poor live side by side. They have abundance, yet many in Africa don't get the rain they need, let alone food. So even if we don't do what God wants us to do, will he still help us?

A mother will say to a teenager, 'I am going to pop out for an hour but I need you to finish your homework.' She leaves and expects to return home to find it done. She returns to find he's done the washing up, hoovered, even run her a bath... Very few of us follow the model of Christ, so why call ourselves Christians?

Even a boxer will pray to God to help him win. Why? Why would God help a man batter and bruise another human for gain?

Christians should know, if the Bible means anything to them, that all humans have a value to God. If you realise that, you'll know he hates violence. Psalms 11 Verse 5 God examines the heart of the righteous and the wicked, yet he hates anyone who loves violence.

Music playing: Chopin's Prelude Op. 28 in E minor. I'm daydreaming. You do that a lot waiting for clients. Nothing specific, quite random really. A quiet holiday somewhere, a Nissan GTR. It works. It's better than shopping. Shopping works for the depressed soul, but there's nothing remotely like sitting aboard a live smoking hot Exocet of a car. Just because someone is sad, it doesn't mean you can attach the 'depressed' label to them. People are so annoying when they make that assumption. 'Cheer up, it may never happen!' I know the world is a nicer place when everyone is happy, but can we simply impose our desires on others?

I hear a civilised commotion developing and look to my right. Oh, the King is on his way back. He looks tired from all the pats on his back. Early night for me then. He must want to return home. I'm confident he'll have a Kentucky or a rack of lamb waiting, or even a couple of game birds with a nice suntan from the oven. He can guarantee they'll be just right, as no one in the family eats before he picks up his knife and fingers. Then and only then, in true Serengeti style, will they all let battle commence.

I ignite the V12 and an array of lights and beeping sounds alerts Houston that we're ready for lift-off. I set the rear TV to the evening news, then disembark to allow my client to board. Doors open and I'm waiting. OK, people bowing. Outside the Dorchester people will stare. A double-decker comes to a halt at the traffic lights, filled with Friday night commuters, all staring, while people are still bowing to him. I just fiddle with my cufflinks. I really should have put my blue ones on... OK, he's in. No, I'm not opening the windows so they can exchange goodbyes for another thirty-five minutes!

'Oh Paul,' the King calls, 'the window isn't working. Is the child lock on?'

I look, and for some reason, the window child lock is indeed on. Good heavens! So I allow him his long kisses good night. Ten minutes later we make our exit. It's beginning to get a trifle busy as the Arab men display their fun side, nocturnally. Lamborghinis, Ferraris in strange colours, like turquoise with pink leather seats, the odd Aston Martin – I say odd because it's seldom that anyone other than the British drive them. Apparently you wouldn't see one in Monaco. The odd one maybe. Or the 'Brick' – sorry, Range Rover. Just a British thing. Oh, and the Chinese. They love British stuff.

A couple of Ghosts are taking up space, mainly because they are driven by individuals. You'll never see a Phantom driven by its owner. If the owner's driving, it's because he's just had a hissy fit and punched the chauffeur, who's gone home by public transport.

As I pull out on to Park Lane, the King calls from the behind. 'Paul, I bought a building down in Peckham to do with my church charity. We have a congregation meeting with some Board members I need to spend some time with.'

'Now, King?' I asked.

'Yes please. We have an hour. Can we make it?'

Friday evening, rush hour... hang on, did he say Peckham? You'd struggle to get from one end of Mayfair to the other in an hour. If you're a black cab driver that would be a nice sum of cash for an hour's work.

I begin to run the route in my mind: Hyde Park Corner, Victoria, Vauxhall Cross, Oval, Camberwell and Peckham. Eventually. The distance could only be two miles but it's the time of day that matters. It's 4.9 miles in a relatively straight line, at an average of 10mph on London roads. It's twenty-seven minutes by the satnav, but that's travelling at what the speed limit on each road allows. Inside London it's 20mph, just outside it goes back to thirty. Double it, fifty-four minutes to be accurate. Not too bad.

Tedious, bumper to bumper traffic. Yes, I'm used to it, but there are some miserable eggs in the boxes all around me. There's a woman with two kids in the car in front. It's twenty-six degrees and her windows are open, no climate control. Kids looked stressed in the back. Not funny. So when I feel like I'd rather be somewhere else to alleviate my discomfort, there's a always another picture to place the one I'm looking at in perspective.

Although I couldn't drive this if I was tired. No chance. All drivers get tired, and you simply have to manage it. You can't just go home. I've had to get use to seventeen-hour days. Each driver will have their own management programme. But in this car, you have to be alert and sharp. It's such a huge car, it's actually a danger. On a family size four-door saloon, the angel sitting at the front of the Phantom's bonnet would reach over the side door and the windows, so in an accident, this could do real harm. Not to mention its weight, just under 3,300 bags of sugar.

'Paul,' the master calls. He's a calm person, which makes it easy to spot when he's getting irritated. But I know what he's going to ask.

'I think I can pre-empt what you're going to ask me and at the moment, there's no bus lane,' I reply. 'But there will be in a minute or so.'

'Ah, great minds think alike,' says the King.

It really isn't difficult to anticipate or interpret a wealthy man's thoughts. As a servant, it's part of the job description. But at times the initial job description extends somewhat. In some cases the job changes altogether. You apply for a chauffeur's position and end up as a butler. Or a cleaner. Or a courier. Or a hedge cutter, which then turns into, 'Oh, you may as well run the lawnmower round.' Or, 'Can you change the light bulb, as I can't really reach it?' See, the rich man wants his workers to earn their cash. No more sitting around waiting, no more lunch breaks. Forget zero contracts, it's zero nothing. Most employers will politely inform you at some stage, 'Oh, it's nothing personal but...' to convey that they are capable of driving their own cars. A horrid, dismissive line, almost as much of a cliché as your spouse reminding you, 'Look, I didn't ask you to!' A nanny will tell you about extra-curricular work. They have to have parenting skills, not forgetting the Nanny is a child herself. Most employers want a 'follow the fashion accessory' nanny. Oh, she must be bilingual. That's a prerequisite! And a social worker. And a psychologist. Must be well versed in rich kid 'never say no' syndrome. Having to accept 'GIMME' as a word. Servants, expect the unexpected.

Crawling past the Oval, I can see a bus lane seventy metres or so on. I hate it, I really do. Great. Police car behind, fighting his way through the traffic on the other side of the road. Wonder if they took one look at the traffic and thought, 'Nah, let's blues and twos it... OK, maybe not, there's an ambulance behind. With the two running in tandem it must be something serious. Right, across the intersection... OK, I am not going to mention the escape route, so see if he remembers. Another police car. Right, this must be serious.'

'Can you see any more police cars, Paul?' asks the King.

'No. Why?'

'I can see the lane,' he replies. 'I don't know why people don't use it. It's just a fine. Nothing serious!'

No, not serious, well does he want to try? This isn't liberated Africa. Is he acquainted with the word anarchy? Great – here we go. The Phantom rolls down the lane. I'm imagining being behind the camera, because whoever it is will ticket you for having two wheels, just two wheels in the lane, but this must appear like blatant disregard. The Phantom's on a stroll, wafting along like it had shares in the bus lane. Drivers are looking on with incredulity. Oh no. I am so embarrassed.

Another police siren… I pull back into line but no one's letting me in. OK. Now I'm begging, 'It's not me, I'm only the driver.' No one gives a stuff. Police car goes by, so I carry on.

We make it to Camberwell and the atmosphere has well and truly changed. There are some streets that are liveable, but not many. From here onwards, there's no ambiguity as to where you are. Like in Kensington, one minute billionaires' row, the next, abject poverty. South London really only holds two splendid boroughs, Wimbledon and East Dulwich. Actually Blackheath isn't bad, just not supported by favourable neighbours.

Heading for the centre of Peckham on the main Peckham Road, police activity is alive. The entrance to a side road had been taped off. Getting closer, the scene doesn't look right. Police with guns pacing up and down and around like mice on crack. As the whole road comes into view there is what appears to be a body on the ground covered by a dark sheet. There's a black youth in the back of a police van, inside a cage, with the outer door ajar.

The King moves to the edge of his back sofa and asks what can I see, and I explain. But for the King, coming from Africa, it's an all too familiar story. You know when people say, 'Oh, I've seen it all before, or worse,' you think, OK, whatever. I believe him when he says it brings back memories he'd rather leave at the back of his mind. To be honest, from the scars on the front of his face, I'm inclined to believe him.

We drive past, slowly, and on to the King's venue. I'm hungry, but all I can see along the sunset strip is deep-fried chicken outlets and they look worrying. Poor chickens. I would love to know where all these chickens come from. Recently KFC ran out! That was amusing. I can't see anything healthy at all. My cashew nuts are not sustaining me and anyway I read the packet earlier and the contents listed nine grams of sugar. Why is their sugar in everything? No salt, but an abundance of sugar. No wonder my stomach has been bothering me. I only take it in the morning with a large cup of peppermint tea. Two teabags, mind, and a tablespoon of honey. So I think the cashews have got to go.

As my mind wanders, all day, every day, it's difficult not to unravel. People watching. Driver watching. Car watching. Bird watching, I can't help thinking, if I keep my mind active, it will keep Alzheimer's at bay. You never know.

The King summons my attention. 'Paul, on the left, can you see the building, like a venue hall? That's the place, on the left.' He's excited, displaying no signs of fatigue.

I always assess my immediate surroundings and even a fool would realise that this car will attract undesirable attention. I couldn't stay here.

'King,' I called. Will you want me to stay right here outside the main door?'

'Er, that would be a good idea. Would it be OK?'

I look back, surprised by his answer. I know it's not my car but, I'd still like to get home in one piece.

'Being honest King, I'd like to get somewhere off this main street if you're OK with that.' But then I'm thinking, even a side street round here can't be much better.

I help the King disembark and he is greeted by two of his wives and other parishioners, all jovial and ready for an evening service, when everyone will end up putting money into his church charity.

So off I go in search of quiet, like Goldilocks going off into the woods, except the three bears were somewhat friendlier towards her. Just hope I don't bump into anyone in this jungle.

I turn to move the car from its spot to realise that I have an audience. We are right across from the market and Burger King. Oh, and a bus stop.

The scene I witnessed not so long ago begins to dominate my thoughts. Whoever was lying on the ground, his family will be there by now, emotions running high. I remember that scene in the movie *Ghost*, when the guy died after an attack and his soul ascended above his dead body, levitating over the scene. Then I wonder if the soul of whoever it was lying on the ground, what if his soul could elevate above himself, what would he say? To himself, to his family. To the friends who probably ran off and left him. To his attacker, if he was on his own. It's dreadful what's going on. There's no fear of consequence any more. Gang violence is unbridled. At the moment, they're at war with each other. What happens when the demons within compel them to disseminate their violence? Cognitive behaviour therapy won't work. It must be difficult for the youth of today to articulate their emotions, except for the one they consistently exhibit – anger. A lot of people display how they feel through music – anger, dissatisfaction, hatred and the heaviest thing to lift in the world, loneliness. When my friend Clive and I meet we listen to a lot of music. I remember a few songs of his, one from his favourite artist, Damien Marley, called *Gunman*.

Long ago I was working for a news channel. One night I took home an executive of the company and a well-known black newsreader. I dropped the newsreader off round the corner in Holborn and took the executive home. He then said to me, 'I'm sure you know who that was and you'll probably have the pleasure of dropping him off occasionally. If and when you do, just make sure he receives the treatment, would you? He's such a lovely fellow.'

I replied that it was strange to see him in the flesh as opposed to on the box all these years.

'He's a marvellous chap. A product of a good environment. It's a shame there aren't more like him. A definite model to follow for ethnic minorities in character and stature.'

Now I'm thinking there's an abundance of talented individuals in deprived areas who either don't know or haven't been provided with the opportunity. I think if you took anyone from the ghetto and took them up to the studios of a TV channel and provided them with the skills required to be a newsreader and to inject a little more incentive, a pay cheque of half a couple of million, no, even half, no let's say a quarter of a million per annum and see if they don't display gratitude. Being on the rocks induces an assortment of physical, psychology and emotion problems. I know. Some make it. A lot more don't. It's a shame there's so much violence between the nationalities. People need to adopt a more collective family unit, like the Asians, because I can feel a storm coming.

Hard Times, Curtis Mayfield

This song is about a brother who left the troubles of inner-city New York to live in unfamiliar surroundings, upstate with family. Curtis Mayfield is another of Clive's favourite singers. Looking out of the window, he spots a brother...

I find a dirty-looking Chinese takeaway and order a vegetable fried rice, with extra egg and green peppers (not the hot ones mind) and a parking spot a couple of streets away. It's early evening, but there's still energy in the daylight. I switched the Phantom engine off, but within seconds the heat begins to push away the cold climate inside the cabin. I think that just helped to close my eyes. I nodded off and found myself drifting in and out of consciousness. You can't just imagine being under the duvet at home, it's so difficult to come back from a deep sleep. Now, you know when you're asleep but not sure if you're dreaming? In my dream I was looking up and out of a glass window and there were five black faces staring at me. *Oh no*, I thought, *have I died and ended up in the wrong place?*

I frown and try desperately to reverse the state I'm in. Then it becomes apparent, the faces are real. Panic mode, trying not appear worried. Check doors locked. Switch engine on, serious face, lower window two inches. Fortunately, they are college students on their way home. Don't kids have uniforms these days? They don't seem to be familiar with the car, as one youth describes it as a Noah's Ark. Another asks if he can move in. Another says his dad would like it. Kids of today are attracted to fast-moving things, supercars, hypercars. This bunch look like they'd have more fun taking a baseball bat each to it. I back up and float off.

I find a place to hide further up the road in Camberwell, a trifle more civilised and my anxieties have subsided. Yeah, I know, should get a lottery ticket. I could have woken up to no wheels. That would have provided comedy relief.

Text message. Who's this from? It's from Clive saying 'keep your windows closed'. Funny so and so. Now he's sending another of his jokes. Chauffeurs send rubbish to each other all the time to jam your inbox. Clive is saying he got a parking ticket, three in a week, with a picture of his car, so he took one, placed it on the table, wrote a cheque. Put them both on the table and took a picture. In satirical mood, he places them all in an envelope and sends them to the Met ticket office. What a plonker! Why would he do that? He waited a week and forgot about it. Two weeks later he found a white envelope on the floor. He opened it and inside was a picture, just a table with a spotlight and under the spotlight was a pair of handcuffs... Clive didn't delay and sent the cheque. Fortunately that joke was mild, text banter can get a little over the line at times.

It's been a long day and I'm growing weary. The fire within that used to thrust me out of bed has begun to diminish. One on one clients can get a bit tedious. The down time is always good and should really be used wisely, but there isn't always down time, so you need to know how to manage your day. Normally there's things to look at, like at my favourite spot, by Peter Jones, Symons Street SW1 at the back of Kings Road. It's like playing tennis with your eyes. Right now I'm on a street that's filled with terraced houses. You can see why the wealthy stay near the West End.

Finally at 2100 my phone rings. The King has remembered he has a home to go to. So I jump into the back and set up the television. He likes it ready as he gets in.

He has wife number two and wife number three with him. They are all jolly – seems like a good evening enjoyed by all. At times, being with the same client all day, you look forward to going home, some space to re-energise. A taxi driver simply clocks off when he wants to, but a chauffeur never knows when he's finished.

Once we're out of Peckham, the wives are joyous that their evening was a success. I know it was spiritual but I'm way too tired to engage. Soon the Two Degrees are louder than the TV. Now conventionally, the wives are under strict instruction not to think for themselves, let alone become creative. The King says something in African, and the exuberance suddenly subsides. It's rare for him to use his native language, and it's a clear indication that they were way too loud.

We hit traffic at Vauxhall Cross, but other than that it's a swift ride back to Harley Street. I drop them off, then go to fill the Phantom up with petrol – again. This will take £1,000 a week, easy. Delighted it's not mine. I throw it back in the garage and take the keys back.

Leaving London always helps the mind. Too much time in the same circle makes it difficult to evaluate. You need space away. Like with a relationship in trouble, you don't linger in each other's faces, to get away, unravel and hopefully things become clearer. It's an hour and a half to drive home. Now that I'm on my own I can put my music on, make phone calls and plan for tomorrow.

I'm hoping there's no traffic. Please no traffic. But it's Friday night on the M1. The rings annoy me, the red ring above that stipulates the speed you can do. For no reason the sign will slow drivers down to 40 and you're looking for workmen, or an accident, but there's nothing. Yet some drivers are whizzing by me, like they know something I don't. As a professional driver, I cannot afford points. The odd fine, fair enough, they're inevitable, but not points.

So that's it – a day in the life of a chauffeur. I run around after the rich and then forget to pay my own congestion charge. Oh great. It's only £12 but if you forget it goes up to nearly £100. Although I drive the clients' cars, never my own, they all take a least a couple of weeks to pay up.

It's a funny life we lead and I've been chauffeuring far too long. But my gratitude toward the job has never diminished, I've never taken it for granted. A way of life is what it is, although it doesn't feel like I have a life at times. This is all I know, and it's way too late in my life to even think of trying another vocation. Although none of us were promised tomorrow, I'll take this opportunity to thank my stars for the air I breathe and I'll be very grateful if I wake up to see tomorrow.

Chapter 5

Of God, mice and men

07:21. Music playing. Eagles, *Desperado.*

Well it's far too late. If you have not met the right woman by the time you get to my age, forget it. Enjoy singleness. Besides, in the shower this morning, I think I found something ugly. I have got cellulite. How the hell? I thought that was a woman thing. Always something.

I am currently at exit 4 on the M1, Edgware junction, heading for exit 2, A1/A41. Roads are busy Saturday morning. Drivers spend all week on the road. Work, courier, school run. You'd think people would relish a rest day. One client I had been working hard all week, so when he got home the kids were in bed. He had two unruly boys. One Saturday morning they kicked off his bedroom door and demanded he spend some time with them. He agreed, but two hours later they were still waiting, so they called their uncle and asked if he could take them to McDonald's. He agreed and said fifteen minutes. The boys got ready and grabbed Dad's wallet. As it was full, they thought, if we take one note, he won't notice, so they took a fifty-pound note.

Dad came down and was ready to go when he saw his brother on the drive. The kids explained and they all went together. Dad's brother drove while Dad decided to pay for the meal. Looking in his wallet, he extracted all the cash and gave it to his brother, as he owed it him for not having his card at the restaurant three nights prior. Now he knew he had one fifty in the bunch and could not find it. He remembered his brother saying the boys had called him and invited him out for a late breakfast at McDonald's. Dad then realised the boys had taken his money, and he was mad. He explained to his brother what had happened and devised a plan to get them back. They drove to McDonald's and slowed down, which heightened the boys' exuberance. They got to the driveway, and drove off. Apparently the boys looked at each other, thinking it was a joke. But no joke, McDonald's was fading away in the rear view. They did this four times, till the boys realised they had been rumbled. 'OK Dad,' they said, 'look, just, we don't see you, we know you paying the bills keeps you out all hours, but what about us?' So the week doesn't stop for some. The weekend is the new week!

I spent ages looking for an Oyster card this morning. Found one, just not sure anything is on it. About to find out. Turning off at exit 2, this is my favourite borough in London, Temple Fortune. It's just so civilised. No parking restrictions, guarantee your car won't get scratched or spat on. I always find a spot to park. Lock up and walk to the bus stop. Ten-minute ride down to Golders Green station. It's a while since I've done this. I conventionally drive to the client's house, swap cars and off. There's some lovely shops along here but hang on, they're all closed. The bakery is normally open first thing – oh, I get it, Saturday and it's Shabbat, one of the priority Jewish observances held weekly from Friday sunset to Saturday sunset. For those unfamiliar with this, a brief description as to its importance. A Shabbat elevator is an elevator which works in a special mode, operating automatically, to satisfy the Jewish law requiring Jews to abstain from operating electrical switches on Shabbat (the Sabbath). An elevator may be marked with a sign noting that it is specially configured for Shabbat observance. There are several ways the elevator works (going up and down), stopping at every floor, stopping at alternate floors, or rising to the top floor and stopping, while going down. Shabbat is regarded with such importance that an individual can't even push the button on a lift. An elevator may be marked with a sign noting that it is specially configured for Shabbat observance.

I believe last week there was another strictly kept observance but an annual one which is never held on a Sabbath, Tisha B'Av. If the ninth day of the month falls on Shabbat, then it's invariably postponed until the tenth. This observance is an annual fast day in Judaism. The fasting symbolises the destruction and lamenting of both the First Temple by King Solomon but destroyed by the Babylonians and the Second Temple was orchestrated by Nehemiah but built by Jewish exiles who had returned from Jerusalem after being held captive for seventy years. Work soon stopped, as the Jews were receiving hassle from Gentile nations around who asked to assist in the building of the temple, but the Jews refused as they felt it should be built by Jewish hands. The Gentiles became offended and began to berate and eventually fight the Jews, who soon became tired of the conflict, left the building work and began mixing with Gentile women instead. Which was strange as the Jews disliked the Samaritans because they were half Jew and half every other nation, yet they abandoned their own wives for Gentile ones.

Many years later the temple was renovated by of Herod the Great (his son Herod Antipas executed John the Baptist) whose brother and successor was Herod Agrippa, but it was later destroyed by the Romans. There was 655 years between the two temples, but the destruction of both are observed on the same day, annually.

The bus stop. It's been a long time. Oh, someone's installed a digital time table. Bus route 102 heading to Brent Cross, one minute or less. Let me see. Yep. On time, I can see a red thing crawling up Finchley Road. My Oyster card had better work, as I heard buses do not take cash.

How lovely. It's arrived and my Oyster card worked. Didn't move any further as the bus was packed. But if this is Saturday, what's it like in the week?

Descending Finchley Road, the pavements are like a ghost town. It's apparent Waitrose and Marks & Spencer don't subscribe to the weekly observance of Shabbat. So does that mean the Jews don't go shopping? Apparently not. Shabbat is part of the deal between God and the Jewish people, so celebrating it is a reminder of the covenant, an occasion to rejoice in God's kept promises. It was the Fourth Commandment and God's intention was to keep it holy. Sabbath candles are lit at sunset on Friday. They represent the two commandments, Zachor (to remember the Sabbath) and Shamor (to observe the Sabbath). The only problem here is that it's a misconception that Christians must keep the Sabbath, since Jesus kept it. Jesus observed the Sabbath because he was a Jew, obliged from birth to obey the law of Moses. Christians are not required to observe a weekly sabbath. The reason – the Apostle Paul urged Jews and Gentiles in his letter to the Corinthians, '*to not accept the underserved kindness of God and MISS its purpose*'! From Friday to Saturday within that duration the Israelites could not leave their locality, light a fire, gather wood, or carry a load. Violating the Sabbath was a capital offence. In Numbers, a man was caught collecting pieces of wood on the Sabbath. The Jews bought him to Moses and under God's command, the man was taken outside, where a crowd assembled and stoned him to death. Exodus 16: '*Everyone must stay where he is, nobody is to leave his locality on this day.*'

So did Jesus violate the law of God? After Jesus' death, his apostles at no time were commanded to observe the Sabbath. It simply wasn't a Christian requirement. Because of what Jesus did for us, the scriptures plainly state that the law of commandments, the Mosaic Law, was brought to its end. Colossians 2 14-1 states:

'Do not let anyone judge you about what you eat and drink or about the observance of a festival of the Sabbath, those things are a shadow of the things to come.' The Pharisees heard Jesus had cured a man on the Sabbath then conspired against him in Matthew 12 verse 12. If Jesus had broken the law of His father he would not have been able to function as the spotless sacrifice for our sins. He would remain unredeemed. To conclude, in Matthew 12.1 Jesus' Apostles pass through a grain field, and being hungry, they begin to pluck grain. The Pharisees question Jesus as to why his disciples did what was not lawful on the Sabbath. We know Jesus was not directly accused of breaking the law, only his Apostles were charged with the violation. But the Pharisees were hoping to hold Jesus accountable for the conduct of his students. Hebrew law made provision for those in need to eat when they passed through a field of grain (Deuteronomy 23:25 and Ruth 2 verse 2). So Jesus demonstrated that not all labour on the Sabbath was condemned. Matthew 12 verse 2 states that 'even the priest violated the law'.

The Sabbath was originally intended to be joyous, spiritually uplifting. But in their zeal to distinguish themselves from the Gentiles, the Jewish religious leaders gradually made it burdensome; they made people a slave to tradition, with innumerable lesser restrictions. For instance a sufferer could not be provided with relief unless death threatened. For there is no other Sabbath rest besides Jesus. He provided the principle to his father's law, i.e. God insisted that 'Thou must not commit adultery'. Jesus says, *'He who looks at a woman as to want her sexually, has already committed the sin.'* He alone satisfies the requirements of the law and he alone provides the sacrifice that atones for sin.

As I walk to the station, I am thinking what a civilised borough this Jewish area is. On the seven-minute bus ride, I notice there are no bins on the road, yet the roads are clean. An air of civility is welcomed any day of the week. They as a people don't really interact with others. It's not as if they don't speak English, but I guess it's their prerogative. Jesus said, '*You will all know my people by their fruits and the love that they display to one another.*'

Jesus ascended to Heaven from the Mount of Olives, which is like a guest-list burial ground as so many want to be buried there, so they can be the first to greet him when he supposedly returns. Or in some cases, when he arrives for the first time! I reiterate Apostle Paul's words at 2 Corinthians 6 verse 1, '*We urge you not to accept God's undeserved kindness (and totally miss the point)!*'

We read the same Bible, so how come they're still waiting for things it says have come and gone? God spoke through the apostle in the Book of Hebrews, where he rages, '*Your forefather put me to the test and kept trying me, despite seeing my works and all I did for them for forty years. This is why I became disgusted with this generation who invariably go astray in their hearts and have not come to know my ways.*'

No doubt the Jews are sincere people. The regularity of their devout religious practices amazes me. Even in this whirlwind of a life we live, they manage unequivocally to display consistency in worship to their God, even though he abandoned them centuries ago. Their form of worship is like disposing of the concept of email and going back to a fax machine. But is it in vain? Are their practices revealing that they are simply slaves to tradition and have missed the point regarding God and his requirements? To become institutionalised in thought and unresponsive to flexibility is a dangerous situation to be in. But with so many religions in the world, who's really doing things the right way? In Exodus, one of the five books Moses wrote, God spoke to the Israelites and they ran and hid, so frightful was His voice. To be in possession of such evidence of the Almighty's existence, He fought their battles for them, gave them the land of decoration, a land flowing with milk and honey. They had His laws given to us directly from him, imploring the Israelites to '*listen to his voice as his decrees are not burdensome, just provided out of love*. Why then would one go in the opposite direction from God? Many today long for his diametrical approach, a visual aid (in addition to the invisible qualities that surround us) to fortify our faith. I suppose, in order to ascertain which religion is even remotely accurate or correct, you could just choose one and ask if they were in charge of the earth and all things on it, would we as a consequence, benefit from their rule? Would the world be a better place? They still live by ancient rules and regulations, and in today's world it should be obvious how outdated they are. Animal sacrifice is still prevalent. People point blank refuse to live like that.

I can hear a beeping noise from this Oyster machine. What's its problem? Reading the warning notice might help. 'Minus ninety-six pence,' oh and there's a message: '*Dear traveller, it's impossible to travel on the Underground with a negative balance. All cards accepted below except Amex, because they're way too expensive and we wouldn't want to take it out on the commuter now, would we!*' What cheeky jobsworth wrote that? Someone who saw the broke man coming I suppose. I top up and head for the train.

OK, I want Great Portland Street on the Circle Line, so I need to change at St Pancras, where the Eurostar terminal is. Right, time to mingle with the commuters. I like how effective the Underground is point to point, just far too many people at once. The Northern Line heading south splits down via Charing Cross, which I do not want. Ah here's one now, Morden, via Bank. Lovely. How clean the trains are. The way some commuters describe them I was a trifle worried. Dirty, mice running riot everywhere. Don't lean on anything. But it looks pretty clean to me. Although people should move aside to allow commuters to alight. Goodness me, move to the side then. Some stroppy people about. I've seen an empty seat. A huge guy has just vacated it, I'm a big guy but he made me look like a toy. I quickly grab it. I understand all who want to get on and grab a seat but please, let a man off first. That's my first visual contact with rudeness today. I make for the seat right up in the corner, but there's immovable arm rests either side, how the hell did that guy squeeze his Happy Meal backside in there?

I turn with a smile on my face like I've won a trophy for claiming a seat, but as I sit, there's a serious scent rising from the chair. Oh my granny, it stinks. It pushes me back on my feet. The fat man's balls must have been cooking in his Y-fronts. I shoot back up like I have drunk a Red Bull and decide to stand. Everyone looks at me wondering what the hell I am doing.

Now this is the bit I don't like, descending into darkness. We are all at the mercy of the train driver and forces loyal to God and the Devil. We are trapped. In wartime apparently, people headed for the Underground for safety, but not any more, we are surrounded by nutters who bring bombs into crowded places.

Looking out of the window it's well dark, the kind of blackness you find deep beneath the sea. I can feel we are descending further. That's because we're arriving in Hampstead, which is London's deepest underground station at a depth of 58.5 metres (192ft). No kind of excavation could reach us down here. We're all doomed!

You can understand why people 'zone out'. Nearly all commuters don the headphones. Some are seriously big, like speakers. Those without headphones are reading murder novels. Let's not forget the word 'mystery' at the end. They don't want others to think they're psycho, or learning how to become psycho, because they may one day audition for the series *Wives with Knives*. Why the love of murder books? One has to wonder what wanders through the minds of these individuals. Actually, it's a trifle noisy in here and I think time will pass quicker If I put on my headphones on.

Music playing: *Goldberg variations,* JS Bach, 998. Seeing as though we are in the murder mystery zone, I will listen to a piece of Bach. Whenever I'm experiencing a bout of melancholy, I listen to this. It restores my heart rate and diminishes my anxiety.

It wasn't long ago when I was listening to Classic FM, the presenter pointed out that the piece was made for the soundtrack of *The Silence of the Lambs*. So I checked and it was the bit where Hannibal was in his cell, 'unravelling'. Remember the scene? The guards approach with his second helping of lamb chops, extra rare. 'Ready when you are, Doc,' says the guard. 'Just another minute please,' asked Hannibal. He regurgitates a pin which will finally extricate him from purgatory, allowing him to once again indulge in a delicacy he has been denied for so long.

I swore I could never watch the next scene again. Let's be honest about the munching moment, it was a long time coming and it was what film watchers were really waiting for. So in the background this beautiful piece of music is playing, just as Hannibal sinks his teeth into the guard's cakehole. It was like when I tuck into a juicy pear, not stopping till I reach the seed.

So, why when we hear classical music in a horror movie, is it associated with a death scene?

Women on the Underground invariably stare at each other. There's never a smile, just daggers. Is it a bitchy thing? Maybe, maybe not, but BITCH stands for 'Babe in Total Control of Herself', which is quite visible these day. Sisters are certainly doing it for themselves.

Euston. One more stop. The train is crammed with people on a Saturday morning and it's only 08:45. Can't all be going cleaning! A young kid pushes past, it's cool, I'll let him off as he didn't stand on my shoes. Good lord, he's huge. He has breasts! Poor kid, his knees will soon be having a word. He looks happy, although sitting down, he can't cross his legs. He may not have a weight problem, probably just can't wait to eat, poor kid.

St Pancras, quick, get off. Phew. Everyone looks like ants. On that last train, there was a power surge and the lights were extinguished, only for two seconds, but it reminds you what darkness really is. I think tonight I will get the bus back.

Walking through the tunnels to get to the Circle Line, I've had three conversations with mice. One popped out in front of me for a chat, like foxes do on the street, it's like they've lost the fear factor. He, no probably a she, wiggled its rear end at me as if asking for some Volvic water, as its lungs were covered in soot. I replied, 'I have some, but then you'll want some cheese to accompany it which I haven't got. Nor have I got anywhere clean for you to drink the water off, to assist in clearing your throat. Oh look,' I continued, 'someone's spat over there, go lick some of that.' The mouse looked up, cleared its nose with its front feet, thanked me for my advice and skedaddled.

One appears from a hole in the wall, the tiniest crack, stops and looks up. I ask, 'You OK?'

'No!' it replies. 'Ratty is around and on the war path.'

'Why, is he hungry and bullying you for your food?' I ask.

The mouse stands on its two hind legs and shouts, 'Food? Where the hell do you see food down here, ya plonker? Pigeons get better looked after than we do and you all hate them as much as you hate us, but ya still feed em! Look, Ratty is just in the, you know, mood…'

'Mood?' I ask curiously.

'For goodness' sake, must you insist on playing dumb? You lot call it mating season amongst the animal world, but it's not a need, it's a necessity in an attempt to annoy the crap out of you humans by reproducing in the millions. I'm running because Ratty is a trifle on the large side. Now you're aware how crap the NHS is, I refuse to wait six hours for suturing after Ratty has finished excavating me. Hang on, can you hear that?'

I look around to see if I can see what he was hearing or looking at.

'It's Ratty,' the mouse whispers. 'Gotta run, nice talking to you.' It runs to the edge of the platform and straight over the top, *Geronimoooo!* I can hear it diving onto the rail track, soon to become another statistic from the wheels of the underground.

Walking on to the Circle Line platform, and to my amusement, right there on the platform is big old Ratty, wandering around in a circle. A train has just gone, so the rear of the platform is empty. He stops circling and stares at me. 'All right?' I ask.

'Well, not really,' he says. 'I wanna get past, if you've no objection.'

'No, none at all,' I reply, backing up.

'What you listening to?' he asks.

'Funny really, I'm listening to some music a friend of mine gave me, this track is called *Rat Race* by Bob Marley.'

Ratty stands intimidatingly up on his back legs and says, 'Oh, you are the funny one, aren't you? If you knew the mood I'm in you would realise it's not Comic Relief I need right now. Oh and by the way, he's still alive you know, that Bob Marley. He's in Ethiopia smoking some of that wacky baccy, you know. Listen, white people see Elvis, I know black people see Bob.'

St Pancras is probably London's busiest underground station. Even way back in 1862 it was a busy trade route with just under twenty per cent of the country's coal consumption being brought through it. The railway station upstairs has now acquired a close associate, the Eurostar, which was a fantastic addition. The champagne bar is fantastic – they could just have added some oysters.

I used to travel to London from the north on my holidays way back in the late seventies as a boy. St Pancras was a ghost town. Remember the old 125 trains? The railway was owned by the public sector and was called British Rail. It was a dead place which smelt of old diesel in a petrol station. There weren't as many people around then. No cameras. Although the setting would have been perfect for a Hitchcock movie in its present state, set in lost time with glamour. Especially with the grand staircase. I could definitely imagine myself descending that staircase in a tux. The red bricks stood in a world of their own. As you walked towards it, you would feel its presence, but you wouldn't give it a second look, you'd simply head for the arches underneath the hotel and make for the exit. Fast forward eighty years, and the whole area is an elevated picture of effervescent life, covered in a blanket of smog emitted by the exhausts of over a thousand of the 25,000 Hackney cabs in the city, hovering in a circle around St Pancras and gradually killing everyone in the immediate vicinity. In the winter, no driver is going to sit in his car or cab all day with his engine off, getting hypothermia. Our winters are long and absolute. Electric cars can't come quick enough.

Great Portland Street. I'm out, I hate it down there. Let me breathe in the fumes from the A40 Euston Road traffic. Thirty motor vehicles cruise by every ten seconds. Right, pick up the keys and run round to the Phantom.

My phone rings. It's in my bag. If it's a friend, the phone will take my focus, but I like to be clear to talk, I'm not one for walking down the street with the phone pressed up against my ear.

Oh, it's Mr Bentayga. I'm required to work tonight. No sleep tonight then. These property developers and bankers party hard. Three-car convoy, me in the Bentley, one of his friends driving the Rolls Royce Ghost and someone else in the Maybach (which is an S Class on steroids), as apparently seven fruit trees will be joining us and have got to fit in the cars somewhere, somehow. Probably sitting on knees. Logistics tonight are going to be fun. All I have to do is make sure I finish this job early. I'm not needed till nine o'clock, should be OK.

I am on the mews at the back of Harley Street picking up the Phantom. As I open the door I hear, 'Woohoo!' I turn to see that the owl noise came from a lady opposite.

'A jolly good morning to you,' I say.

'Yes, just look at the skies, not a cloud in sight. The sun is in jolly good form. I saw you yesterday but didn't get a chance to welcome you back.'

Now the mews, as you can imagine, is small and you can barely get two cars past each other, but each mews house, probably worth in the region of thirty million, has its own double garage, as there is absolutely no parking on the road. Such a close community – everyone who lives here is paranoid. There are no exits at the end of the street, so everyone who drives down here must have a good reason. I remember this lady from last year, she was a trifle reticent at first until she got used to me. She loves to talk, which is strange, as she has volunteered the information that she's ex MI6. I didn't indulge her further, but she loved a chat. Her husband was a decent fellow, a bishop no less, who had abandoned his parishioners and relinquished his post in favour of retirement. It's a strange thought that a man of God actually retires from serving and worshipping his creator. So how come the bishops walks into retirement with a fat pension? Something doesn't seem right.

Recently I was deep south of the river working at a wedding and the church had a notice board which said among other small notices, 'NOW OPEN ON SUNDAYS'. So what had they been doing with the place before? I notice that there are no church bells any more other than in the required place at the required time, like at weddings. Just a thought.

These two had decided time wasn't on their side and thought it prudent to sell up and move to Southern Ireland.

'So this is it then?' I asked. She opened up the garage and there were tons of boxes neatly packed and labelled.

'Oh, you want to see the house,' she said. 'Boxes everywhere. One really doesn't realise what one has until one starts to move furniture.'

I notice a box that said 'ANTIQUES, to be transported separately, handle with extreme care'. It looked like it was awaiting a private courier. I said, 'It seems a mammoth task you've got here, you've done rather well.'

'Oh it's taken weeks, believe me. But we paced ourselves. The house is sold but we were provided with a concession, so no real hurry we thought, but the next thing, time had run out.'

I had to say it. 'So er, is this box heading to the Antiques Roadshow then?'

'No! Although, they could present an entire show with what's in there. Not because of the amount, but for its probate value. Got a special courier coming for that, one that can afford the insurance value!'

It was well wrapped up and I wondered if there was any James Bond gadgetry hidden in there. She gave me a hug and wished me the best of British. I said I hoped the winter over there would be good to her, or she might end up wishing she'd never left. She showed an effervescence seldom seen in women half her age. Delightful, she truly was.

Right, let's saddle up the horses. All 563 of them. Music playing: *Pomp and Circumstance* (Land of Hope and Glory) March no 1, Sir Edward Elgar. Ah yes, turn this up, it reminds me of the last night of the proms at the Royal Albert Hall.

The Phantom never fails to arouse my spirits, even though she resembles a block of flats (not like in Hackney, a block of apartments in Knightsbridge say). However often I jump on her, the pleasure never diminishes. Giddy up old girl. I navigate the bow up the cobbled stone mews, cautiously. There's always a stray pedestrian or resident popping out with their rollers on, going to the bins, or a nanny with the kids, always something from somewhere. Right on to Devonshire Place, right on to Upper Wimpole, right again onto A40 Marylebone Road and right again into Harley. Never fails to draw the necks of an audience. I pass a bus filled with commuters and quietly thank my lucky backside I'm not on that bus every day.

Text message. Who's that from? My phone's always on vibrate with one beep. Can't stand phones ringing. The King's ringtone is loud, which indicates he seldom gets calls as the family deal with the majority of the business. It's funny because those whose phones constantly ring, you never hear them. The phone just gently vibrates.

'Coming out,' texts the king. 'I'm not there yet,' texts the chauffeur. Well, I need more time and it's still nine minutes to nine. He likes the TV on and ready at the right volume when he climbs in. Right. Music off, TV on, oh what's this? *Embarrassing Bodies*, lovely. Switch that right over. How can people appear on TV displaying their bits with extras on them? Why would one do that?

The King's coming out. 'Good morning sir. Delighted to see you looking all refreshed and well rested. You sleep OK?'

'Always, I seldom have a problem sleeping,' says a confident King. I thought, *I bet you don't*. On a long journey, one of the wives massages his feet while he falls asleep, and can he snore! I've heard him in the car, if something wakes him, like the radio, or one of the wives laughs, or the phone rings.

The Three Degrees rotate the bedroom arrangements. Different maid to wash his bits each morning. Family deal with the empire. Back home he's got children in the government. Well sewn up, if you ask me.

'Right Paul, to the corner of Devonshire Place, I need the walk-in clinic, and then to the chemist on Marylebone High Street.' Pulling up at the door of the clinic, two nurses are waiting for him at the main door. He says to me, 'I know, I should have walked.'

'Now, I don't think that would agree with you, would it?'

'No, you're probably right,' says the King. Sometimes it's easy just to give them what they want to hear. I'm hoping nothing is wrong and that he won't suddenly keel over in my presence…

So what will today bring? I'm extremely low on funds, so I must figure something out. Problem is that rich people do not like handing out money, so they make me wait a month before I get paid. It's a nuisance, as I'm always playing catch up. They keep calling, you do the work and at some point you have to risk annoying them for the due balance. Some are really bad payers. They leave it so long, then begin to question whether you did that day with them. They will even fabricate stuff like 'the wheels have been intimate with the kerb'. It's been a while since I've been paid, so I'll find a pawnbroker and release some equity on my iPad. Things get tough, but you have to keep going. Your landlord won't give a stuff where your rent comes from, as long as you pay it. All I need to do now is find a Cash Converter. What is funny is there's even a Cash Converter for the rich. You don't think of the rich that way, running to a pawnbroker, but cashflow doesn't choose its victims.

He's coming back. I jump out to help him in and notice cotton wool and a plaster. 'All OK?' I ask.

'Yes, I just needed a blood test and a prescription.'

'I suppose that will take a couple of days, will it?'

'No, I should have my blood test back in an hour.'

Well, in this day and age, you get what you pay for. Simple.

We head off down New Cavendish Street and all the way down to Marylebone High Street. As always it's alive with shoppers, I love this street. I help the King into the chemist, then find somewhere further down to park nearer to the bank I know he's going to.

It's strange that shoppers have loyalty, like those who shop in St Johns Wood High Street wouldn't go to Marylebone High Street. Those who shop in Bond Street definitely won't shop in Sloane Street. It's just territorial allegiance.

Right, I think I'll run into Pret à Manger. Let's see what I can have. A banana. Cashew nuts with no salt. Water. The almond croissant looks divine, but it will bloat my stomach. No fizzy pop, it would overload me with sugar. Ah, tuna platter. I can just about cope with that. Wash this down with my vitamin D tablets and I'm ready for the day.

Here comes the King now. He's signalling that he's popping into the bank. Cool. I can indulge in some sustenance.

Half an hour later I am fed and watered and ready to let battle commence. Here comes the King with the branch manager, I remember her from last time. The King walked straight to the front and the manager had to politely remind him that over here we form an orderly queue. She's now walking him out. Has he humbled the stroppy madam? As I get out and walk round the car, a guy is on the floor seeking some change. Now I am always polite to them as you never know, one day it could be you. He looks at me and I checked my pockets, but he doesn't bother asking me, probably because he knows I'm a chauffeur and broke. I stand by the car door and wait, as they are still talking. Before I know it the beggar jumps up and stands in front of the King and the bank manager and began his spiel. 'Excuse me excuse me, it's been three days since I last ate and I was wondering if you could see your way…'

The bank manager interrupts him. 'Good golly, three days, I am so impressed, what willpower, jolly well done,' she says. She pushes past and walks towards the car. She then turns to the King and whispers, 'Those people are like pigeons, one simply cannot indulge them you know!'

Driving back to the house, the King is happy. He has obviously picked up his happy pills and checked his current account figures. 'Paul, I will collect wives one and two and then we are going to see friends over at One Hyde Park. Afterwards we will shop in Bond Street and then we should be done for the day. But you can go take a break while we are at Hyde Park.'

See, although we will be in Knightsbridge they'd still rather go to Bond Street. Interesting though, allegiances are strong. But I've been longing for an opportunity to have a nose round that place. I had a client I use to drive, lovely lady. Often she would food-shop down in the Pavilion Village, a quaint but inordinately high-priced light shopping and café area. One minute she would snap at you for no real reason – it seemed she was always snappy before a shopping trip – and after she had finished she would ask me to Bluetooth her phone into the car system and we would drive around playing rap music on YouTube. No lie, she would even sing along to the words, which were invariably about violence, drugs and shooting. If she exhibited this kind of split personality living on a council estate, she'd be locked up. She and her husband (who is thirty years her senior) needed to downsize because of his ill health. He could no longer negotiate stairs, and as the house was listed a stairlift wouldn't work. So they moved from an eight-bedroom home in Belgravia, value £67 million (which she still has and uses only to hoard expensive paintings bought at auction) to a four-bedroom apartment at One Hyde Park, £96 million. So that's the definition of downsizing!

We pull up at the house and he calls the wives on the phone. We wait a minute and two of the Three Degrees appear. 'Paul, I think we need to go buy a present first please, so Bond Street Jewellers on the left from the top.' This excites the wives, as they do not even have credit cards. I think they must submit some kind of offering, probably some nocturnal activity, before being presented with a reward of some type, so shopping is truly a treat. They start yapping between themselves. Bless.

Now I'm wondering which jewellery shop it is, as there was a smash and grab by an armed gang on Monday first thing, before everyone was with it. It was amazing how the owners managed to get the shop fully functioning in hours, as if nothing had happened. I'm sure it's a human resilience thing. I remember the North London riots and looting not so long ago, the damage to the high street was bad. You would expect people to stay at home, out of danger. People were wandering around, probably trying to catch a stray TV. What got me was the press. Imagine the scene. Looting is rife, people ripping off shop door shutters, smashing locks and windows. One guy was running off down the street with a TV which was twice his size, and the Sky TV van rolls up alongside him. He's puffing and panting, and the Sky reporter shouts out of her moving car window, 'Hi, good night for it, what make of TV is that then?' Now the guy turns his neck to see what plonker has struck up a conversation with him, and replies, 'Samsung, in it!' She continues, 'Looks a nice one, do you think it's got a plug with it?'

So I'm sitting outside the jeweller's, but next door, with two of the wives in the back. I don't think with a gift this important he will want an audience, especially if he spent more on this present than he has on them. I doubt they would complain, but it would remain indelibly on their minds. As men around the world know, women hate being rejected or corrected.

Here he comes, and the wives speak in a monotone, in African. They're looking hard at the carrier bag he's carrying. As I open his door to let him in, I can see a box with Rolex written on it, through the plastic. Ah bless, I'm thinking. In his circle, it's definitely not the thought that counts, but the prezzie.

Heading south on Park Lane, I am filled with trepidation regarding my next stop. I've heard so much about it, like mail being X-rayed before delivery. The cars are apparently a lot of one-off specials. OK, I think I'll cut through the park on to South Carriage Drive, which runs parallel to Knightsbridge. A lot less traffic. On approaching the backs of these apartments you can't miss them. Four hundred thousand square feet of the most expensive housing in the UK. Turning left into Edinburgh Gate, the road was moved to accommodate this project. Only money could compel a borough council to sign off something like that. It's true, everything has its price.

Turning into the apartments, a green light and a huge bollard hold me at the front. There is controlled activity on the concourse and a collection of some serious machinery, McLarens, Lamborghinis, Porsches, Rolls Royces, a somewhat intimidating scene. A security guard approaches. As I wind down the window, a voice from behind speaks, telling him to stand down. The people we are there to meet come onto the concourse. The King usually offers his hand to people who come to greet him, but today he pushes past his wives, opens the door and springs out. The man he's meeting is standing in a way that suggests he would make the billionaire King look like a welfare case. It's almost obeisance. A billionaire will only overtly display respect to another individual who is worth more than he is. Simple.

There seems to be some tension, as the man we have come to see has a somewhat red face. They speak in African, and then another resident (as I assume by his demeanour and the way the concierge runs after him) stares at the angry man. The man stares back and says in English, 'You wouldn't address me with that face if we were in my country!' The resident turns on his heels and grunts, 'Showdowns, no one wins, we are all the same here, no one is superior to the other. Just let it lie, I have!'

What all this was about I have no idea. But the whole place resembles a goldfish bowl. Cameras are everywhere. The atmosphere is a trifle stuffy, even suffocating. Serious faces, paranoia everywhere.

'Paul!' One of the wives summons my attention. 'That man we know from back home. He has his own army, but it's his wife who has the cash and she's the wealthiest black woman in the world.' According to the sisters with voices, this family bought out a whole floor here. With four-bedroom apartments starting at twenty million, I really could begin to add up a whole floor.

It's interesting to see how those with serious money carry the swagger. Old English money, European money, Russian money, African money, Asia and Indian. The Arabs are probably the coolest of the lot. But the consistent behaviour, from the majority, is aggressive.

The King's friend squeezes himself into the front seat, immediately disfiguring the shape. I can hear the seat begging for relief.

'Head to the lift,' says the resident. I drive straight toward this steel and glass-windowed lift. They all begin discussing what had happened outside. Now chauffeurs are not meant to listen, so I displayed diplomacy by appearing disinterested. Seriously, these lifts are from another world. The green light indicates move forward. I'm thinking, will it be long enough for the LWB Phantom, but it is, plenty of room. The resident has a key fob which activates the lift, and we descend three floors. That's got to be a hundred feet. From close to open takes three minutes, so it's not quick. Three people in the back, me in the driver's seat and two in the passenger seat. No joke, this guy is huge. All the occupants watch as the light above begins to fade, whilst we descend further into darkness. When it stops, we all wait for the doors open. They do, and it's dark. As we drive out of the lift, daylight-imitation lighting illuminates our way, and there before my eyes are cars I have never seen before – one-offs, prototypes even. Cars people have just played with, bodywork, paintwork, wheels. It's unreal. The most intriguing aspect is that most of the cars are wrapped up in red and transparent bubble plastic with wires protruding, probably for a trickle charger. Oh, there's a body. Someone is washing, or should I say caressing, the car in a sort of bath area. He is washing it like it's fragile.

We drive round in search of his parking space, and words cannot describe this automotive sweet shop. Driving round this huge supercar park, I'm presented with a visual feast of beauty. Two Bugatti Veyrons next to each other, how romantic. An S class Benz, ten a penny, a prerequisite amongst the rich. The 911 is a ladies' delight, or a runaround, so light. The doors weigh less than eleven bags of sugar each and on the turbo, if driven in a town with bad atmosphere, the air comes out through the exhaust cleaner than it went in.

Ah bless, a solitary Nissan GTR, somewhat fading and a trifle dated. Now other cars can blast past it, I'm confident it will soon become obsolete. Shame, the Skyline was a hit. As we drive through slowly, my passengers are rambling while I revel in this visual delight. Oh, the new XF Jaguar. What's that doing in here, with its supposedly intelligent stop-start system? Doesn't work for me. At traffic lights, it switches off. Save the planet. When the air con begins to get warm in the cabin, it switches back on again. So in ten miles across London, the engine switches on and off probably thirty times. How is that good for an engine? With this car, there's no button to choose whether you want it off, it chooses for you. Sounds like diesel cars. The government wanted all to indulge, but now everyone is abstaining.

Oh my, this is orgasmic, look, it's the apex fighter jet, a Ferrari F12, with a wire leading to the boot. Probably a flat battery. Well, even a Ferrari with a dead battery is still beautiful. In the next bay is – hang on, don't see many of them – a Porsche 918, the third fastest car to one hundred and fifty at 10.5 seconds, only beaten by the Veyron at 10.2 and the La Ferrari coming in at 9.8. Astonishing. Just to put that in perspective, the AMG S-65 takes another eleven seconds to reach 150 and a Red Bull F1 car takes nine seconds to reach 190 mph.

We pull up alongside the resident's Phantom. He points to other cars in a line, must be the family's, a Ghost, an Aventador, a La Ferrari which I would have loved to get intimate with, though not in London with all its pot holes and twelve mile an hour average speed. Opposite is a Ferrari F40. Oh my Granny. That one has a clutch which requires an athlete's calf. Imagine that around London in traffic. No thanks!

Next to it is a carbon fibre Aston Martin and next to that a Mercedes SL, pristine, must be a 1940s model, all wrapped up like a baby sleeping. There are 911s all over the place, all of them turbos or at least the GTS model. There are Maybachs young and old.

I'm still daydreaming when the King says, 'So Paul, we will be a couple of hours,' and they all begin to walk off. Now the parking bays are full of colour, but the walls are like our clouds in default setting, gunmetal grey. I need daylight, there is far too much concierge above me, thanks. 'King, if you have no objection, I would rather wait upstairs,' I say. 'I need the facilities.' The King speaks to his friend and then suggests I follow them upstairs. I grab my man bag, lock the doors and run after them.

The resident calls the lift, so it looks like I'll be sharing it with them. He uses a fob to summon the lift, and once inside he has a card to activate the lift in order to choose a floor number. This must be like the MI6 building, I've never seen anything remotely like it. Among the vibrant African conversations, I hear a TV. There's a Samsung on the wall, integrated into the glass, how clever. So he could be looking through the glass without realising a television is there. But one of the wives is in the way. There is some weight in this lift. I'm looking for its SWL (safe working load) advisory statement. I roll my eyes around trying to add up the pounds. Oh my goodness, there's well over a ton in here. Bing! A lady tells us we have arrived on ground floor. No one moves, they're all looking at me. 'Take my keys, the lift will know by the fob which car park you need,' says the resident. The silence that follows means, 'OK, now get out!' Fortunately, I'm quite perceptive where hints are concerned and I don't mind a couple of hours exploring.

I exit the lift. Looking back, I look up and around, then realise there are neatly-hidden cameras everywhere. I thought I'd follow the lift, then realised they're glass and you can see into them, so I quickly turn on my heel and walk off. I have no intention of getting two years in jail for being a peeping tom, but who designed that anyway? It's like that movie *Sliver* where the owner of the apartments has cameras everywhere in strategic positions so he can spy on the residents.

Walking along this corridor, I can see the front desk in the distance. It's a long way and I wouldn't be happy walking that distance in high heels on a night out. Most women's shoes take them from the door to the car, no other walking involved.

I find myself in an unfamiliar world. It's like a scene at the inception of a *Star Trek* movie, except the atmosphere is stifled and silent as a morgue, so all I can hear is my own feet on tiles that are so opulent I questioned my worthiness to trample on them.

'Can I assist you?' a voice suddenly says from the wall. I turn to see a smartly-dressed and athletically-built security guard staring at me. I explain who I am with and say I need the facilities and a driver's room. 'No problem, allow me to show you the way.' He could have pointed to where I needed to go, but I guess I've got 'Mr Nosey' etched on my forehead.

There is classical music gently filling the atmosphere with calm. Hang on, I know that piece of music. Verdi's *La Traviata*, with Renée Fleming singing. You must remember the scene in *Pretty Woman* when the two leading stars fly to the opera and Julia Roberts says to the lady in the box next to her, 'I liked it that much I nearly peed my pants,' and Richard Gere tells the lady, 'So sorry, she meant she liked it as much as the Pirates of Penzance.'

Finally I make it to reception – wow! The ambience is opulent in its extreme form. Not a single expense spared. Irrespective how grand a hotel you have seen, this place would render it a welfare case. Standing at reception, I extend a hand to the architect. The building is first class. As for the atmosphere, well, I remember the words of my client from Monaco: 'The air is invariably nicer wherever the rich congregate. Even so, it doesn't mean you can trust everyone around you, does it?'

The ceiling must be a good forty feet high, with a grand staircase leading up to it. The service charge must be horrendous. I heard that a parking space would set you back half a million. How the hell can a parking space cost more than a supercar? The resident I dropped off had six! I don't begrudge anyone with cash and thankfully I don't have a desire to live like this. Besides, I like country living. I certainly wouldn't mind waking up, looking out of my window at livestock and being surrounded by oil-seed rape. An utterly quiet life.

I was going to ascend the staircase, but the concierge says I can sit in the library opposite, although it has no books in it. It needs two hands to push the seriously heavy glass doors open. Inside the lighting is subtle and once again, pure opulence, so, as I thought when I became a chauffeur, if you can't beat the rich, join them. Behind me is another room and I can hear voices, sounding like posh children. A phone rings and someone answers, 'Yes, I'll be out shortly.' At that an Asian girl appears, a teenager. She strolls past, head up, back incredibly straight and walks out to reception. There's another oriental girl waiting and together they come back into the library. They join another girl round the corner and do their posh adolescent girly thing. Then a tray with what looks like tea is brought in by the concierge. No scones then, I suppose they'd have to pop to the hotel next door for that, quite confident they'll have a credit card. How funny, parents usually feel the need to keep their eyes on their children, but here within this goldfish bowl they are really in the arms of the Bank of England. Nothing's going to happen to them here.

So these children sit down and began to converse. One girl says to the friend who just came in, 'It's jolly nice to see you, how's things, life, Mum and Dad? Do send them our regards, won't you.'

'Of course I will,' says the friend.

The resident girl continues, 'Do you know, my sister and I were talking just before you came and we were trying to work out whether the girl we saw you with at school yesterday morning before registration, is she your friend now?'

'No, why would you arrive at that conclusion?' asks the friend. 'She's actually experiencing a parental divorce, she's going through it, poor girl.'

'My mother always taught me that I have one mouth and two

ears, and in being able to display empathy, one needs to pay more than the usual attention to things heard.'

Silence then prevails for a moment, whilst the sisters reload. 'Far from it for us to impose our views or even to dissuade you from yours, it's just we're not sure you're aware of her grades recently.'

'Yes, she did mention that her grades were somewhat dismal,' says the friend.

'You got the D right, but try deficient,' hollers the second sister. 'She literally got more Ds than anybody.'

'Look, to be honest,' interrupts the first sister, 'apparently the Ds runs as a theme throughout the whole family, or so I am told. So in her favour, we can't really attribute her deficiencies to herself, if she inherited them, can we?'

'No, I guess not,' replies the first sister. 'It's obvious this is not entirely her fault.' The friend seems powerless to impose her opinion and simply nods, probably thinking, 'If I don't, I won't be allowed to sample these scones again.' I was thinking, did I just hear that? Isn't that diplomatic ridicule? Thinking in terms of acts of impropriety, it's like there are two ways to rob a bank, one with a gun and the other with a pen. How would these girls do it? Boardroom bullies, at that age! Amazing.

I think it prudent to stretch my legs, as my internal radar is agitating me. I pick up my man bag and walk to reception. There's a bit of activity. A young lady has two white furry doggies. Full of the joys of summer, they are. Probably a dog walker, the way she's talking to the concierge. Besides, this lot in here surely won't poo pick. Off she goes towards a lift. As it opens, she asks if I want to get it. I look inside and it seems only enough for two people and maybe a small child. It's like a steel coffin. 'You're so kind,' I reply. 'But I think I will stretch my legs.' You see, residents wouldn't ask staff to join them, really. They'd expect you to take the next lift.

By the time I'm upstairs, the lady with the poodles has made it out of the coffin safely and is talking to one of the security men. When I walk past I hear her excitedly say she is taking the 'boys' on to Hyde Park for their late afternoon walk and in an hour they must attend the 'doggie spa', which they love. They are in there for two hours, she says, and she hopes she has enough cash. The security guy says the concierge will sub her, and then she mentions it's four hundred pounds. I stop walking. The security guy asked her what the dogs get for that, and she replies, 'Oh, short back and sides, shampoo and set, fingernails and a ring squeeze.' Yep, my thoughts exactly. What the hell is a ring squeeze? Apparently it's a sort of colonic irrigation for posh dogs. So off she goes, across the south carriageway and into Hyde Park.

I take a look at the park across the road and with the sun glowing in all its glory, it looks inviting. I'm in two minds. There are residents coming to and from the park, each one looking relaxed and tanned. Just at that moment, a car comes up from the lift and security are on their ear pieces. Looks like one of the residents is coming up and has summoned their car. Everyone gets in place. There's a concierge for each door. It's really attentive stuff. As I walk away, as it's not my call to assist, I hear a woman calling my name. It can't possibly be me, but I look anyway. 'How are you?' she asks. I do know her, I worked for her on a temporary basis a couple of years ago.

'Yes, feeling pretty good,' I reply. 'Delighted to see you again, all settled in and happy?'

'Oh Paul, you know me, never happy unless I find something to complain about. I must dash, off to the auction house. Will be a couple of hours, I need to bid on something. Will you be here when I get back?'

'Yes, quite possibly.'

'Marvellous, see you soon. I'll be back shortly.' Lovely lady. A trifle on the batty side, but she's OK. Still rinsing out the auction houses. I once accompanied her and had my eyes opened. Serious business. She bought a painting for fourteen million and didn't even flinch. The conclusion had filtered down to two individuals, her and a phone bidder. I just watched her determination to obtain her acquisition. Nothing like being loaded. She stood, resolute in the auction room, and her demeanour was, no one else will purchase this painting. Once she had achieved her goal, we walked out of there, into the car and off for lunch. She never mentioned it again. It was as if she had gone into a newsagent and purchased a bag of crisps. We got into the car, she plugged in her phone and began listening to rap music on YouTube. I am deadly serious. She was singing along to the words. Strange, you would never have expected it. It's like she was lacking something, although she wasn't visibly deprived of anything. Love, maybe?

I feel somewhat stuffy out on the concourse, security guards tight lipped, camera in constant surveillance mode. At that moment another car pulls up, a Range Rover. Four concierges and security men storm the car doors. On opening them, there's a woman driving with four young girls and three babies. On my way out, I realise the young girls were nannies and the family had three kids and three nannies. From what I've seen, most of these families have a full quota of staff, butlers, chauffeurs, nannies, dog walkers, house maids and cleaners.

I turn to walk off the concourse and notice a man walking north on Edinburgh Gate heading toward the park, with a bird on his arm, the feathered kind. I walk toward him, as I can't believe what I'm looking at. As I get closer, I realise it's my favourite bird of prey, a two hundred mile an hour peregrine falcon. I studied these beautiful birds at school. Only the female is called the falcon and the male is called a tiercel. The name comes from the Latin word 'tertius' which means 'one third', because the male is one third smaller than the female. On the male, the upper part of the chest and throat is immaculately white. The female chest is beige with red markings. Their eyesight is eight times more powerful than ours. They have a third eyelid which is translucent and is called a nictitating membrane, which protects their eyes from dust and dirt when travelling at 200mph. And now I have one in front of me.

The fortunate custodian of the bird is a mature gentleman. He explains that he was in possession of over twenty birds of prey, but the peregrine is his primary passion. So I ask what he is doing here. Apparently one of this bird's favourite dishes is pigeons. Why? They eat crap food, chips and greasy Chinese leftovers. What nutrition does a pigeon have?

I accompany the bird man round the back to watch what he does. The falcon is young and not fully grown, but its talons wrap themselves round his hand and wrist, a stark reminder of this awesome piece of creation. So I say to him that one of the dog walkers will be back shortly, should we warn her? Because I wouldn't want the falcon to snatch the poodles, as his talons look capable of lifting the two of them as easily as I would a bag of crisps. He replies, 'Not likely with her powerful eyesight, if she attacks something, it will be specific to her requirements.' The poodles resemble an ice cream with all the trimmings and appear aesthetically pleasing, but with no nutritional value. Well that's a relief, because its mother probably dotes on it more than her grandchildren, so she'll be relieved. I expect the doggie owners would have checked to be honest. Just to make sure there could be no malfunctions, like say if the falcon had toothache, or even a headache and its radar was a trifle off, then the poodle might suddenly realise it was in a transitional lift, not knowing what was going on, experiencing a knife-like pain in its rib cage from the falcon's daggers. Then as they ascend, sudden hypoxia sets in and the poodle passes out. Terrible thought.

Standing by the main entrance in amazement at this guy, I'm

beeped out of the way by another Brick (Range Rover). As the car rolls by on to the concourse, I can't help but peek at these aliens from another planet, simply to look who's in the car. I can see a guy who looks very familiar in the front seat and think he couldn't afford a place here – it's one of the judges on *Britain's Got Talent*. Apparently quite a few selected celebrities utilise the spa, the state of the art gym, the swimming pool and squash courts. Strangely enough he sort of hangs about as if for applause or as if he expects an audience to suddenly assemble, but he gets nothing of the sort. I mean, he's popular, but not that popular. Eventually, he grabs his sports bag and continues with what he came here to do.

So here's me in pursuit of this bird man, round to the back of the apartments facing Hyde Park and staring in amazement. He's throwing the bird off his arm and the falcon will accelerate right up to the level of the penthouses faster than anything man could produce. He will then place meat on his glove, whistle and the falcon swoops down, grabs a mouthful and takes off again. While they're playing this game, I take a look around and there isn't a single pigeon anywhere – not one. Not even in the distance. They must know that a bird of singular destruction is among us. How strange, because, pigeons have become desensitised to man's existence, like foxes. If you look at a fox, it will stare back and shout, 'Yeah, I'm here, so what?' A pigeon will continue until your car is almost upon it before it takes off. This bird in the sky looks menacing, no wonder the pigeons have scarpered.

The only other time I was freaked out by the presence of 'the birds' was not long ago in a field up in the hills of Henley on Thames, as I was waiting for clients who were on their way back from Ascot. Now I remember engaging in conversation with around fifty sheep, as it was only me, them and their droppings (which I kept annoyingly scraping off the bottom of my shoes) in the field. I was waiting for a helicopter to emerge out of the skies when on looking up I noticed six awesome, intimidating-looking birds, aviating recklessly above me. They suddenly became a menacing picture as they all began to take advantage of low-level turbulence caused by the heat, the trees and atmosphere. This is called 'thermal turbulence'. What happens is that the birds piggyback rising atmospheric currents, which provide them with lift. This enables the birds to fly from this elevated vantage point with reduced expenditure of energy. Man has tried to imitate the bird, just not to its entirety. Helicopters struggle with a strong temperature gradient. When the wind suddenly changes from what seemed to be calm and stable, a helicopter becomes unstable and everyone on the ground wonders what happened. They're as helpless as a dinghy in a storm.

So, somewhere between the surface of the earth and the top of the atmosphere, these red kites found an elevated vantage point amongst the sky waves and began to stalk me. Of course it was food they were looking for, just took me a couple of minutes to realise it. I looked at the sheep, thinking, they're a trifle big to lift, unless two birds lift one sheep. I know they can fly off with a baby, I've seen it on *National Geographic*. Surely they can't lift me, but they could sure peck the crap out of me.

Now I realised I was about fifty metres from the Brick, and didn't realise I had wandered that far. I looked up and they had descended a few feet. No sign of the helicopter, so I ran back to the car, ignoring all the poo I was squashing under my feet. The flipping birds only began to squeal! I'm serious. I could hear them saying, 'If we commit murder, no one will know it was us.' I made it back to the car, opened the door and shouted, 'Of course people will, what about the stab holes in my neck, ya crazy birds?' That's how that man in the Hitchcock movie died. Not me, As I've sought protection from the Brick. OK, I'm inside the car with the doors locked. Fortunately, a few minutes later the helicopter disperses the beggars.

If you drive on the M40 near Beaconsfield, you can see them

hovering above the motorway, waiting for roadkill. They wait till your head is hanging out of the window, then they swoop, as they know an ambulance will take at least an hour to respond. Well, these days, anyway. I saw them on the way to greet the helicopter, but there was a carcass on the road. I saw them dive down on to the fast lane, take a chunk out of the neck and fly off without landing or being hit. It was amazing to watch with their five-foot wing span, talons that deserve a place on that programme *Wives with Knives*. Actually, now I realise why there are no pigeons that side of town.

Only a few weeks ago an Arab hired a jumbo jet and took eighty falcons back to Saudi in first class. They all had TVs and attendants on board. Funniest thing I had seen that week.

I thought there might be some commotion when the dog walker returned, but the falcon just ignores them. It keeps coming back, never once strays. Each time it comes back, it takes in more food and the bird man shows me her gullet where she's storing the food for later. I can't understand how she could fly and eat.

I feel a tap on my shoulder, and it's a security guard, telling me my people are asking for the car. I thank the bird man for his entertainment and head off back down to the car park. The place meets my expectations, but working in a goldfish bowl is a no-no. You couldn't breathe. I couldn't imagine living there either. But it's how the rich like to live, like sheep, all huddled together, although one massive flaw, for all the residents, is that they only have two car lifts, up and down. With the lift parts specially made in Germany, that could cause huge problems. Apparently they break down regularly. Imagine if they simultaneously broke down or there was a fire, the residents would have no way of removing their cars! Hey, not my problem.

I take one last look at the hypercars and a longing stare at the F12. So long, my honeybee. What a blinking machine. Squeezing the Phantom into the lift, my day begins to unravel. There's got to be one thing a day we all do that we can look back on and at least say we enjoyed. Is this how most of us would want to live? No matter how you got your money, you can just come here, seek asylum and find protection in an apartment block like this, where staff attend to your every need, from fetching a water melon to cleaning your shoes. Whatever your requirements in the daytime to whatever your needs nocturnally. Round the clock, the staff are yours. But remember you only get what you pay for. To rent a one-bedroom apartment will cost you three thousand a week with a balloon payment annually for the service charge. Or even a four-bedroom to rent from over a hundred thousand a week. It's an unreality to conventional human beings. But the highlight of the day, for me, was that peregrine falcon. Man could never produce something as liberated as that. It was immense. The colour patterns on its body. The effortless way it ascended to the penthouse. The way its eyes burn a hole through its prey before it hits.

Daylight begins to appear, rising from the belly of the apartments. Through the lift glass I can see my party are at the door waiting. I wonder if the resident enjoyed the Bond Street present, or did he throw it in a drawer with the rest of his unwanted presents? Now what's the chances he's found somewhere else to go tonight? If so, I'm buggered. I'm also trying to decide whether to go pick up my jalopy and bring it back into London or leave it where it is and share a bus ride back to Golders Green with all the Saturday night revellers. Ah, but the Underground runs all night now. I forgot. All good then. OK, moment of truth.

They all pile in and say their goodbyes. The wives seem to have had a good time, by their joviality. As we drive off, I can hear the three of them sucking fragments of beef jerky out from the crevices of their teeth, or whatever they had. They're all chatting away, but I am waiting for what I need to hear. No one speaks of it, so I head straight back to Harley Street, post haste.

'Paul,' the King calls, 'I think I won't be needing you for the rest of the day, I really need to rest.'

'Oh,' I reply, 'If you insist.'

'Now tomorrow, we need to go to the church on the Marylebone Road. We need to be there for ten o'clock, so please arrive at the house ready for nine thirty.'

'No problem,' I reply. Although I'm just a trifle apprehensive, as the last time I parked outside the Presbyterian church in the Phantom, I got hassle. The picture just doesn't blend. A pocket of activists surrounded the Phantom the last time, with disparaging chants about capitalism. But surely lightning won't strike twice. Will it?

Heading up Gloucester Crescent, three or four streets from the house, I begin assembling my thoughts regarding the logistics of my next job. I'm also thinking about a sleep management programme, as it's going to be a long evening. It's not been too long a day, but eight hours driving the long wheelbase Phantom can take its toll mentally. Having to drive in such a controlled and restrictive way can be taxing. My clients refuse to wear seatbelts and hate potholes and speed bumps, so I have to pay more than the usual attention to avoiding them. London is an obstacle course, especially around the West End, and any Phantom driver will tell you how taxing it can be. Clients usually jump on any mistakes. Traffic lights require a lot of attention. To heave the Phantom off the blocks is fine, but when a driver cuts you up or suddenly stops dead in front of you, it's like a lorry in an emergency stop. Like a goalkeeper focusing on a free kick, but the ball is suddenly deflected and it's almost impossible for him to shift his weight in an instant towards the ball's deflected route. If the Phantom hits another car, the nose will simply continue to bulldoze the car in front until its balance returns.

Arriving back at the house, I believe tiredness has caught up with them. All is silent, except for the TV playing to itself. You know what the news of the day is like – once you've heard it, it repeats itself throughout the day. I can hear text messages coming through with the phone vibrating. I just hope tonight isn't cancelled.

As I help the King out of the car, he provides me with further instruction for tomorrow. 'Make sure you come early tomorrow as all of us will be attending the church,' he says.

'No problem. Although, as everyone is going, shall I bring the Viano?'

'No need,' he replies. You'll only be taking me, everyone else can walk. It's only round the corner.' Which makes me realise why he wants me tomorrow – it's solely to stick the Phantom in front of the church. He's a funny so and so. What really does freak me out is the silence and obedience of the women, so well versed in knowing what not to say. As chauffeurs it's none of our business what goes on. At times we are forced to step in if the husband is inebriated and decides to take his bad day out on the wife, who so often plays a subservient, diplomatic role in coping with her alpha male. Women use that label quite liberally – 'I've got an alpha male locked up indoors.' But that alpha male really does bite.

Chapter 6

A supercar sang in Berkeley Square

Returning the Phantom to its home is always a sad occasion. She's beautiful. Look at her nose in the air, so graceful. If the Range Rover had German underpinning, it would have more of a probative value, but the Phantom is wanted all over the earth by everyone who can afford it. There's another occupant in his garage, and it's a 1970-something Silver Spirit with just six thousand miles on the clock, just sitting there gathering dust. Now this one you wouldn't find all over the earth. It was hard work. Kept breaking down. It was huge, with no real presence. The Germans should have got hold of it.

I walk back to the house, hand in the keys and head for Regent's Park tube station. I need to get Oxford Circus, then walk ten minutes to Maddox Street.

I come out of the tube to find Oxford Circus brimming with life. You just can't imagine life without the Circus. I say that because when driving round Knightsbridge earlier, shops were boarded up, a worrying sight. Most shops round there make enough GDP in six months to last the year and pay those million-pound rents.

I try not to window-shop, it just winds me up, although I am seeing fifty and sixty per cent off items in many shops. Shops are closing, is there a pattern emerging?

Maddox Street, west of Regent Street. Nothing significant about it. Its location is a strong point, but there's a chic members-only nightclub that's open from late till daylight, with an Italian restaurant and a celebrity crowd. I cross over the street and roughly fifty yards away, I think I see my companion for the evening. Oh my, she looks gorgeous. Black, with a shine that resembles oil. She's wearing black high heels and showing a cleavage. Yes, even in black, the Bentley Bentayga shines. This is no normal SUV.

Someone shouts to me. The PA calls me over to a bar that's so full people are gathered in pockets on the street. The atmosphere is buzzing and pink champagne is flowing. She introduces me to the finance director and the managing director, who will apparently will be following in two Rolls Royce Ghosts. I hope we don't travel far, because unless you're trained in tandem or familiar with convoy driving, it can get complicated.

The PA walks me back to the car to run through tonight's itinerary. I can feel it calling me. You know that moment you meet someone you finally harmonise with? Well, it's happening. I keep thinking, I hope you drive as good as you look. I have no idea how it drives. All I know is, Bentley made a V8 and a V12. Never been keen on V8 engines, except maybe a Porsche. Their cars always seem natural and right. The Porsche V8 sounds classy and seldom malfunctions. Now I wonder if it will start like the Continental. When that V12 combusts, it's like an earthquake. More probably like the V8, which has a more subtle tone on combustion.

The keys here are huge, just like the car. I do love Bentleys, huge, imposing. Except the Arnage, can't stand that. Large boot, huge bonnet, no room in the cabin. Horrible. The rest of the cars made up there in the city of Crewe are wonderful, beautiful stuff. I know, half German, but so what?

Inside, the cabin is pure opulence, but I could live with it, I wouldn't feel embarrassed. It all fits beautifully. I already love this car. Looking out of the window, I notice a small audience, so I give them something to listen to. Starting up the engine, I hear the delicate but assertive tones of the V8. The 12 is a trifle more aggressive – no, a lot more. Once the automatic choke winds down, I can't hear the engine. I think, that's why, the windows are double glazed, and lower the window. But I still can't hear it. I open the door and hear a faint rumble. Amazing. How graceful. I conclude that this car can't be that fast, especially burdened with its two and a half tonnes of body fat. But it's a lovely experience, all the same. In a car, first thing I look for is to adjust the suspension, as most have too much body roll. With the Phantom, driving it all day around the city, with that long bonnet, over potholes, speed bumps and the obstacle course London is, after sixteen hours, it does become tiring.

I gently roll out from my parking spot towards the revellers. As I am not familiar with the throttle response, I allow the car to roll on idle. It's got some pull, flicking hell! The pub people look at the Bentayga from top to bottom like it's a supermodel on a cat walk. You couldn't demand this kind of attention in the Brick. Nice as the Range Rover is, it's driven by the rich but worshipped only by the underprivileged. The Bentayga steals people's attention. It compels people to turn their heads. This is how the courtship of a woman should feel. Seduction, which then gives birth to desire. Then one becomes consumed by the side effects. It's intoxicating.

I am still rolling, incidentally, towards the traffic lights at the junction of Grosvenor Street and New Bond Street. I'm impressed. Look, I've been driving that long, seldom does my head turn or my heart race from being overwhelmed with joy. Nor have I become complacent and taken this job for granted, because the moment you allow gratitude to fade, you open yourself up to all kind of injurious things. Purchasing this would be like me meeting a lady who owns a five-star hotel group, punching way above my weight.

Sitting at the lights I begin to familiarise oneself. The Bentayga name was inspired by the Taiga, the snow forest of the north of Russia, a beautiful, unspoilt nature reserve, with lakes that are so clear you can see straight down to the bottom. The car's aesthetics were determined by Bentley's internal customisation company. Customers can determine how their requirements are met, at a price, obviously.

OK, enough of that, because the lights have changed. I head straight up Grosvenor Street and slowly over into Bond Street. See if anyone's peeping… hello, a couple of fruit trees smiling and stretching their necks out to make sure I see them. It's nice, but I never respond, as it's not me they want to make acquaintance with. Money will never buy you love, but the Bentley can find you some satisfying company of an evening.

Right, let's see how this drives as a chauffeur's car. Gentle on the acceleration… yes, it's very smooth. There's a bit of body roll, but not as much as I thought. I'm going to adjust the damper controls, see if I can feel the difference. Sure can – now that's a trifle more responsive! It's so alert, it almost speaks to me. Hold on, what's the beeping noise? I pull over to get a text message and one of many lights is flashing on the dashboard. Text from PA: 'Paul, there's three fifty-pound notes in the cabinet, the petrol tank should take that easy.' Right, that's what's flashing on the LCD, I was so engrossed, I didn't check for gas. OK, head for Park Lane. She's funny, the PA. Cabinet? When did we stop calling them glove compartments? Let me check to see if there's a decanter in there. There's a fridge in the back with enough room to store four bottles of Krug reserve and four flutes… Yep! There's three crisp fifties waiting to see daylight, so I limp over to Park Lane for some gas. Six miles left on the LCD. That's nothing, one good push of the throttle and that's gone.

On Green Street approaching the gas station, and at the pumps is another two hundred grand Bentayga. This one's glacier white, with what appears to be a beluga interior.

Opening the petrol cap, I see in big letters, 'FILL WITH SUPER UNLEADED ONLY'. Now look, Bentayga drivers, you're not compelled to fill up with Super Plus every time, the car won't self-destruct, you know. Just mix it – super unleaded until the tank's down to half, then fill up next time with normal unleaded. I have an old 1997 BMW 750i. I mix that with two supers and one normal. You really feel the difference, although I only use Shell or BP. Tell you the truth, a full tank of Ultima BP sends the car demented, like it's taken a tank full of E numbers! On a ninty-nine-litre tank, the difference between normal and super is roughly twenty pounds a tank. As it's not my money, here goes...

While I'm filling up, I'm thinking that in this world where the rich congregate, I can't see too many suffering the ignominy of filling up with diesel. It's almost as bad heading north to Scotland in the middle of January in a Maserati Levante 4x4. A few clients I have just wouldn't entertain the thought, any more than Ferrari would produce a diesel car. Especially now diesels have catapulted from saint to sinner.

Great, the fuel cut-off mechanism has malfunctioned and a bit of petrol has spewed down the side of the car. It's OK, I just caught it. Although I should demand that wastage back! I'll have to bring this to their attention. Could have been worse, I suppose. Nothing a sponge and water won't fix.

One hundred and thirty-eight pounds. That's madness, and this car will require that every two days. Fifty-two grand a year from Mr Arab Man's pockets. No wonder they can spend the whole summer in the UK on holiday. If this was mine, my home setting on the satnav would be a BP or Shell garage, believe me.

Pulling out of the gas station on Park Lane is tricky. You have to cross over a bus lane, on to a fast-moving four-lane highway.

There's no speed cameras, so lots of drivers take this opportunity to open their engines up, but looking north, I notice two cameras focusing solely on the bus lane exiting the petrol station. Trollops! Any car that remains stationary in that bus lane for three seconds or more, it's a hundred-pound forfeit. Nice! Apparently there's a camera near here turning over a million pounds a month. Imagine having the power to invent and implement a concept like that.

The CEO's house is only round the corner, but I need to find a shop first for provisions, as I've got a feeling it's going to be a long night. Looking north on Park Lane, no one's letting me out. Buses passing, taxis, Arab supercars racing past… it's like the old days of Formula One. The smell of petrol is prevalent. I do hope the people in the suites of the Dorchester and Grosvenor house have their windows closed. There's a gap coming, just after two racers. It's a Porsche GT3 and a Lamborghini, a normally-aspirated 5.2 litre Huracan LP6104.

OK, I'm going to fill the gap. I don't yet realise that the Bentayga car races from 0–60 in 119 metres, that's approximately 390 ft. So that's roughly twelve houses in a row. Zero to one hundred in nine seconds and terminal velocity is just short of one hundred and ninety miles per hour. Really? For a sports utility vehicle… wow! It has four-wheel drive, of course. I know what that means, but that's about it, I'm no mechanic. Apparently new technology provides the differential with the ability to vary the torque to each wheel, so in layman's terms, each wheel applies its own torque independently, which allows the wheels to grip the road for superior handling and launching. So this magic carpet is a rival for the Porsche Cayenne Turbo S. I do not believe that. Well, let's say I wouldn't have believed that before I drove it.

OK, let's take advantage of this space, big daddy, giddy up, I need to get some carrot sticks from somewhere. It looks like the Arabs have returned from UAE and Ramadan is over, because the street is busy again. They are definitely back to party. Never did get that fasting thing though…

Radio on. Rock FM? Oh, I'll change it in a minute. Kenny Loggins, *Danger Zone*.

The GT3 moves over to the middle lane, creating space for me to get in between and annoy the Huracan. Utilising some of the bus lane, I punch the throttle. What the hell is this? The Bentayga takes off like it's possessed. Both the Porsche driver and the Huracan driver are staring at my car like I'm some sort of terrorist. At the traffic lights, I suddenly have an audience. I can understand why – this car doesn't look like it could run with the Porsche or the Huracan, but things aren't always as they seem. Remember the film *Quantum of Solace*? In the opening scene when the Renault is keeping up with the Aston Martin, in the cinema I could hear people disagreeing that they could be a match, but they were, the Aston really is that slow. But this beast is a dark horse.

At the lights, all eyes in my immediate vicinity are staring at me like I've done something wrong. I'm incredulous at what's just happened. This magic carpet is alive, with a mind of its own. The two supercars take the right-hand bend south of Park Lane to return north back up Park Lane. I'm already going that way, as I need provisions in Marble Arch. I'm not looking for a showdown. No, seriously, I am far too old for showdowns. The GT3 takes the bend and blue flames pour from its exhaust as the damn thing just takes off. The Huracan is getting way too intimate with my behind, weaving left to right behind me, like a racehorse stuck in the blocks at Newmarket and trying to extricate itself. It's pushing me, shouting at me to get round the bend. Two lanes are clear and all I want to do is understand what just happened. My right foot assaults the throttle and the mayhem commences. The Bentayga begins to behave like it's just been diagnosed with schizophrenia. The Huracan is left sniffing the carbon footprint emitting from my four waste pipes while I catapult ahead to hunt down the GT3.

Speed camera! The GT3 hits the brakes, but far too early. I catch up and I hit my brakes right on the line where the radar sensor starts to activate. As soon as I've toddled past at forty, I'm back on the throttle, pushing past the GT3. I have the passenger window ajar, which I always do on my own, so my own scent (good or bad) doesn't permeate the cabin. Passenger side always for security, as it's a lot more difficult for a reprobate to attack the driver with an injurious substance from the nearside. Air is rushing into the cabin and I can hear the familiar roar of the horizontally-opposed flat six engine of the GT3 taking its revs into the red line to fight me. On my right, the Huracan is screaming for attention.

When the GT3 has broken into its stride, it's a delight to behold, intoxicating and mesmerising. The damn thing pips me to the top of Park Lane and we all acknowledge each other, except the Huracan is a trifle miffed.

I park outside the Cumberland Hotel and run into the convenience store for provisions. I stop and looked back at my companion for the evening, thinking we've only just begun.

Wafting back towards my destination, my heart is still beating, fast. How can one convey that moment of experiencing such sheer, effortless, mesmerising power? With just millimetres of throttle movement I felt myself thrust along on a rush of boost, as if I was strapped to a turbine. It was utterly divine.

I know, but look, every once in a while, you displays a little irresponsibility when a window presents itself – it really does help with a long day. I am an advanced driver, not an irresponsible one. One thing I've learnt as a chauffeur is that you invariably learn from other people's mistakes, not your own. There are way too many obstacles on London's roads that can alter the trajectory of your life, let alone your day, to play games that disregard safety and highway legislation. On the roads, these cars are missiles, Exocets with inertial guidance and rocket propulsion. On the back roads they are weapons of mass destruction. When you hit the throttle, you need to make sure the wheel is pointing north. There must be nothing but clear road in front of you.

Let me calm down and see what radio station is on this powerful-looking juke box. Rock FM, music playing: Queen, *Mr Fahrenheit.*

Queen – don't you just love them, played on a Naim in-car stereo that is probably the most powerful sound system I have heard, with ten speakers. The sub-woofer is sublime.

OK, I'm here at the house in Mayfair to pick up the CEO, who is actually younger than me. That makes me feel old. I'm just waiting, as he is on the phone talking to his PA: 'Oh and please don't forget to book the suite at the savoy for New Year's Eve. We get the balcony for the fireworks and it's the best place on the embankment. They will want a deposit, offer them half of the ten thousand they want for the night. I must have that suite!' He hangs up.

We exchange salutations and head off. The phone rings and on the TV screen, it's his wife's phone. 'Oh great,' he says. They engage in a long argument, I think regarding his whereabouts and his absence. At one point I pull over and offer to get out, but he declines my offer. It's just sad when husband and wife bicker incessantly, and I can hear her somewhat dishevelled and crying angrily. He says good night to his kids and hangs up. He turns his head and looks out the window, and the phone rings again. This time I turn the radio on, just enough to play in the background.

Music playing, Magic FM. It's Amy Winehouse, *Tears Dry on Their Own:*

The alpha male, once again. She's consigned to the house after falling for his charms and he has spoiled her career path and compromised her independence with children. Once he was attracted to her supermodel looks. Now she is just the woman who forces him to stay away, play around and seek solace elsewhere, while she looks in the mirror and sees her face looking weary and full of lines. A woman's sacrifice.

'Paul, let's head over to Berkeley Square, east side, to the restaurant Sexy Fish,' he says. He's a young property developer who rose to the top in double quick time. He works hard and plays even harder. Don't expect tonight will be easy. Sunset closes in on this party town. Which incidentally has come alive with the sound of laughter, buskers, revellers, and musical supercar exhausts. Old men and young girls display their exuberance for whatever they've been promised. I roll round Berkeley Square, slowly whilst he is on the phone, assembling his troops and preparing to let battle commence for the evening.

Approaching the restaurant, the atmosphere is alive. The activity is crazy.

'Paul, find a spot by the door if you can and also can you keep an eye on those two.' There are two Rolls Royce Ghosts sitting quietly waiting to be played with. I drop him off on the corner of Bruton Lane and Berkeley Square, right outside the door. Then I go off in search of parking. Driving up Berkeley Street, the frivolities continue. Top restaurants dominate the street: Japanese, Chinese, Russian. There's the Mayfair Hotel on the right. Two types of five-star hotels, one commercial and the other conservative. The Mayfair attracts the celebrities, a very commercial hotel.

How lucky am I? A Brick is on the move and with his big bottom gone, there's plenty of room for me. At sixteen foot ten, the Bentayga is two inches shorter than the Brick. This car is different in every way. I don't want to lower expectations of the Brick, but its ambitions are decidedly lower than the Bentayga's. With Lamborghini and Rolls Royce getting in on the SUV market, the big boys seem to be around the corner and if Land Rover want to play at this level, they're going to have to offer more than just a few shiny bits of trim. Not only do they cost as much as a house, they weigh nearly as much. Although with a house you won't lose your money so quickly. There's apparently a diesel version for the not so well off. As far as I'm concerned, few cars at any price leave one feeling this satisfied behind the wheel.

The sun sets on Berkeley Square. Looking around, there really is a crazy atmosphere out there from behind my triple glazing, mostly SUVs driven by young rich guys. Is it me, but are the rich getting younger? The Arabs are definitely back from their respective homes, although I can't get to grips with the fasting thing. The Russian women are perambulating the pavements in search for those Swiss-plated supercars. Actually, rewind, how come Christians don't starve themselves? Isn't fasting a good way to detox? I think it was only the Jews who were under the Mosaic law kept that observance. Jesus was in the wilderness for forty days and the devil asked him to turn stones into bread. Although I don't think it was self-imposed starvation, he was miles from a supermarket, what else was he supposed to do? I think Jesus is helping us all to appreciate that no one should expect His followers to conform to the old practices of Judaism, such as ritual fasting.

I think I'll switch the engine on, it's getting warm in here and I regularly like to check that the battery hasn't fallen asleep, because that would be a catastrophe. Now I am starting to see things about this car I couldn't in the daylight. The inside door handles are lit up a sexy reddish-pink colour. The lighting is very subtle. This car is hitting all the right spots. The air flowing from these huge nostril air vents is seriously cold. Some cars just provide enough cold air to keep the heat behind the windscreen, but with this, I could have my coat on while it's in the forties outside. I could drive this car day in and day out and the only thing that would annoy me would be the frequent trips to Shell. It's light and crisp and at moments like this, I love my job. The flight instruments are not as classy an S Class Benz, but the feel of opulence exudes. Outside is madness, but behind these triple thick windows, I'm left alone. No noise, fumes or dirty air. Sitting outside the Sexy Fish I often play a game identifying the angry lions in the boot, engines in the jungle that whizz by incessantly in first gear, guessing what each one is. Whilst the magic carpets, the Rollers, the Maybachs filled with the more mature client, waft on by.

So I'm right at the end of Bruton Lane and an Uber driver is trying to squeeze in front of me. Some taxi drivers get my goat, they really set out to annoy people. Do they do stupid things on purpose or are they trying to make you feel as miserable as they feel? Now he's got his hazards on. Why? So many taxi drivers do it. They pull up on a double yellow, blinding the driver behind them with their hazard lights, and it's so obvious even to a traffic warden a hundred metres away that there's a driver doing something wrong.

I am flashing the taxi man. The full beams are that powerful, I can almost burn a hole through his rear window. He'd best not use his rear-view mirror, these lights could extinguish his eyesight. Good, he's going. Lovely, nice, keep going! Just display a little common sense, that's all I ask.

I look at the restaurant. I bet they're all enjoying a nice piece of turbot, in seasoned vegetables, a hand full of french fries? Boiled Jersey Royal potatoes? They're young guys, I guess that's a matured steak then, that's been marinated in carbon dioxide to preserve its fresh looks and kept in the fridge so it appears like it's freshly cooked. Fine. OK, change that subject. What's the saying – 'Keep colon cancer away, reject the meat today!'

Text message: 'Paul, are you out the front, we are coming out, are all the cars OK?' Here we go.

'Yes, I have been looking after the cars,' I reply. Actually, I haven't been informed where to next. As directed, as per usual then.

Eight minutes later someone pops up at the window. 'It's a bit hot in there, don't think air conditioning is working.' I looked at him with a frown, basically willing him to identify himself. 'Sorry,' he replies, 'I'm the MD of the company, I saw you earlier.'

'Yes,' I reply. 'There were quite a few people, I didn't look directly at you, do apologise.'

'Not a problem,' he says. 'My lady friend likes to sit up front in this car, do you mind?' A chunky lady approaches from behind. 'Is this your lady?' I ask.

He turns round and replies, 'I hope not! Although I do know her, she's in property like us. But definitely not with a bottom like that, bless her!' She says goodbye to him and waves. He waves back. 'Look at that bottom, she's got more crack than Brixton,' he says. I apologise, but he's OK with it.

Apparently the directors are planning to pick up six women in total, some they've met this week and some today. Two tall women, mid to late twenties, appear and stand outside the restaurant. Fruit trees, with no leaves on their bodies. In fact they barely have clothes on. Good job it's a warm night. 'That's mine on the right,' he says, still standing by my window. 'The other one's a lawyer. That smile isn't her default setting, she's just been awarded a settlement in her divorce and it's more than enough to invest in our company and the mad cow has already pencilled in a divorce party.' I thought, no emotional attachment then. 'The other, her father's a billionaire, he's just bought one of our companies. Oh, here's the rest, CEO you know him, there's the FD, going through a crappy divorce, under a lot of stress at the moment. Also under the influence of a judge, he's currently experiencing some "court required quality time" with his kids, basically he sees them when the court says.'

Alcohol, it's like a truth drug, everyone is friendlier when they've consumed aplenty. When the rum is in, the wit is out. Old wives' tale.

Everyone jumps aboard the three cars, but we seem to be four or five ladies short.

'Hilton, Paul. Park Lane,' says the boss. In convoy we make our way up to Park Lane. 'Go to Piccadilly as quick as possible,' says the boss. I take off up Berkeley Street. The ladies are effervescence and talkative. 'Oh, this car is powerful!' says one of the women. She can't stop going on about how lovely the interior is. Now the MD is trying to explain how grateful he is her father paid well over the asking price for the business and she's busy pressing buttons. 'What's this do, what's that? Oh look at this backlight, it's a strange colour!'

Keeping my eye on the two Ghosts, we head up Piccadilly. The boss plays with the radio, as they have called for some dance music. Now see, Rolls Royce clientele are totally different from Bentley owners today. Dance music, I thought, not too flipping loud, please. Great. Spoke too soon. Music playing: *Crazy Love*, MJ Cole (featuring Elisabeth Troy).

In the old days, a chauffeur would have his own compartment with a Chinese takeaway type door slide thing to communicate. Even Lady Penelope had a phone. It kept a division where it ought to be. The noise levels inside the cabin have elevated somewhat. I look at the clock and remind myself I was up and about fourteen hours ago, and the night has just begun. Turning right by the Ritz, I'm squeezing my way past, and the Boss says assertively, 'Keep an eye on the others and oh, watch the wheel, watch the blinking wheels!'

'No problem, I've got this,' I say.

A voice from the back says, 'Hey Paul, don't bruise the twenty-twos!' Yes yes, those beautiful wheels. I won't.

Pulling up at the Hilton I can see a small posse of fruit trees with carrier bags waiting. I realise they are with us. I jump out to assist with door opening, as one's supposed to. All are a vibrant, classy bunch. Nothing much left for the imagination, mind, where clothing's concerned, just as long as all we're happy though.

'Right, Annabel's, Paul, please!' says the boss. Now they've all had a drink, everyone is relaxed and more approachable. The MD and his young friend are very close. I'm not sure they can wait to get back to his place. The cabin smells of woman and it's intoxicating. The difference fragrances collide around the roof of the cabin, and mixed with the alcohol, it's sending me lightheaded.

All three cars pull up at Annabel's. I'm thinking, yes, this is it for the night, I'm going home soon, although I could do with some sleep now. It's nearly ten o'clock. Finally, everyone is out and heading into the club. Oh, the boss is coming back out. I lower the window. 'Paul, just keep an eye on the cars, I don't mind tickets, just don't let them tow the cars away.' Not so much the cash but the inconvenience. He hands me all the keys and goes inside to play. It's unfathomable to me, but by time they've finished, they will have run up a collective bill of twenty grand, just for a drink and a chat. Madness. That's not to mention the membership fee. A normal individual could buy a flat in Heathrow and be happy. Or even a house in Reading with a garden. I know, the comparisons don't really work. There's always going to be a divide, but those who have nothing shouldn't expect a thing from this lot. I work for them and I'm lucky to get my wages. I work on a strict seven-day policy. The way the world is right now, people are getting tighter with their cash.

The back door flies open and the MD pops back with one of the girls. As there's no one else with them, I presume we are not going yet. So what do they want? There's two Ghosts round the corner if it's a squeeze behind the privacy glass they're after.

'Paul,' he calls, 'can we pop back to the Hilton, there's some things left we need to pick up? Take the Piccadilly route.' Why, I'm thinking? It's a straight cut through Curzon Street. But one doesn't ask questions.

The MD turns his attention to the young lady with him, who seems somewhat agitated, like she has ADHD. She can't settle. Fidgeting, running her fingers incessantly through her hair and sniffing, like in a couple of hours she has developed a cold from somewhere.

'So did you get all the items, you know, what we spoke about earlier?' the MD asks her.

'Yes, but one isn't the colour you asked for as they had run out,' she replies.

'Oh, so what colour did you end up with?'

'Well it's not too dissimilar, somewhat darker than what you asked for – problem?'

'No darling, it's just there's a strict dress code and I didn't want us all to turn up and one of us be rejected, it would sort of spoil the night, so to speak.'

Where are they going, I thought? They're all off out after Annabel's – *nooooo!* Well they can get an Uber. This wasn't in the plan!

Sudden noises from the back, pecking noises. Great. Wish I had taken the Phantom. There's a lot more space between me and the back seat. Now some drivers relish an activity like this, as it brightens up their day. At least while Woody Woodpecker is focusing on her he's leaving me alone and I can drive the car in peace. But that's just blinking it, it's far from peaceful. Even though I am looking ahead, my peripheral vision can see the rear-view mirror. So I wait for them to take a breath, then bend it upwards. Didn't want to disturb. If she had seen me move the mirror, in her suspicious head, she might have thought I was adjusting it to see them better, which is exactly what I wasn't doing.

I wonder if I have any headphones in my man bag. They are in the passenger side footwell, and I can't blinking reach it. Now raising the volume may indicate that I am troubled by the rear seat activity. Any movement from me might be misconstrued, her panties coming back up mighty quick and I could be in trouble.

I'm stuck on Piccadilly, the revellers are out in force, the road is jammed with supercars and luxury cars, and only poor God can see the activity in the backs of those limos. Unfortunately, the back-seat activity in my car has increased. I hear a different sound, and I'm in great discomfort. You want to do something, turn the music up or shout, 'Look, you're multi-millionaires, not flipping kids!' I begin inhaling deep through my nostrils. My brain is racing with alternatives, as the traffic has just stopped. OK, let me describe how I am feeling. There are two people in the back of my car, one lighting his cigarette with the car lighter, and the other filling his personal lighter with fuel. She's shoving the nipple of the gas lighter up the jacksy of the cigarette lighter. Now fuel escapes and it's cascaded on to the lambswool carpet. She has just dropped her cigarette onto the same bit of carpet... imagine the scene? Immediate evacuation. That's how I'm feeling!

We are outside the Ritz and I attempt to drop them round the side, by the main door on Arlington Street, but there's no chance. Something up ahead has paralysed Piccadilly. Oh man, they are getting vocal! You know when you've got a piece of fruit that's ripe and delicious, and you're munching your way all the way to the seed? Well the noises are like that.

The traffic is now moving slightly and I'm trying to keep things calm, no drama. It's really a do not disturb type situation. Damn – I just felt the back wheel run over something. What the hell was that? Feeling the pressure, I look in the side mirror. Too dark. I don't look in the back, but the activity is still intense, no change there. I rolled past a traffic light in the middle of the road, and thought I had enough room. Great, I've gone and bruised the twenty-twos!

I manage to skip round two buses which have blocked the exits heading west, and realise that one of them has broken down. I scramble free and race off to the Park Lane roundabout. Now I'm an advanced driver, but stress can still impede your ability to perform. But I am not stressed, just freaked out. Look, I don't care how good a driver you think you are, you couldn't handle this. Even a police driver would have bailed out.

Arriving at the Hilton, there's the usual commotion. People everywhere, like a Saturday afternoon shopping. I pull up at the front door to drop them off. I see the concierge racing over to fling back the door, and search for the door locks among the flight instruments. Not there. Quick, by the door handle. A green light indicates they are locked, just as the concierge tries to wrench off the door handle. It doesn't open, but then he looks at me. I jump out opening my door only. I ask for a minute until the occupants in the back are ready. I can feel his urgency, as it's a drop off, nothing else.

I stand outside waiting, with no cash on me to placate the porter. As I'm standing there, a man and his partner emerge from the casino door. They're not holding hands, he looks grumpy and she is searching for something. Our eyes meet and she locks on. 'Oh no!' I'm thinking, 'Don't look at me, I'm so broke, if anyone tried to rob me, they'd just be practising!' I try to send the word 'chauffeur' in Morse code using my eyebrows, and it registers. It looks like he has taken her out for the evening and it's somehow backfired and she's seeking a quick exit. Wonder how tight she clung on to her jewellery.

The rear door comes ajar and then stops. The concierge makes for the door and I step in between, politely asking him to curb his eagerness. The couple eventually emerge. I stand on the back arch opening the door with my left hand, then utilising my right arm as an aid for her to negotiate the Bentayga's height gracefully. 'We won't be long,' he shouts, whisking her off into the foyer. 'Take as long as you need and don't come back till you're sorted.' Blinking heck.

I reverse to pull up and wait and reflect on what just happened. Music. Put Magic FM on. I can't erase my thoughts. That's it, open the windows. Her perfume mixed in with… no, not thinking about it.

Music playing. Kate Bush, *Feel It*.

But right now, it's sleep I need. I pull the tailgate button and prise myself out of the Bentley. The air hits me and I could fall asleep right here and now. My chauffeur's bag is in the back and I need water and Berocca. Definitely not Red Bull. 'What's that?' I hear you saying. I need my phone to take a picture to read what it is, as it's far too tiny to read. It says, '*This contains pantothenic acid which contributes to mental performance. Vitamins B1 and B2 for physical performance.*' It's got to be better than sugar rush drinks, as the comedown can be draining. I know drivers who drink energy drinks like pop with a bowl full of Skittles for breakfast. How's that supposed to work? However, to accompany my effervescent drink, I have a couple of bananas and cashew nuts. I am so not going to make the Chinese tonight. I could just do with a large vegetable fried rice about now.

Hopefully they will return to the car in a more civilised manner. I really hope they alleviate some of that tension up there. They were just hungry. I should have offered to go and get a bargain bucket so he could rip the wing off something deep fat fried, like he was doing to her. No, I wasn't watching, but it wasn't hard to imagine. Strange, when you hear people doing it in a field and you're like, 'What's wrong with you, get a room!' When a couple are in that zone, they just can't stop. To be that close to a blue movie is even worse!

But what really compels a couple to display that shark attack frenzy? I could see he couldn't say no. He simply didn't have the skills to defend himself. I mean this guy suddenly descended into euphoria like he was locked down, handcuffed, entangled in her spider's web, didn't even realise. That's where it can become dangerous, I've seen it. When tomorrow arrives, he's returned to a civilised state or his caveman default setting, she's dumped unceremoniously after giving herself. It's best to let her tell you it's over. I've seen rejected women turn loopy. Then batten down the hatches. What a merry go round.

I have just got my head down with visions of my duvet, providing comfort to my body, when I receive a text message. 'Paul, could you bring the keys back to Annabel's, we will all travel to the Hilton and press forward from there.'

OK, there's my confirmation. The night has just begun. Nightclub probably. Why can't they just go home and canoodle there?

Approaching the club, all are outside. The boss begins sorting who was in whose car and I help them all into the cars. It's mayhem, as it always is outside Annabel's. Cars want to get past, as everyone's important and got places to go. I notice that the girls have changed, and the men have dinner suits on. Strange, can't be a nightclub then, can it? I speak to the drivers and ask if I am leader. Apparently so. I offer a few tips in keeping up and how dangerous it is to dawdle. The boss says we are late and need to be there in less than an hour for registration… registration? I give him a funny look. He replies, 'Paul, I'll give you the address at the Hilton.' OK, I think. The Berocca has begun to kick in.

After a little messing about and juggling, we are off in convoy to the Hilton. I keep my eye on the Ghost behind me, as we're whizzing though London like the police escorting a Head of State. It's mental. The boss phones the MD explaining that all the cars are going to cause mayhem. On the roundabout it's like a trade route, it's so busy – the Hilton, the Metropolitan with its trendy and hugely popular Japanese restaurant on the first floor, the Four Seasons, the Park Lane Club casino. It's a hotspot. So getting in and out is imperative.

My car is full, so the MD will have to travel in the third car. I direct the driver to pull up at the front door and get out to assist. The couple eventually appear at the front door looking like a Hollywood couple. Everyone looks stunning, but the woman who was a lawyer jumps straight to the top of the tree. She boasts a long satin beluga sequinned open-backed gown which fits her perfectly. I later find out it's a Chanel. To accompany the dress, around her neck is a chain of diamonds in a square with one huge yellow diamond in the middle, repeated, all the way around the chain. Bulgari, apparently. The timepiece on her right wrist is beautiful. She could have owned what she wanted, but she chose what she liked, from the Grande Complication collection, a rose gold diamond-encrusted Audemars Piguet. The screws on the gold band are also made of gold. The AP watch company actually declined the opportunity to support the James Bond brand, as they felt solitary advertising maintained exclusivity. This watch is different and stands out from the rest. I've seen quite a few accessories and I do like those designers who are brave enough not to just follow the crowd. Her timepiece could have bought five Bentleys.

So a convoy of cars totalling one million pounds hits the road. There's a Ferrari 458 Italia joining us somewhere, another member of the gang, wherever he is. He knows the route. Now I am really intrigued.

Leaving Park Lane and heading to Knightsbridge, it's always a buzz to waft on by, even at eleven at night. It's busy. Very busy. Supercars out till the small hours. Coffee shops open, people sitting outside drinking or smoking a bong. Oh, there's Harrods, lit up like a Christmas tree. It's motto should be the same as John Lewis, 'never knowingly undersold', because it never compromises.

I check the convoy is still together. My client is in the front seat, looking behind. 'Yep,' he says. All together. 'OK Paul,' he continues, 'ditch the classical, thanks!' It's my comfort, but I have no choice. OK. Let's see. Capital FM. Music playing: Doolally, *Straight from the Heart.*

'OK Paul, turn this up please,' says the boss. 'I have just had a text from my colleague and he'll find us on the M4, we should collide in around twenty minutes, although he has not yet left Kensington Palace Gardens. Look out for a black 458 Italia. Oh, and the satnav will say exit at twelve at Theale and wiggle our backsides through Pangbourne and Buckleberry. I don't want to go that way, just continue to thirteen and come off at Chieveley and work your way backwards towards Yattendon.'

'No problem,' I reply. 'Could I have the address?'

'Oh yes, hang on, let me put it into the satnav, it's a tricky place, hidden in the middle of nowhere.'

Making it past Hammersmith is always a good moment – end of the A4 and the M4 is in sight. Still a lot of traffic about for this time of the night. Before we know it, we're on the Mercedes flyover. There's the glass building with Mercedes piled one on top of each other. When you see that, you know Heathrow isn't that far. Looking to the left, there's a row of planes heading there on final approach. They look slow, but they're moving at roughly one hundred and sixty miles per hour, so that there is enough wind flowing under the wings to maintain height.

M25/M4 crossing. Now we are moving at a very fast pace, but the convoy is still intact. All in the car very vocal. Right now I'm ready for bed, I don't know where this lot get their energy from. Now the motorway lights have gone, just the cat's eyes for company. I like this stretch of road. There's a plane within a stone's throw trying to gain altitude and running parallel to the motorway. There's a huge jumbo running alongside me now, just taking off. The strobe lights are flashing like mad. There's no lights on internally, because they'll playing 'keep calm' music and everyone will be paying more than the usual attention to any strange noises and listening to make sure the engines are running smoothly. Quite a scary thought really, your life in someone else's hands. That plane is a 747 with four engines to listen to. Must be four hundred people in there. Safe journey then. OK, you can all get the alcohol out now. Four engines means it's going a long way.

I watched this programme on women pilots saying they deserve the same pay as men – no doubt they do. There was a strange moment when they were discussing human performance. One particular flight had just under three hundred people on board, the captain was a man with millions of hours flying time and his co-pilot was a young woman who had not long qualified. With all the training involved you'd say she deserved her spot. But there are people who won't fly with a female pilot. Their prerogative I suppose. I remember how a huge gay singer and performer who is known by everyone was sitting on a jet ready to take off when the captain's voice came over the tannoy with the usual words to reassure passengers. Hearing a woman's voice, the singer summoned the stewardess and asked her to confirm who's voice it was. She confirmed it was the pilot, and he immediately told her to stop the plane, as he was getting off. They did – they turned the plane around. Sad really. In this program focusing on human performance, the male pilot and his female co-pilot were in mid-flight. She was PIC (pilot in command), but for an hour she talked and talked and talked her head off, and neither of them realised the plane was slowing down. It slowed down so much it induced 'alpha max' status. You know on a manual car when you bring the clutch up to the biting point, that point just before it stalls? That's like alpha max on a plane. The pilot told her he thought they were in trouble, and she continued yapping. When she realised he wasn't joking, she pulled back on the 'yoke' (pilot's steering wheel). Now on a horse, if you pull back on the reins, doesn't that mean you have decided to stop? To a plane's computers, it means you want to get off. The pilot was horrified that she hadn't pushed forward to gain airspeed. The plane didn't make it, nor did any of the passengers. The only thing that survived was the flight data recorder.

'What's this junction, Paul?' the boss asks.

'Junction twelve, one more to go,' I reply. That really didn't take long, as all three cars are pushing it.

'WHAT'S THAT?' shouts the boss, and one of the girls shouts over the movie, 'It's the Ferrari.' It certainly was the 456, which shot past like a bullet. The boss phones him to say that if we were on water, we would have all capsized.

'Paul, he'll meet us at the next junction,' says the boss. 'Oh, has everyone got charge on their phones? I have a portable charger in the cabinet.' Opening the cabinet, he takes out his portable charger, but he's horrified. In the heat the charger has exploded. Phone chargers and phones, just don't leave them in the heat.

The clock is close to one o'clock when we arrive at junction thirteen. The satnav sends us round the roundabout and back on ourselves. I haven't been this way before. Past it, but I've never taken this road. Chivalry, Hermitage and the borders of Yattenden have some beautiful scenery in the day, but at night we're surrounded by silhouettes that run across the road in front of the car. I'm worried, as if any animal misjudges how fast we are going, it's over, possibly for us as well as those badgers and the hoggie-type gazelle things, which will take out the Bentley's radiator, easy. No breakdown service around here.

We wiggle in and out of the woods and I'm wondering if it's a house party, with them dressed up to the nines like this. We take a steep bend to the right, then one coming up to the left on a hill. It's pitch black. Satnav displays 300 yards. Really? What, in the blinking woods? A Phantom pulls out just ahead of me, then the Ferrari follows him. He is now in front of us. The satnav concludes its journey. We take a sharp right and on the right there's a thirty-foot driveway and twenty-foot high gates flanked by two Olympic flames, burning brightly either side. There's a queue. We wait. There are two athletic-looking men, one inside the gate, one in front. Now the cars in front are showing the gate men their phones. The men should move aside and the gates should open. The Ferrari moves up to the gates and stops. The gate man approaches, but the boss jumps out and walks over to the Ferrari. He shows the man his phone and comes back. What the hell was on that phone, a password or something?

As we wait for the gates to open, the front is lit up in subtle lighting, just enough to reveal the entrance. Seventy yards past the gates, the lightly-coloured pebbled driveway begins to darken as the lights fade and the driveway heads off into the twilight zone again.

As we drive, the crunching of gravel beneath my twenty-two-inch diamond-cut wheels reminds me that this is as far as a Bentley will go off road. I suppose it's off-road ability is irrelevant really. We take a left-hand bend and I can still see the house. Trees flank the driveway both sides, as far up as I can see. One hundred metres or so on we take another left-hand bend and lights appear over the driveway again. There's the house. The bricks look like huge champagne-coloured breeze blocks. At the front door are two doormen and two valets. Everyone disembarks. The boss takes bags out from the boot. One of the doormen approaches and asks if we can be swift in coming in, as others are arriving and the cars need parking.

'Paul,' calls the boss, 'I'll text you when we're finished. Probably be a couple of hours, not sure, will call.' Then off to play they all go. I speak to the valets and they say they will show me where to park the cars. We take the Ferrari, the Bentley and one of the Ghosts – the other Ghost is left behind. I'm thinking, oh well, this is where my role ends. As I drive off I look to my right into one of the windows and my party are putting different face masks on. What on earth?

We drive round to the back of the house, where some serious machines are sitting in a dimly-lit car park. Very strange. There sleeping chauffeurs in some of them, others are empty.

In the distance I can see upstairs and downstairs, where there is a lot of activity. But it looks formal, calculated. Maybe it's still early. Actually, maybe it's time to get a little sleep. I turn the radio back to Classic FM to see if the music can assist in me getting off. The armchairs provide the support and I leave the passenger side window open for air. It's so nice to be left alone for a while...

You know when you are asleep, but you're not sure, then you wake up all dishevelled, not knowing where you are? Oh, I'm still in the Bentley. The radio has gone to sleep. Daylight is finding its way through the clouds. I'd better see if the battery has fallen asleep. The Bentayga bursts into life. Thank granny for that.

05:37. I release a yawn, a long one. Actually, I could do with some mouthwash. Now you would have thought that this house, being so splendid, would have some Listerine in those posh Portakabins, but no.

Music playing: Dean Martin (featuring Helen O'Connell), *How D'ya Like Your Eggs in the Morning?* I'm gonna have me a coupla fried eggs, over easy. Hash browns. Two of them. Beans and toast, no butter. Yuk! Maybe some fungi, isn't that mushrooms? But first, I so need to stretch my legs. So I slowly disembark and allow the morning air to refresh my body. It's about thirteen degrees. I'm surrounded by acres of neatly-manicured land, like a golf course. The trees look like they were strategically planted. What a way to start the day. Breakfast on the veranda, overlooking this beautiful, stunning scenery. I walk on the grass, as the path is too noisy. I hear an engine start up – sounds like an Audi R8. It is, summoned to pick up its weary owner. Once the V8 sound diminishes, I continue to walk toward the back of the house. Looking upstairs, there's still activity. How come there's no curtains on the windows, can't they afford them? I feel I should put my jacket on. Actually, what am I doing? What if a couple of Doberman Pinschers come running? I could never make it back to the car. Oh well, I'm here now. Have you ever had the feeling you're out of bounds? Hang on – why am I whispering?

I can hear music. Instrumental type stuff. There's a window, let me pop over. Twenty odd feet away from a window and I feel a hand on my shoulder, no lie! I turn around and it's a an athletic-looking man with a gold mask on. What the hell? He's scared the living daylights out of my backside. He leaves the mask on.

'Hello sir, can I be of any assistance?' he asks, in a slow, deep, calculated voice.

'Hi, er, I was convinced that the male facilities were in this direction,' I reply.

'No sir, you're slightly off course. Allow me,' he says, and moves out of the way, so I can walk first.

I ask, 'So how were last night's frivolities, successful, I trust?'

'Splendid sir, did you not care to participate?'

'After the day I'd had, energy was the last thing I'd choose to dispense with,' I reply.

'Quite,' he replies. 'The Portakabin is right in front of you sir,' and he points to the spot. 'I trust you'll be returning to your vehicle after being satisfied by your visit, sir?' I take that as a warning. But I have no idea how he knew I was there. He just appeared from the trees and the mist. It could be worse, it could have been a couple of Dobermans. Was he looking at the CCTV all night? He probably has infra-red.

Back in the Bentley, I feel safe, so I put the seat heater and the steering wheel heat on. Damn, I'd better check my phone… nothing. He's probably fallen asleep and forgotten me. That's nothing new. Looking around the car park, there are a few more spaces, as some cars have already left. This is usually the worst time for hanging around, but it's good for uninterrupted sleep.

Text message. Finally. 'Come to the door in five minutes.' Brilliant. I'd best have a check around the car. Oh, the wheel. Looking at it in this light, I can't see much. Maybe I didn't bruise the twenty-twos after all. Let me check in the back. The carpet's a bit dishevelled but nothing… oh no. On the passenger side, tucked under the seat is an unidentified object. It's a very delicate lacey pink. You're joking! I'm not picking that up. But what if I forget and the boss's wife picks it up? Do I use two fingers or just grab it with my whole hand? Sod it, I'm leaving them. Got to go.

Pulling up at the house, my client is waiting and he doesn't have a mask on. He appears wrecked. His waxed hair is usually so neat and all in place. He has tried to cover his shirt with his jacket, but in opening the door he bends down to get in and his jacket opens up and there's blood on his shirt and scratch marks on his neck. I'm sure he's not been shaving. Driving to the gate, the same two men are still on the gate. Need I ask? No, none of my business. Long as he's happy. Just doesn't look it. Very strange.

'Back to London Paul, quick as you can!' he whispers. I'm quite happy with that, I'm due to start my next job with the King in three hours.

Sunday morning and the road's clear. It takes an hour, but we are back in London now. He doesn't say much, just exhales a lot and nods off a couple of times. Pulling up at his place he thanks me but never offers a tip, he never does.

Parking up the Bentley, I quietly thank it for a fantastic evening. I reluctantly hand back the keys and remove my rucksack from the back. The boss shakes my hand and I can see he just wants to get inside. He says, 'Before you go, there's some rubbish under the seat, could you bin it for me?' I open the back door and those pink things are just lying there waiting for me. I'm not happy. What if I'm stopped and searched for being out that time of the morning? Or I fall ill with them in my bag? I could have pinched the off someone's washing line. This is bad. I use two fingers to prise them off the floor and push them to the bottom of my bag. I say nothing, and head for the gates. 'Send your invoice in the mail and the office will deal with it Monday,' he says. I look back at the Bentayga and wish I could take it with me.

It's 06:56 on a Sunday morning and the London streets are civilised and peaceful. Very dirty, though. I wonder if I'll have enough time to go to a McDonald's. To a driver who's on the night shift, that familiar M sign provides solace. I'm limited in choice though – Egg McMuffin and hash browns, or at lunch time a Beanburger with fries and chilli cheese bites.

Great Portland Street is too far to walk, so I'll run down to Green Park. Walking over Piccadilly, I can see the Ritz and the concierge out front, cleaning the debris of Saturday's nocturnal activities off the pavement. Looking the other way, they're doing the same thing at the Park Lane Hotel. I really like that place, for me it's the second most pleasurable four-star behind the Cavendish.

All civilised down here. On the Jubilee Line to Regent's Park, but I'll stop at Oxford St McDonald's. I must eat something. I'm trying to remember where it is.

Out on Oxford Circus, I have the place to myself. Street cleaners are out in force. The odd bus strolls by. There's the sign, opposite Hanover Square. I'm excited at the promise of junk food, I'm that hungry. Look at the state of this place! What's with the pay for your food? McDonald's have changed their system. One woman on the till, eight people in the queue. McDonald's doesn't need a 'cook to order' service, it has enough hungry customers to have food ready, like it used to. OK, so let's punch some holes in this massive computer. No wonder there's no jobs, McDonalds employs thousands of staff. How are they going to account for the workers they dismiss when they render them redundant because of 'artificial intelligence'?

OK, made my order. Let's count the minutes. Looking at their food holders, they are all empty, is that to avoid wasting food? I don't know. Eight minutes later, she calls my number. 'Big breakfast double sausage and double bacon and a Coke!' she calls. That's definitely not my order. I walk over and show her my ticket. 'This is yours,' she asserts.

'No it isn't,' I say. She takes the ticket and walks off. See, the old system, I would simply whip my beanburger off the shelf and I'd be eating it now. Why do people complicate things?

She returns with the right order, and I ask her if I can make an addition. She asks what, and I reply that I didn't see any

Chilli Cheese Bites on the menu. 'That's because we do not sell cheese bites, you need to go back to Burger King. We do have Mozzarella Cheese Bites but they don't begin till ten o'clock, sir.'

Well, that told me. Not really a fan of Burger King, except for the onion rings and salad. Now they've always had an 'order and wait' service, because they don't have McDonald's' traffic. I think they're bigger in America though. Their flagship restaurant in the middle of Piccadilly Circus was given to them by McDonald's. They let Burger King have that prime spot because they didn't need it, but still, with all that traffic, Burger King have always operated the 'order and wait' service.

I watch everyone in the restaurant drinking all those sugary drinks, the different coffees. I have to stay well away. A couple of years ago, my doctor referred me to an ENT consultant at the Royal Berkshire Hospital. Actually, it's a lovely place if you're allowed a choice. My problem was that I had fat protruding into my eye, like a cloud of fat forcing its way out from the socket. So this surgeon explained from my blood results that my cholesterol was seriously high. I was mortified. His suggestion was to remove the eyeball, leave it hanging by its internal threads onto my cheek bone and cut away the cloud from behind my eye, cauterise it with something hot, then shove my eye back in. So I ask, 'You won't forget to line it back up again will you, oh, and will it hurt?' I really didn't have the stomach or the appetite for it and I knew there were a lot of risks. The consultant mentioned something about a cardiac arrest because of my cholesterol level. I thought, I talk to many things but a heart attack is a conversation I don't want. I've seen people have them and they are not nice. I can almost hear my heart saying to me, 'Oh, you're listening to me now, huh? You didn't want to listen when you were sitting at the bus stop, munching on that pork chop, did you?'

When you see a heart attack it's like the victim is bending down, begging for one more chance. His heart is talking back. 'You're in a state right now, why wait all this time before having a conversation with me?' says the heart. 'You've never asked me how I feel, how I'm doing, nothing. You call God's name all the time and you don't even believe in him! When did you call me or check up on me? So here we are and I suppose you're looking for some quick answers. Are you gonna live? Can I get something for the pain? Can I have some reassurance? What about my family, can I have one last call? Will they even listen to me, as they all have been begging me to look after myself?'

Since that warning, I've cut out nearly everything I had to cut out, and my cholesterol is where it should be, low.

I relax and nod off for an hour and now I have to muster the energy to go to work. As I'm packing up my things and placing my rubbish on the tray, a woman approaches and began asks me how I am. Her clothes are not clean, but she's dignified all the same. She says, 'Hi, can I sing for you? I know you'll like my voice.'

'Er, no thanks, please don't,' I reply. 'How can I help?'

'I apologise if I've bothered you, it's just been a long week, and my problems seem to increase.'

I interrupt to save her from the ignominy of having to explain herself, and it's frustrating when people refuse to get to the point. Working for all these impatient clients, it's probably rubbed off on me. So I ask her what she needs.

'Oh, anything you have spare please, God will bless you. You do believe in him, don't you?'

'Yes, of course I do, I try my utmost to live by his standards,' I reply. I open my bag to draw out the small amount of cash I know I have in my man bag, which is inside my rucksack.

'Thank you so much, I'm dying for a cup of tea,' she says.

I pull the contents of my bag out and on to the table. 'I don't think I have much, but you can have whatever I have,' I say, looking at her.

When I look down to open my man bag, there sitting on top is a luminous pair of finest Rigby & Peller ladies' underwear. A thong. Right there in the middle of the table. I'm horrified. She just stares at them and so does the security guy behind her. I'm quietly struggling to erase last night's immoral episode from my mind. I give the lady what change I have, then throw everything back in my bag and get up and walk.

It's a lovely morning and I have a fifteen-minute walk to the Phantom, north through Portland Place, west up Devonshire place, north on Harley Street. I'm twenty minutes early for work, and all raring to go. Seldom do I witness such enthusiasm from churchgoers, these days anyway. So I pick up the Phantom and bring it round.

I can feel London slowly waking up. The weight of traffic on the Marylebone road is consistent. This is why London is good for the depressed soul, you can never get bored, as there's so much going on. I am conscious I haven't had a change of clothes, but I haven't actually been working in factory all night, so think I will survive the next few hours.

As by convention, they all come out of the house together, the King and his three wives, but only he gets into the car. It's like he's saying, 'You're all used to the heat, now walk!' Helping him into the car, he seems jovial and well rested and he's smiling like he's just got the cream. All fine and dandy.

Driving round back up to Marylebone Road, we meet the wives walking up. He doesn't wind the window down and offer some health and safety advice regarding the inappropriate height of their heels and how unstable they look on them, or beg them not to attend McDonald's before church as they would only fall asleep mid service and pass wind involuntarily. They can't even change their minds and go home, because none of them has a key. This polygamy thing seems terribly one-sided.

Pulling up at the church, my usual instruction is to wait, not in the car park but right outside the church, half-blocking pedestrian access. Helping him up the stairs, two clergymen rush out to greet him. I think, how nice, they're coming to assist me, but one of them stops and rubs his hands together, as if he's saying, 'Great, we can get the roof done now, and maybe, if there's any change left, those gold candelabras we saw on the Metropolitan Police auction website. You know, the one where they confiscate goods from criminals.'

'Hmm,' says the other clergyman. 'Yes, I had a peep myself and I did notice a couple of his and hers Rolexes that were going remarkably cheap.'

After disposing of him to his spiritual pocket-cleaners the Three Degrees come running up the steps. Well I say 'running', forget that. Anyway, the clergymen just turn on their heels and walk through the door. Hey ho. So I return to the magic carpet that sits floating outside, awaiting people's comments. 'Oh, isn't that car huge!' 'Is a member of the Royal Family in there?' 'Is that your church?' 'Is the Rolls the preachers' car?' 'Or the bishop's, even?' Once I had someone say, 'Don't you wear a hat? You would look finished with a cap on.' The role of a chauffeur is subservient enough without looking like a complete joey.

I had a position with a seriously wealthy middle-aged man who lived next door to one of the Beatles down in Surrey. I made it through the interview and turned up to work for a trial, but this antagonistic so and so insisted I wore a hat. I forgot to bring it, as I wasn't used to wearing one. Halfway through the day, he stated that a prerequisite for the vacancy was to wear a cap. I explained that I had left it at home, and he stated in no uncertain terms that I should not turn up tomorrow without it. That day, he had all the cars, Phantom, 458 Ferrari, a lovely AMG S class Coupe, but you know what he wanted me to drive to the Chelsea Flower Show? A twenty-year-old Lexus, his best friend he called it. He kept it to remind him of when things had been tough and it was one thing that didn't let him down. Lovely, thanks for sharing the story, but he wanted me to park outside in this car with a flipping hat on? That's when I knew he only wanted to mug me off. Just no reasoning to it. When he commentated later about getting back and giving his shoes a once over, I was grateful to remember that a trial day isn't just for the employer, it's for the driver too.

On a hot day, I have the Phantom engine running outside the church, because you need the air conditioning on, yet no one has ever said, 'Switch yer engine off!' Because you really can't hear it. The V12 is huge, but so quiet people stand by it and think it's off. I can see why people ask questions as It appears hypocritical. The only thing this Phantom lacks is a number plate saying 'PRAYD4'.

I suppose those with money don't really care what others think. But what happens if we meet our demise? Do we not want to leave some sort of legacy, or even a good name for ourselves so we are not forgotten (in a favourable way that is)? Even Jesus asks us to remember him with the observance of bread and the wine. Not sure how often, but I do know we don't celebrate our anniversaries and birthdays every week.

There was a famous man, Alfred Nobel, born in 1833 to a family of engineers in Stockholm, Sweden. In 1850, he met Ascanio Sobrero, the inventor of nitroglycerine. Intrigued by nitroglycerine's unpredictable tendency to exploding under pressure or heat, Nobel became interested in finding a way to control it and make a commercially usable explosive. In 1857 he filed his first patent, for a gas meter, while his first Swedish patent was on 'ways to prepare gunpowder'. After years focusing on improving the stability of the explosives, in 1867, at the age of thirty-four, Nobel invented dynamite, which was much easier to control and safer than nitroglycerine. Dynamite was an immediate commercial success, it was patented in the US and the UK and was widely used in mining.

After further developments, Nobel amassed a fortune from his many inventions, of which dynamite was the most significant. His philosophy was, as he put it, 'My dynamite will lead sooner to peace than a thousand world conventions ever could. As soon as men will find that in one instant whole armies can be utterly destroyed, they surely will abide by golden peace.'

In 1888 Alfred's brother Ludwig died, and a French newspaper mistakenly published Alfred's obituary instead of Ludwig's. Reading his own obituary, Nobel was appalled to discover what the public thought of him. The newspaper condemned Nobel for inventing dynamite, giving him an infamous nickname by reporting, '*Le marchand de la mort est mort*' ('the merchant of death is dead'), and stating, 'Dr Alfred Nobel, who became rich by finding ways to kill more people faster than ever before, died yesterday.'

To Alfred, this obituary was a warning. What he read horrified him. He had spent his life alone inventing things, and was deeply disturbed and concerned at how he would be remembered. This unfortunate event inspired him to make alterations in improving his public image and to be remembered for a good cause. Shortly thereafter, he established the Nobel awards. Today, everyone is familiar with the Nobel Prize, while relatively few people know how Nobel made his fortune.

Thinking about how your obituary is going to read can motivate you to rethink how you're currently spending your life. No eulogy ever says he/she dressed well, lived extravagantly, took fabulous vacations, drove an expensive car or built an expensive home. I never heard anyone praised for being too busy at work to find time for their children. A call to someone who is lonely, a listening ear to a person in need, long walks with our children, saying thank you to a spouse, are the essence of a life well lived.

Thinking of my obituary, would it indicate that I am thinking of others, that I actually care what people are thinking?

I wonder how coming to church could fortify that. Do all those people in that church think anything of the one next to them? Actually I don't know what the church stands for any more. If it wasn't for the Apostle Paul, churches wouldn't exist. He was like an overseer to all the congregations he set up in the first century. We see in the latter part of the Greek scriptures the number of letters he sent warning the congregation to maintain God's standards. Be aware of wolves in sheeps' clothing. He stated that the church was supposed to be a safe haven from the unrepentant wrongdoer, so everyone in there right now should be sincere. No rapists, no thieves. You should be able to leave your belongings in the church and come back and find them. You should not be in fear of attack. That sounds like a stretch to imagine. So what is supposed to bind Christians together today? One of Apostle Paul's letter, this one to the Galatians chapter 6 verse 2 says, '*Unlike the mosaic law, the law of Christ unites its adherents to live more by conscience and principal.*' So if God provides the command, 'Do not commit adultery', Jesus' principle would be, '*anyone who looks at a woman so as to lust after her, has already committed adultery in their heart*' (Matthew 5:28).

So the path of freedom obviously lies in obedience. But I hear many people say that they are sincere and they live a good life. So putting sincerity into perspective, what does God think of sincere people? Well let's look at Noah. God overtly displayed how he found pleasure in Noah and his family, who stuck by him. He and his wife paid their tithes, were nice to the neighbours. But what of the community? They still 'took no note' – even in the face of all the evidence that God was blessing Noah and his endeavours. They could not help but notice the animals streaming into the ark. But we should not be surprised at their apathy. People today likewise take no note of the overwhelming evidence that we are now living in the final days of this world system.

Back to this church and its followers, I don't attend because the whole church thing doesn't add up. Jesus said, '*My people will be known by their fruits and the love they display to one another.*' I just don't see this. Not knowing who I am sitting next to, it's scary really, although the church is meant to be a safe haven from the unrepentant wrongdoer, they are there in disguise. No wonder church attendances are falling, most seem so disillusioned. As Jesus said, 'Look at my sheep without a shepherd.' A couple of centuries after the first century Christians had gone, apostasy set in. Then over the years, the Bible was kept in the language of Hebrew and Latin, so the clergymen were in effect 'fossilising' the truth in it, until in the Middle Ages a few people who recognised what the clergymen were doing set about trying to translate the Bible into a language for the common people.

Now we have Isaac Newton, almost a candidate for sainthood, buried in the grounds of Westminster Abbey, as he's held in such high esteem. For Newton the world of science was by no means the whole of his life. He spent more time on theology than on science, and wrote about 1.3 million words on biblical subjects. Yet this vast legacy lay hidden from public view for two centuries until the auction of his non-scientific writings in 1936.

Newton's understanding of God came primarily from the Bible, which he studied for days and weeks at a time. He took special interest in miracles and prophecy, calculating dates of Old Testament books and analysing their texts to discover their authorship. In a manuscript on rules for interpreting prophecy, Newton noted the similar goals of the scientist and the prophecy expositor: simplicity and unity. He condemned the 'folly of interpreters who foretell times and things by prophecy', since the purpose of prophecy was to demonstrate God's providence in history when 'after (prophecies) were fulfilled, they might be interpreted by events'.

A member of the Anglican church, Newton attended services and participated in special projects, such as paying for the distribution of Bibles among the poor, and serving on a commission to build fifty new churches in the London area. Yet he seldom made public pronouncements regarding his theology. He is remembered instead for his pioneering scientific achievements.

So these individuals understood that God has requirements of us in order for us to have a relationship with him. We cannot be drinking out of two cups, his and his adversaries. No matter how sincere the person, God expects them to display the intelligence he gave them and to go find the source of the air we breathe, the food we eat and the creation put here for our pleasure. We have free will in accordance with his will, whether we obey him as ruler, or simply don't – that's our choice.

A tap on the window makes me jump. Looking in the mirror it's one of the wives, the least favourite one, although I think she does have character, unlike the other two.

'Let me in,' she says. I unlock the doors. 'Ah, it's lovely in here,' she says. 'It's so hot in that church that two flies came in, flew around and one said to the other, "Let's go find some other church with air conditioning, sister!"' I do like her, she isn't as stand-offish as the others. I offer her a small bottle of water from the fridge, which is chilled to perfection. She took it, sat back and began to cool down.

The climate control is a serious piece of workmanship in the Phantom. It could be forty degrees outside and I could sit in the driver's seat with my jacket on. Nice and cool.

'So how was church?' I ask. But what I really want to ask is, 'Why are you in the car on your own?' That never happens. If they have fallen out, I really don't need a storm on such a lovely day. She lets out a breath, then throws her head back past the head rests and on to the back shelf, no doubt to allow the cool air in the cabin to refresh her. With her eyes closed she says, 'They'll be out soon, let me know when you see them please.'

Now, I have no objection driving male or female, although with a lone woman in the car, my radar is somewhat more alert. A man can create a storm and you know it's coming and you deal with it, however aggressive the situation becomes. But a woman on the other hand… they light fires, and you won't realise until it begins to burn your face. Hell hath no fury and all that. Crime reports often claim that women are usually detached from their victims. They know many ways to kill a cat, whereas a man won't have the patience to mess about and will just meet the problem head on. I've had many colleagues who have fallen foul to a female, thinking he understands her. She's so nice to him. She even gives him a kiss on the cheek, or a rub on the arm and he utterly misconstrues what she's trying to convey. They have a knack of making a situation appear like the world's about to end, then sit back and watch you run around like a chicken that jumped in to the deep fat fryer by mistake. I have worked for some utterly beautiful women, with hearts of gold. It's just when they suddenly change wind direction and you're not expecting it.

I take a glance in the rear-view mirror to see if the family are coming out. Her eyes are looking straight at me. Her eyes fill the mirror. I decide to vacate the car and stand outside. It's hot and noisy. The King appears at the top of the steps and I ascend to greet and help him. I stand back a little till he's ready, so all the churchgoers can indulge in their goodbyes. Oh no – I forgot her in the back. *Leave her*, I'm thinking, *not my problem*.

He summons me over to help him descend the stairs. 'What a lovely service,' the King beams. 'You should have joined us, it was elevating.' I keep quiet but display a plastic smile. When someone's having their moment, if you can't contribute to enhance the conversation, you keep quiet. He continues, 'We have some developments for this week. Take Monday and

Tuesday off, but Wednesday, I need you in the morning as I need to conclude a deal in Canary Wharf. Afterwards it's back home and then to the airport as I have some urgent business to deal with in the States.'

Brilliant, I think. He still pays me for the week, so now I can confirm with my other clients. It's working out well. Getting to the car, he notices heat coming off it. 'Is the engine on?' he asks. 'You know the insurance wouldn't pay out for the car if someone stole it?'

'No,' I say, 'there's someone in the back.' I open the door and his wife was sparked out on the back seat. Bless her, it was definitely her turn on the rota last night to provide his master with whatever his requirements were. Though she doesn't appear like a woman who requires Alka Seltzer to reverse the alcoholic abuse from a mad night. Poor woman looks like she's been up cutting toenails. I bet that's it, he waits a while on the rota till it's her turn, and what does she get? 'Oh, my sunflower, you're the best at pedicures darling, so I thought I best wait till I see you again. Don't forget my bunions honey, they've not been pampered for a while, you're so good.'

Many cultures are so different from our own, there's no right and wrong about people's ways, we just have to respect and roll with it. She makes her exit via the other side and he gets in. They speak in African and she wanders off to meet the others. 'OK Paul,' he calls. 'I need the chemist quickly on Marylebone High Street.' As the horses are already fired up, we waft along two streets to the chemist.

If I had some cash spare, I would most definitely purchase an apartment overlooking this cosmopolitan street. I love it. There's a few other streets like this, or on this level – Chelsea Market and Chelsea Village Square, St John's Wood High Street, Pavilion Road village. The super trendy Notting Hill High Street. Hampstead High Street. The inflow of cash is pushing wealth out beyond central London. It's alive and vivacious, just an uplifting street. Obviously, to enjoy it, you'll need access to a bit of cash. A new credit card maybe, but that won't last long. A rich partner is what you need, as you'll feel compelled to shop every day.

Seldom does a driver obtain a parking spot where he needs it, so about five shops down, I pull up. I will help him back up the street. Walking up the street he really is in a good mood today. I would have loved to be a fly on his wall last night – well, maybe not, I don't do bunions. Especially not on a Sunday before lunch, thanks. But what I will have is a couple of bananas from Pret further down. I'm thinking I won't eat much, as in a few hours I'll be going home to hug my bed. Yes, shower first. Take some Night Nurse and gone for twelve hours. Funny how we don't miss things till we need them. Water is another, we get dehydrated, feel ill and most of the time, it's just water we need to replenish us. A glass an hour of bottled water though, not tap, as there are too many sick people, and it's got to be coming from somewhere.

Here he comes. Running back to the car, I have just realised something – I left my bananas in the blinking shop. Seems he's got his medicine. Actually it's a bag of pills and it's heavy, no wonder he asked me to carry them.

'That's really it for today,' he says. 'Just park the Phantom and drop the keys back to me please and I'll see you Wednesday 09:30.'

I'll be grateful for the day next two days off. As he is only a once a year client and the others are regulars and fickle, if you're not around, then there's a million other harbour sharks waiting to jump into your seat.

As I help him out of the car, he thanks me for his day and I take the Phantom to bed. Would I have liked to drive it home? Nope! I will happily hand it back, thanks. She's way too high maintenance.

I am now heading back to Golders Green and wondering how my car is. Er, no I'm not. I have Mr Monaco tomorrow, I need to be at LHR T5 by half five in the morning. I'd best go get the car. Actually, ringing his PA would be a good idea.

Finally, ten minutes later, I get through. So I'm taking the S Class 500 for tomorrow. It's in an underground car park in Ebury Street, Victoria, which is where most of his cars are. Just reading her text. Keys will be left with the porter at the desk. Cool. There had better be petrol left in the car.

OK, Victoria Line down to Victoria Station. On the tube I take my phone out as I have another message of instruction. This client is into property developing, and he's just finished one of his properties and spent millions sprucing it up. Last night the place was let out as an Airbnb. Four floors and it's finished to the highest spec possible. This place is in the Chelsea area. I've been asked to go around and have a nosey, as last night, the party that rented the house for a weekend wrecked it. Police were called to an out-of-control party and the police found over a hundred people in the house. It was wrecked and the card used to secure the booking was stolen. So I'll pass by and check the place is locked up.

It's been a while since I used Victoria Station, and I forgot how mad it is. Underground, trains to the south east, and just round the corner we have the National Express coaches that travel the country. Actually, the last time I was here, me and my best friend went on a rare night out to the theatre to see *Wicked*, the follow-up to *The Wizard of Oz*. Fantastic night and there was even room for my legs. OK, a quick dart across Buckingham Palace Road, turn left at Santini restaurant and I'm there.

The porter walks me round to the car and lets me in. 'The gate opens automatically on your way out,' he says. OK, where is it? There she is, the latest shape S Class. Definitely my favourite all-round car. No delusions of competence, just does what it says on the tin. She's a little dusty, but never mind. Good, it's got a full tank. The 500 is not my favourite engine. I believe Porsche produce the best V8s. OK, let's wake up these horses and go on an inspection.

I so love this car. So easy, it does my job for me. Each model grows in stature. They just get better and better. I owned an S600 in the shape before this and the only thing it lacked was four-wheel drive. I didn't want to get out of it. The V12 in that car was awesome. It was powerful and I don't know where it found grip on take off. The 500 has guts, though no real difference to the 350 diesel in power, and you'd get 200 more miles of petrol for the same money.

Working my way down Royal Hospital Road, I see the house. Looks like nothing aesthetically, but worth twenty-eight million. All outside appears normal. I need to park up somewhere, but there's nowhere to park except double yellows. You pay all that cash for what? To look out at brick walls either side of you?

Walking over to the property, it's all quiet. Let me take a look in the window. It's like a war's kicked off and bombs have been dropped on the place. I can even see bricks have been removed from the walls of the dining area! Rubbish and hundreds of wine glasses everywhere, must have been some party to want to kick the house down when they finished. Who would want to be a landlord? Just going to send a quick text to say the property is locked down and all OK. Should be an interesting day tomorrow. I think now I will go check on my car, which should be safe – the area is probably the safest borough in London – then head home for some sleep. The journey should be somewhat easier with this beautiful car. Most would say, 'Why make cars with the S class capability and limit their speed?' That's because they were not made for British roads, although they handle much better than cars that were made here. The S class deals with British roads with ease. But where it really excels is on the road to the Côte d'Azur – as it's the only place in Europe I've driven to, I can offer my opinion. It was divine. Once you've driven one, you wouldn't settle for anything less.

I arrive in Temple Fortune, five and a half miles north of central London, to check on my jalopy. She's not happy, she's covered in dirt, and it's only been a day. You really wouldn't want to hang washing on a line. All's well and the M1 is only round the corner, joining at junction 2. It's a beautiful day, and I can see families in their cars heading off to wherever they are going – some shopping, some to spend time with family. There's a BMW X5 towing a trailer with a jet ski on it, heading south, well obviously the seaside for them, have a safe trip then. After a hard week people deserve to blow off some steam. It's lovely watching families spend time together, albeit in traffic and on the motorway. Who cares? They're together. All credit to the parent who has probably struggled through the week with one problem after another, then muster up energy to take the family out.

Chapter 7

Mr Monaco and the fruit trees

It's 04:58 on Monday, and the weekend's over already. Working weekends is not ideal for those of us who are getting older. I usually have Mondays off, but today I'm all messed up and I've only got half an hour to get to Terminal 5.

Right, I need some calm music today. It's nice listening to instrumentals, but it's even nicer to sing along at times. Magic FM, the chauffeur's station. Music playing. Kate Bush, *Saxophone*.

Is that dolphins at the beginning of this song? Jolly well sounded like it. I think it was released in 1978 on *The Kick Inside*, which is a fantastic album, and wasn't it her birthday last week, along with Emily Brontë on the same day?

Right, I need to look at flight information for Terminal 5. Strange, that word – Terminal. Doesn't that imply the end? But how crazy to associate it with an airport. '*A point of connection for closing an electric circuit*' or '*a disease predicted to lead to death*' are the concise dictionary terms. So why for an airport? I do hate going to them. Dropping off is fine, but having to go in and pick up is tedious. But today, I asked the client to meet me at the top, he jumps in and we're off. No hanging around. No unattractive emotions, like bawling, no watching public displays of affection

(I think I've been on my own too long), no watching a long snog goodbye, or hello, as the case may be.

Normally he flies into Farnborough, a lovely mini-airport, or Luton's hub for private aircraft. No hassle, no waiting around. It's what the wealthy like. Exclusivity, not having to share their privacy with people of less importance. It's a peaceful way to travel, allowing aircraft owners to utilise the airfield for their toys, enabling them to come and go as they please. A few airfields that used to be somewhat derelict have suddenly been renovated and brought up to the standards required by the Civil Aviation Authority. Money has been thrown at these little airfields and they are great places. Especially the café, a great greasy spoon with none of the stress of the class A airports.

M25. Look at all the blinking traffic already! Where am I? A404, great. Now sitting in traffic with twenty minutes before he lands. OK, squeeze past this car, a little on the hard shoulder, then race up the slip road past everyone. Get to the top, yes, lights on green, race straight down the other side. Now that's a good half a mile. I remember once a while ago, I did the same down at the M3 exit, not realising there was no straight over, and it swung round back on to the M3. It took ages to get back. Wasn't happy!

Now I am panicking. When my client disembarks, he only has a man bag, so it's straight through for him. Just passing M4, the exit for LHR Terminal 1 to 4. Next one, phew. Straight over a roundabout, as I need to sit right at the end of the set down. His plane touched down ten minutes ago. The baggage in the hole moment provides you with an extra twenty minutes for the quick ones. Right, pull out my iPad. Find my apps, and now I am looking for Flight Radar Pro, which enables me to locate the aircraft and inform me of its speed and distance, so I can track the plane all the way to the floor. Once it's connected, I can see an abundance of planes of all shapes and size in the vicinity. Look at all the planes just off the coast over Southampton in holding stacks, lining up to follow Heathrow's corridor. 650 arrivals a day, every day and an equal number of take-offs. The day starts at 04:30 and seventy per cent of aircraft comes from the east, over London. Two runways. The northern runway is fifty metres across and its length is 3,902, meters which is just under two and a half miles. The southern one is two miles long. They run from the west on compass heading 270, and the east on 090. A compass is divided into four sectors of ninety degrees, which is named the quadrangle. So nearly fifteen hundred aircraft movements a day, that's just unreal. Imagine when they build the third runway. If there's a problem and Heathrow is closed, where on earth are they going to go? There are some big planes coming in, with empty fuel tanks. Perish that thought.

So where is my flight? Great, it's not only landed, it's landed early. I can see a few planes on the ground, so I tap one, and an Emirates flight pops up with particulars, how many on board, where it came from and so on. There's a smaller plane, BA, that looks more like it. Oh no, police coming over. OK, I'm going. I'll have to drive round again. I hope this isn't going to be a merry-go-round. Ten minutes later I stroll back onto set down. That policemen had walked further down, I drive straight to the end and I still can't see him. I'm going to have to get out. You forget how soundproof the S Class is, outside is well noisy. He's not where he said he would be, so I look to my left. At the entrance I can see a small individual. Is that him? As I run closer I can see it is. He recognises me whilst sucking on his favourite Marlborough Light, and he looks grumpy, no change there then.

'I do apologise,' I said. 'I must have heard you wrong, I'm at the other door.'

'No Paul,' he replied. 'I needed to fill my lungs with some polluted air.'

'OK,' I said, 'I'll see you in the car.'

Just at that moment a guy with a sweeping brush and tools literally pokes my client in the ribs. 'Hello?' he shouts. Mr M slowly turns his head and asks him what the hell he wants. 'Can't you read? No smoking.'

'Of course I can bloody read,' says Mr M. 'That's why I'm not at Heathrow Airport cleaning floors, you cheeky beggar, get lost, go on!' *Great*, I thought, *that'll cheer his day up.*

Ten minutes later he makes it to the car. We exchange our salutations briefly, as he's not into pleasantries. 'Paul, head for the Dorchester, I've booked a suite there,' he says.

'Isn't check in after 14:30?' I ask.

'No, I booked for two days yesterday, so the room is mine.'

I'm thinking, so he booked the suite at eight thousand for last night, although he knew he wasn't using it? OK, no probs. I have a client from the UAE who last year stayed at a hotel in Knightsbridge, took five suites but only used two. Her bill came to five hundred grand. I suppose spending like that just makes everyone around know you've got the power.

So, off to the West End we head, wondering what madness will come today. He's quiet now, but he changes as the day goes on.

From Heathrow to the centre of London took just over two hours. It gets worse. Outside the Dorchester, things are rather calm. This hotel doesn't conventionally wake up till the latter part of the morning.

'Paul, can you run over to Belgravia and pick up a suitcase for me from my PA and bring it back here? I need a change of clothes. When you're back, Just buzz me and I'll come down.'

I receive a text on my phone. A client has come through to me from my agency, and he's just checking all OK for tomorrow. I'm hoping so, as today is going to be long.

Down in Belgravia, the house has almost been turned into an Airbnb. This one has been finished beautifully. All the houses he has are worth upwards of thirty million, all chosen from five postcodes. She then spends millions bringing them to a standard that qualifies the property for that postcode.

Now I'm racing back to the Dorchester, as everyone wants to meet at the damaged house, to take an inventory. I'm calling him but he's not answering. My guess is he's taking a nap or has gone down for breakfast. Whatever he's doing, I'll just stand by, passenger window open whilst I listen to the madness. What can I think about? Let me check my phone. I have Mr Happy tomorrow. Some people say, how can you just drive all day every day? Some weeks I could do a couple of thousand miles a week. Well, the cars really help. They make a long journey easy. Get stuck in traffic, stick the TV on. No noise from outside. If my back gets stiff, I put the 'massage my back for an hour' switch on. Music systems or plug the iPod in. No added stress of filling up with gas, oil, replacing tyres from my own pocket. What can get a trifle tedious is the client. I can get on with almost anyone, but some people are just unnecessary. Some clients are so spoilt they will literally stamp their feet, as they're so used to getting what they want.

Take the client I have tomorrow. Now we know Europe hates us, you only have to watch the Eurovision Song Contest. But say we don't get a Brexit deal. We get offered five times the conventional deal for our food and produce, then say we disagree. Europe sticks two fingers up to us. We need their food, yes, they need us as we import 850,000 cars from Germany, we purchase our cherries from Spain, we drink an inordinate amount of champagne, more than France, they could put prices far higher, and we cannot legislate for that. So imagine no shipments for three days. Imagine food!

The client tomorrow, his wife is lovely, a vivacious, outgoing woman. He bought her a Porsche as a present recently. I asked him why he bought her such a powerful car, and he replied, 'To give her whiplash, old chap. What else?' She really is a delightful lady, although she's not performing her diplomatic skills to placate the alpha male very well. At a restaurant recently, she couldn't hold herself together, and it appeared she was drunk, so he displayed his displeasure by shaking her arm, and giving her a couple of slaps round the chops! To the horrified guests, it appeared like abuse, but she was actually hooked on anti-depressants and he was trying to straighten her up, as she was incoherent and struggling to hold her knife and fork.

Looking across the set-down of the Dorchester I can see a man looking around, and realise it's my client, Mr Monaco. I race across to see if it's me he's looking for. Pulling up, I lower the window. 'Your clothes, do you need them now?' I ask.

'Yes, I'll take them up with me. We'll head to Chelsea in a while,' he says. So as I had to drive round on to Park Lane, I thought I might as well quickly grab a sandwich. I race round to Shepherd Market, where there's an OK sandwich shop that's been there for years. My only problem is that they use their fingers to pick up the salad, the same fingers that handle the change. I order a Mexican tuna salad on toast, two slices of toast, the tuna on half, and lettuce on the other, although I'd prefer baby spinach. On top of the lettuce is cucumber, tomato, grated carrot, and sweetcorn. Put the other piece of toast on top, cut it in half and that's it. I won't eat it straight away, but the toast won't get soggy. To accompany the sandwich, I take a packet of plain crisps and a bottle of water. I so fancy a cake, but I'm sitting in the car all day and the sugar will wreak havoc internally. It's tough, but I've got to do it. The price of that meal is just over five pounds, unlike Starbucks and Costa, where it's a fiver just for a large coffee and a croissant. Five days a week and over the year it adds up to £1,250 just for a coffee and croissant. World's gone mad.

Text message – OK, he's coming down. I drive straight into the set-down, jump out and throw my sandwich into the boot. Oh no – they didn't put any red onion in my sandwich. Actually, it's probably best as we will be driving people all day.

In the car, he seems to have cheered up somewhat. He was on the phone to someone who put a smile upon his face and concluded with, 'I'll see you later.' Well, it didn't sound like business, so it must have been a woman. Actually a girl, as he likes them young. He doesn't like music on in the car, in fact I don't think he likes music at all. He's always in trainers and jeans and hates wearing a suit. It's his desire to remain as inconspicuous as possible. He once stated he could never marry because he's far too wealthy. He lives in Monaco because it's far from the madding crowd and in his words: 'The atmosphere is invariably better, where rich people congregate.' So although he lives on his own, his life is directed the way he wants. He's got loads of friends, celebrities. His pockets are deep, deep enough to have recently bought four houses over the thirty-million pound mark and spend another twenty million each sprucing them up. Yes, he has his idiosyncrasies like most of us, but we don't all walk into the Dorchester favouring a bagman who looks like he just spent last night in a Primark doorway. His prudence stems from the fact that life on his level does have its challenges, and being discreet goes a long way in keeping yourself from injurious things, I suppose.

We arrive in Chelsea and as usual, parking is a problem. I drop him by the door and he asks me to bring his bags in. I end up parking on the next street, then walking back.

Getting to the door, the builder lets me in. Inside are a few people who Mr M had summoned to take an inventory and provide quotes for the damage. I couldn't begin to describe the scene. Carnage, road traffic accident. Like arriving back at your white Phantom parked on the Kings Road and your spouse has sprayed all over the car in red paint, 'CHEATING SO AND SO'. Or it's been attacked by a pocket of anti-capitalist activists. Champagne glasses were everywhere. Food was on the walls, the floor, just not in the bins provided. Police said there were around a hundred people at this party. On walking in there was this crystal chandelier hanging down from an eighteen-foot high ceiling. I think Tarzan had been using it in a physical education exercise. White marbled floor, trashed with marks of all kinds and what appeared to be a stiletto excavation exercise. Bricks had been dug out of the walls. The only thing they didn't do was set it on fire, and this was the whole four floors. For him, yes, it's only money, but as a businessman, surely it's about your reasonable rate of return as well?

I leave them to formulate a plan of action. Walking back to the car, I can't help but wonder why anyone would be so animalistic. The privilege of a being a weekend custodian in such a grand house should induce a little gratitude.

I look at my client and he appears horrified. He's quite calm and collected though, processing things in his mind. I have other clients who would be a lot more vocal in their quest to find the culprits. That's one thing about a London, there's always someone bigger and stronger where muscle is concern, but it's no longer about loyalty, it's who pays the highest.

Text message: 'We are coming out.' Best get back. Pulling up outside, Mr M and his PA jump in the car, still deep in shock.

'Paul, can we go to Connaught please?' says the PA.

Mr M interrupts, 'No, one only goes there for dinner, it's not a lunchtime venue. Cicchetti, Piccadilly, will be much better.'

I head towards Piccadilly. London has warmed up by now and the roads are in full chaotic mode. His phone rings. He looks at it and continues talking. A minute later, it rings again. When he picks up, even though the phone is in ear mode, we can hear the caller. I don't know who she is, but she's shouting, 'You're not the only rich man in town, please don't mess me about!'

'Look, of course not,' he replies. 'I've just had a very trying morning with a bill attached in the region of five mill. I'm going to lunch and it's near you, so I'll see you shortly.'

That sounds like one of his little fruit trees. Possibly a bonsai.

It's much better since they dispensed with the bus lane on Piccadilly as you can drive both ways from the Circus and I can drop him straight outside, as opposed to round the corner on Regent Street, St James' side. My mind's always working overtime trying to calculate how long at a particular time of day it's going to take to navigate through London.

Piccadilly is its usual hectic self. Approaching the circus, I always wonder who picked up the bill for Neon Lights Corner. There's so many kilowatts burning there twenty-four seven.

I pull up at the restaurant and they jump out. 'Paul, we'll be an hour.' No problem, I think. I race off and take a left at Fortnum & Mason down Duke Street, as I'm looking for a spot to stop. I nearly forgot, I have my lunch in the boot. I finally come to rest on Charles the Second Street. Dive in the boot and see what state my sandwich is in. Yep, the toast has kept the sandwich dry and the water next to it kept it cool. I must give thanks for this. *Bless the hands that prepared the food and the hands that cooked the food, and thank God for providing me with the tools to enjoy my food… Amen!*

Well. That sandwich deserved a knife and fork, maybe a couple of toothpicks. No sauce made it taste better, just feel the salad's natural flavours. I'm so cheap it's unbelievable.

Just had a text from my client for tomorrow. She had a friend she introduced me to one night last summer and it didn't end particularly well. We were all at a venue in a posh part of Buckingham, and me and a friend were taking clients backwards and forward to the venue from a local hotel. The party organiser hired an American singer and there was a pianist. Splendid evening. Can't remember for the life of me what it was for. However. I was listening to this talking about why she was so upset and her husband was displaying beastly tendencies toward her. As I was trying my utmost to listen amid all the noise, her friend popped over. Early to mid-fifties, powerful, rich, ex-Bond girl. She had the world at her feet, put it that way. She had the long, strong hair, the 'is she, isn't she' look. She was in an exceptional mood, because she had received the settlement figure she felt was necessary to keep her in the standard she had become accustomed. I didn't recognise it, but she was in the mood to let off some steam. You see, we chauffeurs are trained not to see emotions like this. It's seldom our eyes collide with a stray. You have to be in the right place at the right time. And when you do recognise the signs, you're supposed to ignore them. Now have you ever witnessed what happens when a man rejects a woman? For us chauffeurs, it could be bad, especially if we misread the situation. She's hungry and requires satisfaction, and she's not offering a vehicle to someone without a conversation. I don't mean chat. So next thing I knew, she took herself and her spider's web perfume off to work the room. I thought nothing of it and carried on working.

My colleague and I found a few minutes to sit down and reason and he said quietly, 'Paul, I saw you.'

'Saw what?' I asked.

'You, losing it around that woman. Forget her. She's in a different league. She's part of that crowd, you know, the richest two percent who had a share of seventy billion in the last year. What could you possibly offer her?'

'Well, thanks for that reference, I'll be sure to give you a call when I need a job!'

Weird thing was, as we were talking, the woman stormed over. 'Can one of you drive me home?'

I jumped up and said to my colleague, 'Catch you in a bit.' Then I grabbed his keys, as he had the Bentley and I only had the Benz. As he jumped off the table to tackle me, I threw the Mercedes keys at him and ran. I ran around the marquee, but on her long legs she'd already scarpered. So I ran out the front, where she was waiting with a right face on her. I opened the rear door, she pushed it shut, she wanted to get in the front. So I held down the button to lower the windows and allow air into the hot cabin.

My colleague had said earlier, 'That dress, she just threw it on, how could she just come out with nothing underneath it?' He was right. I just wished now she had got into the back!

On the way home, I mean her home, she was quiet, but shaking with anger. I pulled a small bottle of water out from my door well and offered it to her. She looked at it, then looked at me and took it. 'I thought the evening looked amazing,' I interjected.

'Shame that in such a fine house there are such NASTY PEOPLE!' she finally opened up. It transpired she'd had a face to face with one of the family members of the host and her anger stemmed from the fact that she couldn't punch who she was arguing with, which would have released that pent-up aggression. So she still had it. Shaking, biting her teeth. For the next ten minutes she remained quiet, other than left here, right there, straight at the roundabout and don't hit the badger.

No one does country houses as well as the UK. Her house was well hidden, deep in some trees surrounded by greenery and livestock. I pulled up to the door and reversed the car. With her finger she wiped a tear from her cheek, then opened the door and held it to speak to me. 'My jacket's on the back seat, can you bring it in?' Then she walked off towards her front door. Why couldn't she just grab it herself? Then she left the front door ajar...

My phone was ringing, I looked at it and it was my colleague, wanting the Bentley back. I threw the phone in the car, grabbed her jacket and headed into the house. I walked from the front door, through another door and across this shiny black Valentino floor. How can a floor make you feel so good? She had a massive kitchen in white with a cooker with gas rings that only accepted pots and pans.

She extinguished the main lights and touched three subtle halogen lights distributed around the kitchen. I pulled out a bar-type chair and sat down. 'So, you feeling remotely better?' I asked.

She slammed the double fridge door, took a huge block of ice and threw it in one of her sinks, then asked, 'Drink? I've got most cocktails, but I'm not in the mood, so something straight.'

'Er, bottled water if you have any,' I said. She wandered over to another fridge, which was filled with soft drinks and loads of alcohol. She brought me a bottle over and a glass that shined like daylight. She pulled up a chair and sat down, facing me. 'Well I do hope you sleep better and that you don't take this evening's negativity to bed with you,' I said. She just stared at me with her deep blue Caribbean eyes. She looked powerful in that dress. 'I think I'd best be getting back,' I said. She stood up as if to display herself to me. I felt her womanhood, and it was overwhelming. I felt weak, my energy zapped, my head spinning.

I checked my drink, and it wasn't fizzing or discoloured, what the hell was going on? She walked round me, getting closer. She leaned down in front of me, no bra, her nipples protruding angrily through her blouse. Oh, someone help me. I swallowed hard, began taking deep breaths. I think my cardiac muscle had taken its eye off what it was supposed to be doing, because instead of beating rhythmically, the beats became irregular. I stood up, trying to extricate myself. But her perfume began to reel me back in, suffocate me. I looked at my phone. The rings had stopped. No one was looking for me any more. 'I really must be going,' I said.

'No need,' she said. She was using that 'I get what I want' voice. I felt uncomfortable. Seduction only becomes a sin when repeated or practised. She sat me down. 'Relax,' she said. She pulled open a drawer and took out a small knife. Reaching over to her fruit bowl, she stabbed a Golden Delicious apple. She removed the skin, then with the knife she sliced off a small piece and slid it into her mouth with the blade, staring at me. It would be rude to run for it. I couldn't help thinking of that TV series *Wives with Knives*. It was probably too late. I was about to meet my demise.

Her hand reached out and touched my face. 'Life can be really strange at times, you know,' she said, looking at the fruit bowl again, she stabbed a fat, black, juicy grape in its rib cage, twisted it and detached it from the colony. Still using the knife, she removed the grape from the tip and popped it into her mouth. Her laser eyes stared right through me, and at that moment my central nervous system shut down and was taken over, like when you take a couple of sleeping tablets and they suddenly hit, and you have no control, it's over. She moved her face closer to mine, and her perfume smelt strong, as if concentrated. It was infiltrating my veins, my arteries and my sinuses and dancing round my head. I was doomed. Her lips collided with mine, like the gentle liaison between a space ship and its docking port. 'Houston, I really do have a problem.' She force-fed me the grape, like I was a helpless chicklet on antidepressants. I needed to escape. She had disarmed every fibre of my spiritual morality. Her left hand reached under my chin, and seemed to lift me up as if I was weightless. I was being guided north, to the next floor of the house...

But now my phone's ringing. Why is it on silent? Mr M, let me see what's up. 'Paul, we're on our way out.' Thank goodness I'm round the corner. Regent Street is very busy and I'm having to bob and weave my way up to the top of Piccadilly. He could have given me ten minutes, then come out. He knows I can't simply park on Piccadilly.

OK, I'm here now. Turning the corner, he's standing on his own. Imagine if I'd been further away. I pull up and he jumps straight in. 'So Mr Paul, how are you?'

I'm thinking, what's up with him? Oh yes, he's had a drink. 'Yes, good thank you,' I reply. 'So sorry about the Chelsea house, it was so beautifully done.'

'Yes, unfortunately we business people have to put up with the odd reprobate. It seems like each time I come back they seem to increase,' he says. 'I have a friend who took his family over to South

America recently for a break and a family member was kidnapped. He ended up paying a few million to get them back.' He looks out of the window like he's searching for answers. 'Do you know, the world has always had its conflicts, Middle East, all over the place, look at Syria, it bleeds whilst everyone else bickers. I've never known the world to be in such a constant grip of violence, it's like we can't extricate ourselves from impropriety and violence. A friend of my just came back from Africa two weeks ago. He made some business acquaintances and together they established some common ground. They set up a business plan, he went over to execute the plan and his private jet was about to take off when his plane was surrounded. Somehow he made it back home with his life. He's got the Learjet. They confiscated it on the tarmac. Er, go left here. So, when you coming to Monaco, Paul?'

'Actually, Wednesday is looking good. Is it starting to resemble London?' I ask.

'No, not remotely. For one thing there's no flipping council estates. And the air is invariably nicer where just the rich congregate. It's so different to London, poor living next to the rich will always cause divisions. It just winds people up and devalues houses. You've got Holland Park with Notting Hill one side with Shepherd's Bush to the west and Ladbroke grove to the north supporting it. Love the area, but as it's not in London's top five areas its sort of has its limits.

'Wednesday I thought you were with the Phantom guy? I can wait another week, just I have to swap the cars quick, else I incur penalties. It's obviously not the cash as I'd rather give that to you, it's just complicated. So you think Wednesday?'

'Absolutely,' I said, 'I take them back to the airport, as he has urgent stuff to do in the States, so as soon as I send him off, I'll go pick up the car and head for the Channel Tunnel.'

'That sounds fantastic. As you know, I hate the 945-mile drive from Calais to Monaco. By the time I've got from here to

Folkestone, I've had enough. You know I parked the car up last time and took the train? I think you were in Potsdam, Germany at the time, as I remember, and I couldn't find anyone I trust to swap the cars. The French drivers hate driving British right-hand drive cars and the British drivers hate driving on the right. I just can't bloody win! The French drivers all seem like they're struggling with anxiety or sexual frustration as they keep smashing up my cars. You know the white Roller, this idiot rammed it into a lamp post when nothing was coming. I was charged with damage to the street furniture as well. So Wednesday, stay for a couple of days, I'll make sure the Monte Carlo Bay hold a suite for you. Remember last time you arrived at one in the morning, you ordered sea bass? Just do it again, they serve food twenty-four seven. Is that a definite then?'

'Yes, absolutely,' I said. 'I'll be leaving before the afternoon traffic starts. Calais by seven, Monaco by three.'

'Fantastic, so I'll see you Thursday morning. Actually if you want to, bring a lady friend with you, although she'll get whiplash the speeds you travel at. I know you push it Paul, no one else gets down here that quick, it took me two full days once. I thought about abandoning the journey and finishing it on the train, but I carried on, only because I didn't want to leave the Bentley anywhere.'

'Thank you, but no thanks, no lady friends in the pipeline.'

'Well I told you, come to Monaco, I'll look after you, women want guys who are liquid anyway. You know what the Chinese say: "When money runs out, woman runs out." I don't care what women say, they all invest emotionally in everything they do. Go left – LEFT HERE! Head up to Windmill Street. OK, I'm going in here, make sure your phone is on as I'll need you by the door when I come out.'

'So you're not coming back on your own then?' I ask.

'I jolly well hope not. See you soon.'

As he walks off, I search for a parking spot. Then I realise I can hear a beeping noise every ten seconds or so, and pull over and start looking. In the floor in the back is his phone. No! He's going to need it. Oh great, that means I have to go in. I get out and run across the road. The sign outside says, 'We have the most beautiful women in London!' Yep, I thought, that's where he's gone. On the door are two gorillas. I ask if they saw my client come through here. I describe him and they both acknowledge he just went through. I say he's left his phone and he'll need it. One bouncer suggests that maybe he didn't want disturbing. The other says, 'It's OK, run on in, but if you stay, it will cost you.'

Oh my days. What a sight. I try to focus on looking for this guy. Ah. The bar, where else.

'What you doing in here?' he asks.

'Your phone.'

He checks his pockets, adamant he's got it. 'I thought I had it,' he says in shock. 'Thanks. Now you're here you may as well have a drink. It's OK, just one and I need to be out of here. I can't find who I'm looking for.'

'Erm… OK, I'll have a fizzy water. Thanks.' *What am I doing in here?* I keep asking myself.

'OK, it's work Paul!' Great, that's it then.

Music in background. Tina Turner, *Private Dancer*.

While he's getting the drinks, I can't help feeling out of my depth. Then I see someone who looks familiar. I'm looking at a girl who came to some mad Arab party a while back. I picked up fifty women that night, frogmarching them down Sloane Street two by two with the Sheikh's main bodyguard and a lady who ran the show. This girl was second row from the front, and I recognise her as she appears somewhat apprehensive. At the bar she has recognised me too. I ask if she's OK and does she remember me. 'Yes I do, but it was a while ago now.'

'That night, were you OK?'

'No,' she says. 'I didn't want to do it, as clients have a reputation. With taboo subjects. You must know?' I replied that I couldn't share the nocturnal activities of Arabs, I just work the night shift.

All the girls collectively had a share of a couple of million pounds for an hour or so of work. It was enough to sink a company, dependent on its creditors. But that's another story.

The neon lighting's affecting my eyes and I want to leave, but my client taps my arm, saying, 'You're not supposed to touch the girls.'

I say, 'Yes, but I know her.' He's looking around like a kid in a sweet shop. I feel like I'm in a goldfish bowl and I'm very uncomfortable.

He spots a girl he's familiar with, one who will take what he offers with no back chat. 'I've been calling you,' he says. She comes over. Where've you been? Trying to ring you. She mentions that she lost her phone. She says that in order not to create suspicion, he has to have a dance with her. She starts to dance and whispers sweet nothings in his ear. She knows not only that her rent is about to be paid but she can probably go on holiday too. He runs off to find an alcove. She turns rounds and asks if I'm coming. 'No, please tell him I'll be in the car.' She nods.

I turn round and run. At the door, the doorman put his hand out in front of me. 'You owe…' he says.

'Look, see the guy I was with, he says put whatever I owe you on his bill, no matter how much, and could you send one of the waitresses over with a bottle of Krug, he'd appreciate that.' He lets me go. If you're looking for trouble, this really is the place.

I run back to the car, forgetting I didn't buy a ticket for it. I didn't expect to be in there that long. The sun's beating down and by the time I get back to the car, I'm sweating buckets. The 500 is such a pleasure to possess, even for just a day. I love the car. Sitting inside, the aircon goes on, full. I look at the windscreen and see no ticket. Relief.

So now I have to contend with him and his female behaviour. I know what he's like, he goes demented. He completely loses it. That fruit tree he was with, you should have seen her face. Like Christmas and birthday had all come at once. The strange thing is, when they're gone, he calls them 'professional rinsers' and he's seldom satisfied.

I take a glance at my rear-view mirror and there he is, running down the street. Anyone would think he was the girl, with that beam across his chops. He seldom smiles. He has one of those faces that when he smiles it looks like he's trying to hold back a gust of wind. Don't suppose he can help it. I remind myself that this playboy is worth two point one billion pounds, yet he looks like he couldn't spell it. You do wonder by his behaviour how they accumulate such an amount. He jumps in the back, excited.

'Did you see her, what do you think?' he asks.

I tell him one, that I think that he will need some sort of protection if he thinks he's playing with her and two, a government health warning might not go amiss, she could seriously be injurious to one's health.

'You are funny,' he says. 'Actually, she reminds me of that Aston Martin advert.'

'Which advert?'

'You know, the one with the half-naked model leaning over the kitchen table in their new advertisement for pre-owned cars: "you know you're not the first, but do you really care?" Classic!' I'm thinking that one of these days he might stumble across a joke that's actually funny.

He keeps looking back. She's coming in a moment. 'Here she is, now take us back to the Dorchester and quick as possible,' he says.

She jumps in and begins chatting. My ears switch to garble mode. All I hear is her telling him her bosses might shoot her for this liaison, after all, he's their client. 'They do support my mortgage you know, when you're not here.'

He replies, 'But I think I pay half the year's worth in one day, so I can't be that bad.' They laugh and began to munch one another. Great.

'So where are we going?' she asks.

'Back to the Dorchester. I know you love it there.'

She doesn't like that. 'Oh, I thought we were going shopping,' she says. 'I thought you were going to cheer me up.'

By her reaction, I can tell that she is fully aware that promises get broken after the man has had his needs met. And he's definitely a fall asleep straight after type man. But after a few minutes of wrangling, he caves in. 'OK Paul, can we go to John Lewis, Cavendish?' I'm thinking the only thing there is perfume.

She interrupts. 'Listen, I'll get my friend to meet us there in a cab. You remember her from last time?'

'Oh, Miss Frosty Pants!' he says.

'Yeah, but once you got to know her, you both got on quite well. She's a little rough, because of the high society type cavemen she has to deal with, a top judge has small change compared to you, so just tell her what you want. And she didn't mean to break your finger last time.'

'Well, it was only fractured, you know I have a high pain threshold,' he says.

'Oh yes, honey, I do remember, like the thirst you have for a good spanking!'

'So, you've brought some assistance today, what's your friend's name?' she asks. She's talking about me.

'Who, him? No, he's my driver, although, if you kill me, he will testify that you were the last to be seen with me.'

'Oh honey, the only time us women want to choke you men to death is when you're being unnecessarily TIGHT! Now, I know you're not remotely like that. You're quite safe darling!'

If this was a TV programme, I would switch it off. What the hell am I listening to? I begin to speed up. I have to get them out of the car before he explodes.

'I've texted Miss Frosty, she'll meet us in the perfume counter in ten. Incidentally, she's out of a particular Dior perfume and she's also missing her Coco. She says there's a bar across the road and I'm to get you a cocktail called DNR.'

'What the hell is that?' he asks.

'Not entirely sure honey, although in medical terms it's short for Do Not Resuscitate.' They both start laughing out loud, but I'm confident that she was serious. She actually spoke like she had undergone execution lessons, sorry, elocution lessons. Probably has an economics degree and has most definitely learnt the art of placating an alpha male. She is stunningly beautiful and looks like she could empty a man's pockets from a hundred yards. Well, I can't wait to see her mate!

Right, get your credit card out, I bet he'll blow five hundred on perfume. At least they will be happy and I can get rid of them. She doesn't look the type to waste her day on a couple of trinkets and some perfume.

We pull up at the side of Debenhams on Hollies Street W1. The wheels haven't stopped turning before her door is open. I jump out to assist and she's right behind me. She taps my shoulder and says, 'Beautifully driven, I didn't feel a thing, darling.' She's got manners too. Most wouldn't give you the steam off their urine. So off they go and flipping heck, he looks like her daddy. Some people just don't give a toss.

Roughly ten minutes later, a taxi pulls up and the driver jumps out to open the door. But it's not a black cab, it's an S Class 350D. Uber have S classes on the fleet, so probably one of theirs. This stunning brunette steps out, looking like she's fresh from the Côte d'Azur. Early twenties maybe, even gives the driver a tip. She looks Greek or Italian, strong, two-tone highlights though. The requisite diamond Rolex, outfit's probably Emporio Armani lunchtime wear. I'm thinking is that her friend, because if it is, he's in trouble. No it can't be, the driver's opening the shop door for her. OK, yes I'm curious.

I hear beeping noises and look in the back to see his phone half way down the seat, beeping like mad. I'd best take it in to him. A quick look around for a traffic warden – none. I jump out and run through Debenhams' doors and straight into the ground floor perfume department. So where are they? I walk over to the Chanel counter, where I can hear laughing. That's them, but why is he sitting in a Dior make-up chair?

The girls have already accumulated several bags each, in such a short space of time. They are all laughing as Miss Frosty applies blusher to his face. I have to interrupt. 'Apologise for interrupting, but don't you want your phone?'

'Oh heck, where was it?' he says.

'Down the side of your seat.'

At that moment the woman on the Dior counter leans over and says, 'Excuse me sir, that's five hundred and seventy-eight pounds please. If you've no objection, do you mind sliding your card into the slot?'

Mr M withdraws a card from his wallet. 'None at all,' he says.

While he's waiting for the display, a gay guy on the Dior counter says, 'Excuse me sir, after you've finished there, would you please oblige me with six hundred and twenty-nine pounds please?'

Mr M replies, 'Oh yes, no problem.' He withdraws another card and shoves it into the Dior card machine. Such excitement, the sales people delighted, the girls warming up. I don't know what to think as he uses both hands to simultaneously enter his pins on two machines.

One of the girls remembers my role. 'Hi darling, would you mind awfully?' She hands me the bags of shopping. I take that as my cue to leave.

Back in the car, I wait patiently for the madness to continue. Hopefully now, we can go back to the hotel and I can have the evening to myself. Actually, I feel peckish. After witnessing that lot, I've sort of worked up an appetite. Behind me, Oxford Street is heaving. Where do people get the money to shop all day every day? I bet the women are mostly on refund shopping. Bought last week, good excuse to come back this week and exchange it. No wonder shops are closing.

OK, we're off again. Here they come, the kingpin with Dolce and Gabbana. He looks delighted. Maybe now he can have his pampering time. But even I didn't realise make up and perfume are so expensive. They all jump in, full of the joys of Oxford Street. 'Paul, do you know… what was the name?' he asks the young ladies.

Miss Frosty looks at me and says, 'Hi, could you take us to Lowndes Square, the corner of Motcombe Street? The Louboutin boutique. I've already rung ahead, they're expecting us. They don't like people just turning up.' Oh I knew it, one of my favourite shops, obviously not for me, it's women's shoes. Now when you see a woman wearing Louboutins you think, what the hell did she have to do for him to get those? But if they're all right with that stigma, who am I to stick my nose in?

'Can we have some music on? It's like a morgue in here!' he says. I look at him, because I know he hates music.

'What, the jukebox is broken is it?' says Miss Frosty.

I touch the screen to bring up the radio. Magic FM. Yep, they seem to like this.

Music playing: Tina Turner, *'What's Love Got to Do With It?'*

'Oh, I love this song,' says Dolce, as she was the first.

'Hang on, put this armrest up,' says Frosty. 'What's in here? Look, it's a fridge, and an empty one. Where's the champagne?'

'I'm not in this car long enough, I won't see it again for a while, unless Paul brings it to Monaco on Wednesday.'

'You're going back Monday,' says Dolce.

'Yes, well in the morning. Oh and Paul, I need to be at Luton Signature for six o'clock, my Challenger will be ready to take off from there.'

'What's Signature then,' asks Dolce. 'Is it another name for Luton Airport? And can we come to Monaco?'

'No, it's a private jet airport attached, but they all use the same runway.' There's no reply to the 'coming to Monaco' question. I expect he'll have a pocket of Côte d'Azur fruit trees of his own down there.

I pull up outside the beautiful shoe shop down at the bottom of Motcomb Street. The ladies run inside, like they already know what they're after. I think this is one of my favourite spots in London. I just love it. Waitrose, my favourite shop, is behind me. The produce is always second to none. In fact I'll run inside and grab some nuts. I don't have long.

Inside Waitrose, it's as civilised as a store should be. Right, I need some cashews, no salt. A bottle of Volvic, some Perrier and a bunch of bananas. Hit the checkout and gone. I cannot afford a ticket today. Walking by the shoe shop, It looks like they are still in there and I'm surprised that he stayed in there with them. In *Pretty Woman*, the guy left his card and a pizza. I wonder if he's running two credit cards concurrently. Those shoes start at a thousand pounds a pair, minimum. Oh, here they come. Dolce has two bags and Miss Frosty has three. OK, so in this short space of time, that's ten grand he's spent. Like Superman, these women must have a cape with an 'S' stamped on it covering their 'Little Miss Indestructible Womanhood' to be deserving of this kind of pampering.

I jump out to help with the shopping. As I open the boot, the girls throw the bags in and go and sit in the car. He's in the middle and they're bestowing kisses on him like you would give a new-born baby. Loud ones. I turn round and he's drunk. You wonder to yourself, shall I intervene, but something says, the girls couldn't spend all his two billion, so leave him alone. However many Louboutins they buy, he won't starve.

'So honey, as it's Miss Frost's birthday, can we go for a bite to eat and a drink?'

'Absolutely. I don't fancy a DNR cocktail though, but you never said it's your birthday.'

Miss Frosty interjects, 'How were you supposed to know, it's OK. None of my family in London, so just us two tonight?'

'Oh well, we can't have that, can we?' he says. 'Are you sure I can't get you a birthday present? I'm so sorry, allow me to express my delight by buying you both dinner.'

'You're on,' Miss Frosty says, stroking his hair. As Dolce moves forward, to look to see if there's any water in the front door well, I hear 'PING' and another 'PING'. He's pinged her across her bottom. I wait for a response, as she's leaning through the middle offering him a bird's eye view of Scotland. 'Oh, he's becoming a trifle boisterous,' says Miss Frosty.

'Yes, it would appear he needs taking in hand, what do you say Dolce?'

'He definitely deserves a good spank himself, just, as long as he doesn't come anywhere near me later with those teeth of his, he'll give me a hysterectomy!' Dolce grabbed his hair in the palm of her hand and kissed him on his cheek. I heard a rip, from the roots. I'd be crying if she pulled my hair like that.

'Hey, listen to this,' said Mr M. 'I've got a joke. Little Red Riding Hood decides to take the short cut home through the woods, right? OK, so, Mr Big Bad Wolf jumps out on her. Riding Hood says, "Wolfy, what on earth do you want?" Wolfy replies "You, Riding Hood. I'm gonna throw you on the floor and shag you senseless." Riding Hood replies, "Oh no you ain't Wolfy, you're gonna get on ya knees and eat me, just like the book says."' Everyone falls about laughing. That was actually one of his better ones.

I take the left turn coming out of Cadogan Gardens and head south down Sloane Street. Wrong blinking way! There's congestion at the junction. 'Can we do one more stop?' says Miss Frosty. I look at my client, and he seems disturbed that this pit stop is going to disrupt his afternoon.

'OK, can we make this the last stop, as time is ticking?' They both hold him and begin bestowing kisses all over his chin. Then they all get out and walk straight into Cartier.

So I'll sit out here for a while, leaving the aircon on. It's jolly hot. I forgot lower Sloane Street had its own shopping quarters as it's a good way from the top to where the main shops are. Sloane Square is a stone's throw away and is a great shopping area. I can see the shop assistants running around, there's one at the window in the bracelet section. The assistant's eyes have been briefly diverted as a bunch of youths stroll by whistling at her. They all have their shorts and trousers hanging down over the backsides, so their cheeks protrude. The assistant is laughing, but do women really find that attractive? My mother would have pulled my ears off if she'd seen me walking around the house like that.

I've been thinking lately that a holiday would be nice. Not had one for years. I think Scotland would be a dream for two weeks. Or even Bournemouth and Sandbanks for a week. Rent a boat, take time, watch time slowly disappear. I have clients in Sandbanks, it really is a lovely place. Everything so clean. The sea, I can hear Will Smith singing *Miami*.

That sounds like Sandbanks to me. Haven't I got some food in the back? I jump out and run to the boot. Bananas. I take a banana and a bag of cashew nuts and return to my seat.

Actually, I'm looking forward to Monaco on Wednesday. It's a change. He asks me all the time to relieve him of his French drivers who are driving him potty having to pay for all their smashes. 'They're so frustrating,' he says. But I wonder what my down time would be like. I don't speak French. Don't want to be like that record 50 Cent sings, *Window Shopper*. Then again, he does have an apartment waiting for me. Long evening walks along those southern beaches.

I do live on my own. Nothing and no one to think about. Life, it really does come down to just a few short moments, could this be one of them? So – leave the UK, like all the wealthy people. Abandon this place that's been so good to me, provided for me, in so many different ways. The NHS I've so frequently taken advantage of and taken for granted because it has always been there. I support this country with my contributions through taxes, parking tickets and bus lane subscriptions. Why abandon a country that's bleeding and swear allegiance to somewhere else just because it appears to be the easier option? Although life has become incredibly difficult, the government simply experiment with people's lives. There's a new power every hour, they've no real idea. The biggest question in the lives of the British people, and the decision was given to them? I hear people asking, 'Why us? Why couldn't you give us something easy to make a decision over, like letting us decide when we pay child maintenance or our own bedroom tax, or give us power over the DWP and unemployment benefits?' So why would I leave others to fight over what's left? Besides, there's no Waitrose supermarkets down there and who wants sunshine every day? There's nothing wrong with gunmetal-grey clouds and a bag of fish and chips drenched in curry sauce and a glass of Dr Pepper. Is there?

Finally, they're coming out. I jump out to assist, opening the boot thinking they will want to throw stuff in, but the girls walk straight to the doors. They're all delighted. We head off back to the hotel. 'Can we cut through the park, driver, I love going through there?' asks Dolce.

'No problem.'

Driving past the apartments at One Hyde Park, the girls pay more than the usual attention. Their necks are transfixed. I do wonder what they're thinking.

Pulling up, Mr M summons my attention. 'Paul, end of the road today, I've got dinner here, the casino's over the road, my suite's upstairs and your job is done for the evening. Thanks, but I'll need you outside at 4am, my jet's now at Luton.' Dolce leans over and kisses me on the cheek. I jump out to relieve the boot from the weight of shopping (well, in monetary terms).

What a mad day. I'll head home, eat, shower and early to bed. I'm happy with that.

Chapter 8

Mr Grumpy and Mrs Lovely

Saturday morning, 03:08. Sunrise not for another hour and seven minutes. It's crazy going to work at this time, but when you jump into a hundred-thousand-pound car, it does tend to make it all OK. It's dark, although a half-moon is throwing out a little light, bless it. Only me in the middle lane of the motorway, passing the odd articulated lorry, but I have a million cameras, one every fifty metres. It's horrible. Trying to hold this car at seventy is like trying to hold back a racehorse in the blocks.

Right, switching to autopilot. Because if your foot forgets and starts to squeeze the throttle past 75mph, the big yellow camera will zap you, three points and a fine. You could lose your licence on this stretch of road alone. OK, setting auto pilot to 69mph just to make sure. Radar switched on, in case I fall asleep. If I did, I wouldn't hit a car or head towards a bridge, it would just stop dead. The steering wheel monitors your pulse beats from your wrist and if it slows down, the car screams at you. 'Drowsiness detected, take a break, have a drink, the AA.' That's not Alcoholics Anonymous by the way, although it appears that way.

The lane departure warning is on, so if I wander, the steering wheel brings the car back in between the two lines of the lane I was in. Great, so the car is armed and I could effectively fall asleep.

The autopilot is great. Because of man's short attention span, it's far too easy to speed.

I think I'll change the lighting in the car. It's white at the moment, a single light that travels around the cabin, very subtle though. Let's see on the screen. Blue. Not that one. Red. No, purple… OK I like this, very subtle. Yes, that will do. OK. Wake up! Where's my best friend the radio? Need to sing along to something. Magic FM.

Music playing. Randy Crawford, *You Bring the Sun Out*.

I'm running though today's itinerary in my head. Take Mr M to the airport, take S Class back to London. Pick up my car, then off to Hampstead Garden Suburb, Magistrates' Court, then wedding in Ascot, then on to Penny Hill.

Good, coming to the end of the M1. Twenty minutes to get to Park Lane. I've gone past Luton and I'll be back here in an hour and a half. Bet the traffic will be nasty.

Phone ringing. 'Paul, are you on your way? I need you to drop one of the girls home.' So that leaves me with ten minutes to get to Park Lane.

Yes, of course I made it. Just texting him that I am outside.

'Drive up to Notting Hill Gate, drop off and race back please, I have an allotted time for take-off, just don't need the hassle today.'

I pull up onto the set down, right outside the door. No doormen at this time. To my left, a line of around nine privileged supercar owners have secured coveted spaces outside the Dorchester. They're all the colours of the rainbow. Blood red Phantom, black Aventador. A yellow LaFerrari. A blue Bugatti Veyron and a white Phantom… oh, she's here. Best jump out.

'Morning,' I greet her gently.

'Hey, you OK? It's so early for you, sorry!' she replies in an undertone. Her dress was not as crisp as it was yesterday. Her hair needs assistance. Her make-up needs redoing. But she has just sprayed some fresh perfume on, she must have, it can't remain that strong all night.

'So where we heading?' I ask.

Music playing. Roxette, *It Must Be Love:*

'Oh yeah, can you drop me off at Notting Hill Village please? That's so kind, you're such a darling. Have you any water in front? Oh, actually, can I use the ones in this other door?'

'Go ahead, can I get you anything else?' *Like flipping what?* I ask myself. I'm not Waitrose and I don't have a toilet, so what the hell am I offering?

'No, I'm good thank you so much,' she says. 'We had a fabulous night, I personally did rather well at the casino.'

'Oh, splendid, so a good night all round then?'

'Oh, absolutely!'

I want to know where the other magpie is, but I think I'll leave it. Maybe she's hanging on to him for another day's shopping? Or she's fallen in love with him? Nope, not these two ice cubes, you can see their mission statement would be '*the first rule of gold digging is never fall for your victim*'.

'Don't forget your presents in the boot, will you?' I say.

'Oh, gosh, well done for reminding me!'

I think, *I bet you are.* Good job I'm honest, a reprobate driver would have taken them round to a colleague of hers and tried to get the same kind of evening she had.

'My house is just over there by the zebra crossing,' she says. We pull up and I run round to help her out of the car. Well, I don't actually run, I just casually walk round and offer my arm to hoist her out.

'What about your friend's prezzies, shall I take them to her?' I ask.

'No honestly, I'll give them to her later. You're so kind. No doubt I'll see you around, do take care of yourself.'

It's a bit like that bit in *Pretty Woman* when she's leaving the Penthouse feeling like a new woman and gathering all her new clothes and trinkets like they're the most important things in the world. See why women love shopping? It must be true that shopping is a cure for bipolar disorder.

Phone ringing. 'OK, ten minutes, downstairs,' I say. He just puts the phone down. I race back to Park Lane thinking, at least someone's happy. I mean, for a fruit tree to get looked after like that, you can't really blame them. After all, it is her prerogative and it was a good day's work well done. Funny how life changes and pimps aren't around any more. Woman can do what they want. Good luck to them, just remember at that level, you'll need a cape with an 'S' written on it.

Pulling up at the Dorchester, there he is, just waiting. I pop the boot, he throws his bag in and jumps in the back. 'Paul, don't spare the horses, Luton as quick as we can and we need to show passports, because you're driving me straight on to the concourse and right up to the doors of my jet. Please tell me you have your passport?'

'Yes, I always have it with me.'

I select the manual option on the transmission, as when I have to drive quickly, I like to be in control of the gears and it's a lot smoother drive. I'm wondering though if I do have my passport.

'Paul, how're we doing?' He's pressing me for time. This is when a driver consults the parameters of the things surrounding him. How much he needs the job, what time of day it is, type of car. The M1 is getting busy, should be a clear run to Luton though.

'So Paul, Wednesday, what's the plan?' he asks.

'I'll be with you around midnight.'

'Great, I'll book the room for a late departure unless you're staying a couple of days or for longer. Choice is yours.'

'I do appreciate it, thank you.'

Approaching Luton, he reminds me we don't want the main airport. We have to take a left to the VIP and private section.

It's very strict – you drive through the gates about forty metres and stop. Everyone disembarks and walks inside to display their particulars. Once all is accepted, you drive past reception and follow the lines for a few metres and then you're allowed to drive on to the concourse and straight to the main door of the aircraft. Yes, I do have my passport.

I help him from the car and thank him for yesterday's entertainment. He doesn't comment or moan that he blew seventy thousand in fifty-five minutes. He ascends the stairs and look at home boarding his private jet. For me, another job done till next time. I drive out of the gates, wave to the receptionist and head back to London. I wish I could keep the S Class. I could drive this day in, day out.

The drive back to Victoria takes around an hour and a half. I park up the S Class and race back to get my car, which incidentally takes another hour and a half. The house I am going to is in the next village to Golders Green, Hampstead Garden Suburb, a fifteen-minute ride through probably the nicest area in London. I'm over the Bishops Avenue side, which is where I first worked. The street is a mile long, with houses starting at around fifteen million and going up to seventy million. A lot of them are second, third or even fourth homes owned by heads of state who seldom use them and in some cases, the houses just rot away, with pigeons and mice as the sole occupants.

I turn down one of the side roads and think that to be honest, they all resemble each other. The one thing that strikes me is that most houses here have driveways filled with cars, so people are in – I'm not surprised, as I wouldn't want to leave a home like these unattended. But the weirdest thing is just about every house has its windows and curtains and blinds closed. Look at that, nearly every one. So how do they see who's at the gate? That's another thing, on the outside they all resemble high-security prisons. The gates are all seven to nine feet high and not an inch of their ground isn't covered. If your name's not down, you're not getting in.

I pull up outside the house I'm working at today, I know them well enough. Like all the others, it has four cameras bearing down around the front door. All the houses have a few visible cameras. There's room on the drive for me, as it's residents' parking everywhere. I put my hand out to press the bell and the door opens. The housemaid answers the door and invites me in. Her English is weak, but she manages to offer me a drink. I hear Mrs Lovely call to me, 'Paul darling, we're in the kitchen.' I call her that because she genuinely is a lovely individual, but years of tyrannical behaviour from Mr Grumpy has taken its toll and she's now dependent on pills to control her anxiety.

When I walk into the kitchen she greets me with a hug. Her daughter is strolling around as if she owns the place. She spends most of her time abroad with her dressage horses and taking part in competitions with her girls her age who have a lot more money. She sought, found and now cultivates a life she thoroughly enjoys and has no desire to leave. There's just one problem, she's not paying for it and she certainly isn't earning. The Bank of Mum and Dad is beginning to display signs of weariness, and most of their conversations start with the sentence, 'So, what are you going to do with yourself?'

'Ah, Paul, so you're going to favour us with your company today, splendid! It's been a few weeks I know, so sorry we've just been so busy.' She walks off into her vast kitchen and sits back at her table to finish her breakfast. 'We won't be long, I'm here, my grump of a husband is currently sitting on the loo, supping his porridge, either watching the CCTV for outside, reading a naughty magazine or wiping the inside rim of the toilet with his manhood. Oh, and my daughter, as you can see, is invariably unhappy when she returns home, and now look, she can't even feed herself as her mind is so preoccupied. You wouldn't believe how talented she is. Darling, what's in that bowl?' she asks her daughter.

'Cornflakes and Rice Krispies, Mummy.'

'Oh splendid darling, at least you've made an effort, although we've an abundance of food in the fridge you know, and there's cupboards over there with lots of stuff in them just for you. Hey, and if you ask our lovely housekeeper, I'm sure she would have no hesitation in cooking it for you.'

'Oh Mummy, must you insist? Please do stop going on!'

'OK darling, I just love you, you know that, but for all the nutrition that's in your bowl, you may as well eat the box.'

Her daughter (who is now at an age where she is displaying unattractive traits not too dissimilar to her father's) gets up and walks over to the radio and raises the volume. Music playing. Cyndi Lauper, *Girls Just Wanna Have Fun:*

'So what's the plan for today?' I ask Mrs Lovely.

'Well, we're off all over the place really. I have the hairdressers on the Fulham Road, and as you know, my husband has to attend Westminster Magistrates' Court for drink driving. How that's going to go, I've no idea. How embarrassing, it's all in the media all over the country for everyone who's acquainted with us. Imagine if we had a son, he'd no doubt influence him with his careless attitude. I know it eats away at him, no son and heir to amend his tarnished image. He'll end up a king of all he surveys, but dying powerless and alone.'

I'm ignoring her. She has a pathological tendency to wander.

'Oh, and then we have the wedding and the reception is at Penny Hill Park. And whilst you're here, we need you next Saturday, as we have a wedding and then a boat party along the Thames in Henley, so please keep that free.'

Fifteen minutes later the husband appears. Wedding attire on but with cuffs and collar needing attention.

'Paul, what a delight to see you, we have been so busy you know.'

Mrs Lovely interjects, 'Yes, darling, he's fully abreast of how wonderful he is and what the itinerary is for today.'

I see things haven't changed here. The chance to resuscitate the passion they once had had long since gone, but they still have an amicable relationship, along with the hypocrisy.

'Well as I'm not needed, shall I wander off to whence I came?' says Mr Grumpy.

'Oh darling, please don't be so dramatic, leave the drama to its allotted time, 7pm to 9:30. Paul, you wouldn't know this, but not only does he eat his breakfast on the lavatory he watches his soaps in there too, can you imagine?'

'Mummy, must you insist on provoking Daddy?'

'Ah bless. Now there's allegiance for you. In Daddy we trust. Yet when Daddy declines an increase on your credit cards, who do you come to?'

'See, I knew all along I had some use.'

Since I've been away, nothing has changed. Their love for one another has sunk lower than the Titanic and appears irretrievable. He'd often joke on my arrival, 'Watch out, she's hormonal and on the ropes, don't expect any civility!'

'You know, when we were younger,' says Mr Grumpy, 'after an altercation she'd invariably regret it and provide some sort of mitigation like, "Oh, I'm sorry darling, just time of the month. You know how it is." To which I'd boomerang with, "I see why you women get your monthlies now, because you deserve them!" These days she spouts off a load of nonsense and I must concede that it's her age. It's the only thing that compels me to remain under the same roof.'

Feeling the need to arbitrate, I try to provide a distraction. 'Sir, if you've no objection, allow me to adjust your collar.'

'Oh, well done. The only assistance I get round here is from the dogs. If you wouldn't mind doing my collar supports and cuff links, Paul. The judge is going to think I'm dressed up for his benefit. I just hope for his sake, he displays an ounce of intelligence.'

'So what on earth happened, were you drunk?' I ask. I lift his neck northwards to insert his collar supports

'Oh, my dear Paul, well, it went something like this. We were at the Waterside Inn you know, over in Bray. We'd had a wonderful evening until my dear wife decided it was going too well and thought she'd put a spanner in the works. Life pops up and bites one occasionally. You see, it was my conscience, damn emotion, it simply deserted me when I required it the most. It just left me with no car and no dignity, and I know someone called the police. I drive that route all the time after dinner and never had a problem before.'

'Your arms sir, I need to lift them,' I say, adjusting his sleeve to receive his cufflinks.

He continues, 'This police office revelled in detaching me from my Range Rover. Loved it, he did. I pay his wages, and what respect do I receive for it?"

'Do you need assistance with your tie, sir?'

'Er no, actually, I don't want the judge thinking it's for him, don't want to appear overly contrite, if you understand my meaning.'

'Right, darling,' says the wife. 'Please don't make me late today, it's my friend's wedding and I need to be there on time. I know you don't like accompanying me to things when it's not your friends.'

'My dear, I will be on time,' he assures her.

'So you're confident you won't get locked up then?'

'My dear wife, I don't know what pills you're on today, or what you're supposed to be on, but can you check please?'

'I hate tablets and pills. In front of a guest, how dare you! Must you insist on being so beastly?'

'But Mummy,' the daughter interjects, 'since when has your disgust for prescription medicine risen to the surface? When I was a child, you used to dip your finger in a bottle of Night Nurse and run your finger over my tongue to shut me up!'

'Hey, I've had some of that stuff,' says Mr Grumpy. 'It knocked me out till the next morning. It's a druggies' favourite you know. I cycled to Boots, locked up my bike and walked to the counter. I asked the man for some Night Nurse liquid. He looked at me and said, "Seven pounds, please. And it's got paracetamol in it. Make sure you're near your bed when it takes effect." I realised that as I was sweating, he thought I was a druggie.'

'Look, I have a very important appointment shortly, can you please HURRY UP darling!' says his wife.

'Will you please desist from calling me that?' he says.

'Calling you what, darling?' she says.

'That, darling, it's so disingenuous. We both know damn well how and what I mean to you.'

'That is not remotely fair, I resent your inference to being labelled untruthful.'

'How can you stand there and sprout such rubbish? Our relationship, yes I agree, is of a peculiar nature, but from our infancy we were intended for one another, darling.'

'Yes, and soon we're heading for the divorce courts. You think I don't know you're expecting your mother to pop her clogs to fund your latest habit?'

'Daddy.' His daughter cautiously approaches. 'May I tax you for some change? Well, notes, Daddy please.' He pulls out his wallet, deeply exhaling. It's full, notes all tightly pressed in. He pulls out a fifty without dislodging the others. She takes the note and stares at his wallet, as if deeply unsatisfied.

Having made his point that he's not a money tree, he turns to me. 'Paul, let's get out of here. Your friend's coming today, my wife's best friend who's just had a divorce party without knowing her settlement figure yet. Sure the cash will be enough for you and her when she gets it?'

'Yes, I know you're punching above your weight, she's a formidable woman, strong, seriously intelligent and soon to be backed up with more money than anyone really needs. Her only problem is that she invests so much, her emotions simply become confused.'

'Paul, I see your radar is in good shape. I wouldn't deny that with a woman like her by my side, I could conquer the world.'

'But the question is, could you conquer her?'

'But sir, I spurned her advances!'

'You know, all she said to her ex was, "Darling, we're struggling and I have no money, I can't carry on, so please let me sell one of your cars so I can have a bit of cash to spend." He replied, "I have a splendid way you can have a regular income. If you remove the sex ban you've been enforcing for the last six months, blaming it on your menopause, then maybe we can get rid of the nanny." That was it, red card!'

'Yes, But didn't she take you for dinner at the Jumeriah Hotel in Sloane Street?'

'Yes, but that was so I could thank her and apologise to her.'

'Oh I see. Well how did she take the rejection? Women hate being corrected or rejected. When a woman offers, who are you to decline?'

'That's just it. I offered the meal, and paid for it.'

'Good golly, in the Rib Room at the Jumeriah? You have ideas above your station son.'

'Yes, I realised that when the bill came.'

Life in that house is not easy. I feel for them both, but what can I say, other than wish them the best? The husband would say that it's not healthy for a couple to peer incessantly at one another for over twenty years. He definitely feels rejuvenated around younger girls. I know, I've seen him. He feels trapped.

I pick up the keys left for me. I thought we were taking the Range Rover but it looks like we are taking the wife's car, a Volvo

XC90. This job isn't always about having the best, sometimes just about getting there safely. This will be an experience, as I've never travelled in a Volvo. Apparently they're called 'airbags' because there's no car safer.

I jump out to help them both to get in. 'How do you like my car, Paul? Lovely, isn't it?' she says.

'Yes, it's splendid.'

'You're such a fibber.'

'Give me a little longer and I'll give you my answer,' I tell her.

'Right. Paul, head to Seymour Place first please, as the Westminster courts are on the Marylebone Road. Just you can't park there and then my wife is going to... hang on,' he turns round to quiz his wife, 'so what's this important meeting you're going to?'

I'm never sure if she has a short attention span or she really does simply forget things. 'Oh darling,' she says, 'did you know seventy percent of the British people hate paying inheritance tax, although the interesting thing is that only three percent of us do pay it.' See, she's so random. 'Oh, and incidentally, when you can spare a minute to discuss our daughter, I'll be waiting.'

'Do you have any intention of providing me with an answer today?' he says.

'Yes darling, I have a hair appointment on Fulham Road.'

'That's your appointment, your bloody *hair*?'

'I do recall bringing it to your attention, twice.'

'Forgive me love, it's just you made it sound like you were meeting the Prime Minister.'

His phone rings, providing much-needed respite from their point scoring, as it was really giving me a headache. Or maybe it's the Volvo.

'Paul, how long to my hairdresser please honey? And does anyone know what the forecast is today, I heard for later it was threatening.'

'It'll take a while yet, sorry,' I reply.

In London a driver should always overestimate the time. It saves one a lot of hassle and makes you look good turning up early.

Mr Grumpy is becoming agitated on the phone, as it keeps cutting out and he's talking to a business colleague. 'What's your number? Actually, call me on my spare.' He turns to me. 'Middle of the UK and I can't get a bloody signal. Are we in a third world country? There, my iPhone's cut right out.' He smashes the phone against the window in fury, again and again. Remnants fall to the floor. 'Airtime providers, you're so big you can't even remember how many customers you've got because you don't care, and you expect investors to prop up your company when you offer this crap service!'

He turns to his wife and reminds her that he is being dropped off first. 'What are we, two minutes away, Paul?' he asks.

'Yes sir, nearly there. I trust things will go your way today. Should be OK, shouldn't it?'

'You know it's not the impropriety that determines one's trajectory, it's how one rectifies it. We all make mistakes, but the trick is to learn from others' mistakes, not your own. Remember, we all have two ears and one mouth. Listen a damn sight more than you talk. Pay more than the usual attention to things heard, old chap. I will be OK. I trust that this judge is capable of displaying the odd moment of common sense.' His wife remains silent.

We pull up outside the court and I jump out to assist him with his jacket. 'Wish me luck, as I possess no class whatsoever,' he says. He looks through the window at his wife and says, 'If I'm not back, then start without me.' Then he walks through the doors.

'OK, so which part of Fulham Road would you like?' I ask, but I do not receive an answer. I glance in the mirror and can see that she is wounded.

'Just allow me a minute would you, put the radio on or something,' she says. I fiddle with the Volvo sound system and find Magic FM.

Music playing. Guns and Roses, *Don't You Cry Tonight:*

She digs deep into her bag and withdraws a blister pack of tablets. She turns to open the fridge door just above the armrest and withdraws a bottle of water. She seems to be dependent on those pills, holding them as you would a long-lost friend.

'Did you notice how they gang up on me?' she says. 'Look Paul, I have no desire to appear indelicate by implicating you or lobbying for support. I just need to extricate it every now and again from my system. My husband treats me like a pair of comfort slippers at best, and something beneath them at worst. My daughter, who I'm so ashamed of at times, rattles on about how hard life is on the extended budget we provide her. I pointed out to her that she thinks those horses she plays about with and all the pomp and ceremony that go along with it grow on trees. We told her she could start funding your own life. I'm afraid I implied that she can't be my child with her level of ambition, so far below my own.'

'Oh you didn't!'

'Yes, I'm afraid I did. Hey ho, many a true word spoken in psychosis.'

I will leave her to assemble her thoughts and take immediate inventory of her prospects.

She continues, 'Yes, I do want a divorce and yes, if my mother were to die, of course I would benefit as I'm the only beneficiary, but my fundamental objective is to fight him. All I want is a couple of million.'

I choke for a second.

'What's up?' she said.

'It's just the way you said all you needed was a couple of million. You made it sound like getting a couple of bags of crisps!'

'Well, it's all relative in the world we live in. I hate the word "money" but how on earth can we progress without it?' Her phone rings. 'Oh it's my daughter, she must need something. What is it darling? Or have you rung to continue with your vilification?'

'No Mummy, I just rang to say I do love you, just that you do make a rod for your own back at times. You and Daddy at loggerheads simply intensifies the pressure that's already consuming the family.'

'Oh, so it's me, I'm the problem am I?'

'See, off you go on a tangent, again. I've just spoken to Daddy.'

'Oh, really, and what's his problem now, beside himself?'

'Well, his intention is for me to come home, so he can set me up in my own property business, but he's just not getting it, it's not a job, Mummy.'

'So what the hell is it about?'

'Look, I need you to persuade him to provide me and my fiancé more time down in the south of France to make up our minds, as you really don't have an inkling what's it's like for me.'

'Hang on darling, have you been taking my medication? This cannot be my daughter speaking. I'm livid. I've never known you to be weak. Not my daughter!'

'See, this is what I'm subjected to, you can't even listen, can you!'

'Oh do shut up! Are you not familiar with the saying, "a whining wheel does nothing but demand all the bloody attention"? You cannot be my child when your ambitions are so far below my own.'

She put the phone down and stared out of the window. I'm thinking, isn't there another saying: 'Give a child everything they want and they will despise you?'

We pull up outside the hairdresser and she's still staring out of the window at nothing. I sit and wait quietly. A traffic warden approaches and I signal to her with my finger to just give me a minute. She can feel something is amiss and displays a certain amount of intellect by backing off to the wall behind her. Strange how when you're experiencing pain, the world just continues regardless. It doesn't give a stuff. Like yesterday, I saw a guy knocked off his bike on the embankment as I was travelling the opposite way. I couldn't stop or turn around, and as he lay on the ground, the world just continued.

I hear a teary voice from behind. 'Thanks Paul.'

'Are you ready?' I ask, handing her a small bottle of water.

'I have to be,' she replies. She continues to stare out of the window. 'He's a fool, you know. I would have happily lived quietly and contented in his shadow.'

After about half a minute of silence she grabs hold of her handbag and I get out to assist her. Opening the door of the hairdresser, she touches my face and walks into the shop. I turn and walk back to the car, thanking the traffic warden for her patience. If I'd had cash I would have given her some. Never seen such patience from a warden before!

Right, I'd best make my way back to Marylebone, let's see if Mr Grumpy has met his fate.

The Volvo is definitely an everyday car, but it's charm itself now that we are acquainted. It's comprehensive, coherent and playful. No longer the cumbersome lump they have always been seen to be. But I am suing Volvo for blinking whiplash! Travelling briefly on the A406, London's North Circular, we were in the middle lane and I didn't know, but it has lane assist which is automatically activated. I knew something was wrong, because as the car wandered to the edge of the lane, the steering wheel pulled back and freaked me out, I thought it was something I was doing. The lane assist kept rectifying what the computer thought was a problem by yanking the whole car back in line. At one point I wanted to change lanes, so I yanked it out of the middle lane and the computer did not like it and yanked it back, with venom. If another car had been to my left, we would have collided, because there's no side distance control. You forgot that one, Volvo! Yes, the car has side impact protection, but why no side impact avoidance? Volvo claim that their vision for the future is that while 1.3 million people worldwide die from a road traffic accident annually, the day will come when none of those 1.3 million will be in a Volvo. That's some promise. And this car is way too sensitive. Just after the tug of war with lane assist, someone pulled out in front of me and the computer just took the brakes from me, so my client was pulled sharply to the end of her seat. In the Land Rover Discovery, the avoidance system is only activated when you push the cruise control button, but the Volvo's is switched on all the time. I did feel I had an abundance of time to react, so the computer was a trifle premature. But seriously, who's being picky? It has four wheels and I'm fully aware that if a lorry hits me, I'm safe.

I get a text message from Mrs Lovely: 'Unreserved apologies for bending your ear, but a huge hug for listening to me.' It's strange, you wonder how someone with so much money could feel so isolated. You forget rich people are still mortals, and they get tired, sad and emotional like the rest of us. Incidentally, being sad shouldn't be misconstrued as depressed. It just means feeling or displaying sorrow. I feel my client is displaying signs of melancholy. But imagine feeling like that and having no food. You can see why a lot of people are on the edge.

Text message from Mr Grumpy: 'Are you outside?'

I'm hoping that the judge has looked upon him mercifully, but with what he's in for, I doubt the outcome will be anything but favourable.

I pull up outside the court and return his text. What a noise from all the traffic. Sitting across from the Landmark Hotel, I never realised the weight of traffic, it's horrendous. The door flies open and Mr Grumps jumps in. 'What a bloody palaver!' he roars.

'All sorted, sir?' I ask. 'Did you see the judge?'

'Yep, I saw the judge but I think he saw straight through me! No, NOT all sorted. He was somewhat combative. They've left the bench to deliberate, and I needed the facilities anyway.'

'So did the judge not look upon your mitigation favourably?'

'I think I am about to find out, Paul. I believe in a court situation, the only ones who ever win are the lawyers. Do you know, the gallery was filled with unemployed bystanders, armed with their blinking iPhones. Why aren't these individuals at work? My private life is not for any Tom Dick or Harry to indulge in!' (I'm thinking, but didn't you make it public business by your behaviour?) He continues, 'You should see them sitting there with their bags of popcorn with me providing comedy relief. Actually Paul, I could do with a coffee.'

'There's a coffee shop on the next street,' I say.

'If you could, I would be so grateful.'

'You sure you don't fancy something stronger?' I ask flippantly.

He pauses and actually thinks hard about it. 'Hmm, I'm tempted,' he grumbles.

'A Jack Daniels would fortify you. Apparently added stress will kill you well before alcohol does.'

'Thanks. I think a flat white with sugar and some sort of biscuit, if they have anything, will suffice. I'll run to the gents and see you back here in what, five or six minutes?'

'No problem,' I reply. As a matter of fact, I'm delighted to extricate myself from his incessant blaming of everything and everyone else for his problems. Driving round to Baker Street, I know that he knows they are going to take his licence, and he's resigned to it.

When I bring back his coffee, he is standing outside, drawing hard on a cancer stick. I actually thought maybe he had packed them in. He jumps in with his cigarette still lit. 'You're a star, thanks Paul.' He takes one long last draw, flicks it against the wall and blows out the smoke into the cabin. Lovely!

'What's these?' He plucks the biscuits out of the bag.

'Oh, custard creams, it's all I could find.'

He rips open the bag and begins to munch, hard. I watch the crumbs miss his mouth and cascade all over his lap and down the side of the chair. I know he will just brush the crumbs off his lap onto the floor.

'Actually, my favourites are bourbons, didn't they have any of those? Not saying I'm not grateful, although they're not the original make, but no, these will do.'

After ten minutes he's finished his coffee and runs back inside. Text message from Mrs Lovely: 'Paul, how's things going, has he been seen yet?'

'Yes, all going OK, just waiting for the judge to arrive at a conclusion.'

An hour passes by before I see his face again, bless him. Oh, here he comes, author of his own misfortune. He is not remotely happy. He flings open the rear door and throws his jacket on the back seat, then clumsily gets into the front. 'Right, let's go and pick up that mad cow of a wife of mine!' he snaps. I don't ask him the outcome. That face of thunder conveys all I need to know.

After about fifteen minutes he says, 'Paul, I think I'm going to need you around for the next few months, can we discuss it later?' Now this is one thing I like about being rich. They take holidays when and where they want to. They eat where and what they want, while the poor eat when they can. When adversity strikes, like now, he can laugh in the face of the judge and just hire a driver. Life continues as per usual. I see why most rich people don't call upon God. They don't need him.

'I take it the judge made no concessions then?' I ask.

He removes a cancer stick from the cluster in the box, places it between his lips and holds it there, studying the end of it. He flicks his lighter till it fires, then draws on the flame until the cigarette is alight. 'I just wanted the judge to display some common sense. Instead he breached my human rights and tried to disrupt my freedom by banning me for two and a half years and fining me three thousand pounds. How on earth does he intend to benefit from that? I explained how my conscience simply deserted me when I needed the blinking thing the most. What was it the Apostle Paul said… *'For I do not do the good that I wish, but the bad that I do not wish is present with me. But if I do what I do not wish, then I am no longer the one carrying it out, but it is the sin that dwells within me.'* To be honest, I've no idea where to find it, I just know that line exists. Could even be Shakespeare for all I care.'

No, not Shakespeare, it was definitely the Apostle Paul's words in his second letter to the Corinthians, chapter 8. Well, I didn't expect that, but what was even more surprising was that, analysing his pensive demeanour, I realise it wasn't about the fine or the length of the ban, it was standing up in front of the judge and being told what to do that he had the problem with. His face actually resembles a spanked bottom. Not good. I shouldn't laugh.

'Paul, can I use your phone to call the wife?' I hand him my phone and beg him to remember that it's not his. The remnants of his old phone are now in the glove box, awaiting surgery after he smashed it against the window earlier.

'We're nearly outside, how long before you're done with your important meeting?' he says to her. Ah, lovely, they've picked up where they left off.

'On my way out,' says his wife.

When we pull up at the hairdresser's, he's still grumpy. He's acting like a man who's seeking recompense, but as his adversary is a judge he can't just exact revenge. Like last weekend when I ran into a night club to inform my client I was outside, and a female reveller was in the middle of an altercation with a doorman three times her size. She was spitting insults at the guy and then she slapped him hard across the chops. The girl recognised his weakness – he couldn't hit back and she knew it, hence her confidence.

Mrs Lovely jumps in and immediately recoils at the smoke fog in the car. 'Darling, if you've no objection, would you mind extinguishing that, please? So how did it go in court?'

'Splendid honey, all good. Paul, let's head to the church in Bagshot,' he says.

'And can we not spare the horses, it's my friend's wedding and we must be there on time,' says his wife. 'Darling, your cigarette? Please spare my hair. Besides, I thought you were giving up. You said you were thinking about it. Thus sayeth the man who keeps a safe distance from any exertion.'

'Have you finished?' He takes in a last draught of nicotine.

'Oh come on darling, you still think cleaning your teeth is exercise!'

Mr Grumpy lowers the window and flicks the cigarette onto the pavement. I half expect a woman's voice from the Volvo computer to admonish her for fly tipping.

The roads should be driveable – M4, M25, M3. First I'll check there are no nasties on the M25. But we're OK. The journey takes around forty minutes and we are in a lovely part of the country, Bagshot.

'I'm hungry,' she says. 'Paul, can you find a Waitrose or a Marks & Spencer and bring us a couple of sandwiches and crudités?'

We pull up at a cute church in between Bagshot and Windlesham.

'Darling, you did put a couple of bottles of champers in the fridge, didn't you?' the wife asks.

'Yes. Actually Paul, when we come out could you pop the cork off one of the bottles, as we'll have guests with us?'

They both eventually disembark and wander off toward the grounds of the church. I race off to find a decent supermarket. It's been a while since I've been to a wedding. Always good to visualise the body language between the couple. Is it really love or just convenience?

I return fifteen minutes later with some dips and stuff. I'd best text them to let them know. Mr Grumpy pops out, sits in the car and lights up a cigarette. 'This is so boring,' he says. 'Now I've got a blinking headache. Have you got any paracetamol, Paul?'

'Er, no, sorry.' So he begins rummaging around in the back. 'Ah, she's left her make up bag.' He rips the bag open, causing items to fall over the back seat and floor. 'Found some!' He rips two small tablets out of a blister pack and gulps them down with a glass of some wine he found in someone else's car boot. 'I mean, these are *her* friends, I've no idea what the hell I'm doing here, other than getting a flipping headache. I've so much to do!' He takes one last draw of his cancer stick and then flicks it onto the neatly-manicured grass. 'Here's the bride, I'd best go. Paul, don't forget the champagne and there should be four flutes in the fridge too.'

'No problem, just go and express your delight at the couple's happiness. And enjoy yourself!'

'Paul, I am only happy when I am making money. See you shortly.' And off he goes, in search of someone to punch.

Ah, the bride has just turned up in a 1940s Bentley. Black exterior and blood red-interior with white-walled tyres. It's delectable. Space is made for the bride to glide through to the entrance of the church. Utterly divine. She looks beautiful. The doors close behind the guests. The moment of truth for the bride. Has she prepared enough, is she ready, will anyone declare an impediment, or will it all go smoothly? Commitment and sacrifice will spring to her mind. I can only wish her good luck.

Forty minutes later, I feel much better for my forty winks. One has to take advantage of down time. Switch the radio on. My company in times like this. Radio 3. Music playing: Barbara Hendricks, *Bachianas Brasileiras no. 5*.

Now they're all venturing out for photos. The bride and groom appear genuinely and blissfully happy as they walk out of the church and straight into a fresh blizzard of confetti. The guests seem genuinely happy for them too. The couple can't keep their hands off each other. Their old Bentley wedding car has the boot open, with the shelf hanging down, which enables the driver to rest some champagne and a couple of glasses on the shelf. I think it's time I imitated them and laid out a spread and some champers.

Fifteen minutes later, they arrive back with two friends. One is the lady I know from the hotel, the one I took out. I lay the spread out, crudités and dips and grapes and four glasses, and the setting appears almost as nice as the bride's car. The wife is talking to her friend and the husband is talking to my acquaintance. Everyone is drinking, yet my acquaintance takes an odd moment to stare at me. The husband notices and comes between us. He says to her, 'So have you met our wonderful driver Paul?'

She looks at me. 'Yes, I have had the pleasure.' I turn to her, hoping she will accept my salutation. 'So how is Paul?' she asks.

'You know, I'm splendid, the sun is shining and I've been watching the ceremony. Can I fill you up with some more rosé?'

'Don't mind if I do actually,' she replies. To be honest, the atmosphere is somewhat strained between us, because I declined her offer of an evening together on a night when she was feeling emotional and apparently needed to feel like a woman. I didn't oblige for whatever reason and ran out of the house. As the moonlight lit up her face, her eyes changed colour and I felt she wanted to exact some sort of injurious punishment on me. I remember feeling this sudden compulsion to run before I was pushed down the stairs.

'So,' she says. 'Do you remember what it was that spooked you that night?'

'Oh do please inform us what you saw in the shadow of the night that compelled you to hotfoot it, Paul,' says Mr Grumpy.

'Look, I just felt that I wasn't the only claimant to her affections,' I reply.

'But you went out to eat, right?'

'Yes.'

'Hang on, so, she declined a starter, what did you order for main then?'

'Well, I ordered turbot.'

'Oh, did you now!' He giggles. 'Expecting her to pay, no doubt. Rule number one, you never expect a woman to pay for a meal, no matter how much they bang on about equality. No wonder you're on your own. So then what happened?'

'We ended up in the Red Room till gone three,' she interrupts.

'I do remember, I was there. I recall the barman calling for last orders, and you finished your drink and wandered off.'

'But, you knew where I was heading. I left you the suite number!'

'Seriously Paul, humour me?' she says.

'With what?'

'The mood was set, the ambience at the Grosvenor was captivating. I'm no super model, granted, but a model at least, yet you walked past the lift? I wasn't asking for commitment, and if you had got the rest of the evening wrong by being selfish upstairs, then no biggy, it was just a window that we could have taken.'

That evening still dominates my thoughts. There's nothing bad to erase from my head, but now she's demanding closure. Yes, it was a mind-blowing evening and I get dizzy spells from it. My mind was all over the place, I remember singing to myself.

Thinking music: Bobby Womack, *I Wish I Had Someone.*

Mr Grumpy begins to display his short temper, not unlike a mortar bomb with a short fuse. 'Well it doesn't look like he's going to spill any beans as to why he declined my wife's friend on a night when she required company. I mean why the hell did you just run off? I'm dying to know.'

'Look,' says his American friend, 'if you've no objection, this is a conversation in progress between A and B, and really doesn't implicate C. So could we just have a private moment?'

'Oh, yes, well go ahead then, is she only our friend?' says Mr Grumpy.

I feel I have breached protocol by interacting with this woman in this unconventional way. And I'm feeling uncomfortable. But for some reason, she is demanding closure. Whilst all the others are enjoying the moment, sunshine, laughter and champagne, the American lady is seeking to assuage her disappointment in me by getting an answer.

'Go on then,' she asks, staring at me. I pour some more champagne into her glass as if stalling for time.

'Well, OK. In your en suite, there were some man's clothes.'

'Yes, my ex-husband had been that day, and decided to shower as well as picking up the last of his stuff,' she said.

'But in the walk-in wardrobe, the man's clothes hanging up were designer stuff and completely different in waist size.'

'OK, a friend of mine who pops over from time to time. He felt it advantageous to leave a change of clothes, so what?'

'And in the bedside cabinet, the half-cut glasses and nasal spray and inhaler that looked like some kind of breathing apparatus. Did someone die in your bed or something?'

'My, you did peruse my abode well in such a short space of time.'

'Well, is he a platonic friend too?'

'You know, you really are asking the wrong questions. He is a friend who at that time was in Portugal seeing family. Is there anything else?'

After that exchange we agree to differ, as the wedding guests are wandering off to a posh spa up the A30. I pack up and shove all concerned into the car.

Ten minutes later on the other side of Bagshot, we arrive a supposedly world-class spa. Waiting on the driveway a few metres from set down, I watch as wedding guests get dropped off by their chauffeurs. Once again every type of supercar litters the estate. Mr Grumpy has been nodding off in the front seat. In fact, his snoring is so loud I thought at first he was teasing. When I realise that nope, he is sleeping, I think, *Wow, poor wife having to sleep with that.*

The American lady begins shaking him on the shoulder and he jumps out of his skin. He doesn't look right.

'Sir, how are you feeling?' I ask.

'I'm not bloody sure what's going on, I feel very strange.'

'Has he got food poisoning Paul?' the wife asks.

'I shouldn't think so, from his symptoms,' I reply.

'Well he must have taken something.'

'Actually, he took some tablets from your make-up bag for his headache.'

'Oh no!' says his wife. 'Which ones did he take?'

'He took some little white and orange tablets in a pack which I thought were paracetamol. Why, what are they?'

He appears to be declining rapidly. Then he becomes really grumpy. He snatches the make-up bag out of her hand, forces his hand into the bag and pulls out three or four blister packs of tablets. 'These!' he says. Then he throws them in the back, shouting at her to identify them. She doesn't reply. He searches in the make-up bag looking for a box. He finds one. 'Mirtazapine!' he shouts. 'What the hell?' He reads the pack. 'Take only two a day.'

The American woman consults Google. 'They're an anti-psychotic drug,' she says.

'A what?' His wife is visibly shaking and jumps out of the car.

'Where are you going, I haven't begun with you yet!' says Mr Grumpy. I jump out to help all disembark. Mr Grumpy is furious. He races after her.

She turns and shouts back, 'I didn't ask you to raid my vanity case!'

'Right, I demand to know what the hell my wife is on. You'd better start being honest with me right now!'

He grabs her by the arm, as a police officer would grab a junkie, and frogmarches her past the guests and into the venue. I turn to the two other ladies and say, 'I will be parked just here, maybe someone can get him a glass of Red Bull, in an attempt to reverse the effects.' They agree.

Never a dull moment. I do hope the wife is OK. I know why she appears spaced out most of the time.

I am parked up near the front entrance, being inconspicuous. No woman will notice me in this car, not like the Bentley or the other clients' cars. Yes, I'm aware it's not my attention they crave. I've had women just open the doors and get in, offering themselves, until they realise I'm just a chauffeur. In the Volvo, I'll be left alone.

Oh, hang on, the wife is coming back. I stay still, looking at my iPad. Not sure of the situation, so I'll wait.

'Hi Paul,' she says as she jumps into the back seat. She begins rummaging hard in bags looking for something. 'I'm so sorry about earlier, you see what I have to put up with?'

Trying not to take sides, I reply, 'How is he?'

'Oh him, he's in a back room drinking coffee and trying to reverse the consequences of rummaging through a woman's bag. Actually, it hasn't shut him up, but the drugs have definitely neutralised him. He looks like a German Shepherd, just without the teeth!' (Smiley face.) 'He actually looks like a boxer who has finally lost his killer instinct. Ah, found it,' she says triumphantly. I look round to see her rip the lid off a 100ml bottle of Chanel Coromandel and begin spraying it like her life depends on it. I seriously thought she was digging for more tablets. That stuff smells delicious. I haven't seen that particular one. Just googled it – only available at the boutique in Westfield Kensington. She's still squirting. She must get through three of them a month. I know she wears another perfume for the evening. Imagine spending roughly a grand a month on petrol, then a grand a month on perfume!

'Right, Paul. I'd better go back in quickly, but not before I change these bloody shoes. Oh and be a darling, grab my other blouse from the boot, there's a cow inside I despise and feel compelled to trample on, she's wearing a top not too dissimilar to mine in colour and designer.'

'Do you require anything else in the boot whilst I'm there?' I ask.

Removing her top, she says, 'Er no darling, nothing, but do run along, they'll be sending a search party for me imminently!'

Walking to the boot, my eyes are assaulted by her womanhood. Flipping Nora, she could have warned me, given me a chance to swing my neck out of the way. I pull the door ajar and stick my arm in the cabin. 'Paul!' she shouts.

'Yes?'

'I can't reach!'

I have no choice but to dip my head down into the cabin. She grabs hold of my wrist and says, 'Excuse me, am I so deeply unattractive you can't even look at me? Or is it you only like American women?'

'That's totally unfair,' I say, looking out of the front of the car.

'You've seen me undress in the car before,' she says.

'No I jolly well haven't – well yes, but I put the mirror up.'

She smiles and gives me back my arm. I'm relieved, as the perfume and her womanhood permeating the cabin are impeding my ability to think! I walk round to the other side of the car and wait till she's ready to alight.

'OK, how do I look?' she says.

'Splendid,' I say enthusiastically. 'Just like the John Lewis slogan, you're never knowingly underdressed.'

She hits me twice, gently, on my face. 'I'll be back, darling,' she says.

I won't deny that at times this job can be very pleasant.

I must have nodded off after that. It's about an hour later, the sun has penetrated the cabin and I awake to feel perspiration running down my face. Quick. On with the air conditioning!

I sense someone approaching and lift my head up. It's Mr Grumpy staggering to the car. I lean over to let him in.

'I've had enough,' he says, throwing his head onto the headrest. 'Are you aware that people take this stuff just to feel the way I do right now?'

'Well if you feel anything like you look sir, then that's a trifle worrying,' I reply.

'Now I have more of an understanding of why she walks around like a drunken cow all the time. I must get her off these tablets. This is ridiculous, how is one supposed to function? Do you know, she now believes I took them on purpose. The temerity of her!'

'Make sure you consult her doctor before you take them off her won't you?' I remind him.

'But why would I do that? I need a fully functional wife!'

At that moment a wedding guest with a screaming five-year-old – at least he looks five years old – comes between the cars and stands by my side window telling her son off.

'So go on, why should I have to tell the doctor what I intend to do to my wife?'

'Well apart from the fact that she'd be attempting to please you, we might underestimate her withdrawal intensity. It could leave her with all sorts of side effects, like anxiety for instance. So for medical reasons, he should know.'

'Well, she can go on her own. I don't need that kind of embarrassment, he'll probably think she's on it because of me.' Isn't it mad how tablets can turn a normal individual into a raving junkie? 'Oh my god, look at that!' he says, looking past my window. The mother with the screaming child is right outside the window trying to cuddle her boy and calm him down. But when I turn, she's breastfeeding him. As our windows are blacked out, she can't see us. She has picked him up and is leaning against the next car.

'A comfort feed,' says Mr Grumpy. 'I mean, what a waste. She's gorgeous.'

'I'm sorry, but I fail to understand.'

'Look,' Mr Grumpy says, 'if I was her child, I'd be feeding on those breasts till I was sixteen. It's why men get mad when women whip them out in the street, because we want some. Especially as lovely as those, they weren't really meant as a plug to shut up stroppy kids, they were meant for us!'

'Er, I'm not entirely sure,' I reply. 'Although I'm delighted that you're feeling better.'

'What a waste,' says Mr Grumpy again.

The lady eventually returns to the venue and Mr Grumpy vacates the car in search of some Red Bull. Great. Now for some peace.

As the day goes on, the sun makes me drift in and out of consciousness. I drink some water to refresh myself and begin thinking about tomorrow. I have the King in the morning and Mr Monaco in the afternoon. I must check my room at the Monte Carlo Bay Hotel.

Actually, I think I will stretch my legs. Just as I grab my phone, I feel a presence at the passenger side window. It's the wife on the phone. I wait and realise that I haven't seen the American woman. I think that was a door long since closed, and I'll never know what was behind it.

The wife jumps into the back and digs into her vanity case type thing. Yep, another squirt of perfume. 'How's things Paul, have you eaten? Do you need anything?'

'Seriously, I'm good, thank you. I may go for a walk in a while.'

'Jolly good idea. He's not very good and he already wants to go home.'

'Shall I take him home and come back for you later?'

'Let's see what happens, but that is an option,' she says. 'The spa and hotel is lovely, probably the best in the area. The service isn't brilliant but it's functional. The parents of the bride have just been told that their pyrotechnics display will have to be dismantled and cancelled because the owners of the estate adjacent to this park have stipulated that they will not allow that sort of noise in their vicinity. Can you imagine?'

'No, I wouldn't want to. So whose is the estate?'

'Apparently, members of our lovely and immediate Royal Family. There are some very unhappy guests fuming because no one from the hotel informed the newlyweds that there would be no nocturnal entertainment.'

'I bet.'

'Right, well I'll run your suggestion by him as I think it's a good idea. He's probably better off at home than wandering around here displaying a slapped bottom. I'll be back shortly with a conclusion.'

I decide to stretch my legs, but really I want to peruse the 120 acres of grounds. I've heard the swimming pool is the business and the ambience at night seductive, albeit without the illumination of a firework display. Walking down the drive, I find a rock to sit on. I can still see the main entrance, but it's under a tree and the shade is more than acceptable. I can't have the engine constantly running to keep me cool and contaminating the wedding guests. I really don't fancy walking. I know, I don't do enough of that. What am I afraid of, that I'll fall over and break an ankle so I can't go to work? I do ask questions constantly. I'd be on my own, and who would help? No one, hence why I am extra careful. I suppose because I'm fat as well, exercising is difficult, to get up at a certain time and give commitment to something you're not obliged to do until the doctor tells you 'exercise or die!' 2k? OK, a 1k run. I think I could do it. On a bike! Or in fact, round here actually. The setting could actually provide an incentive. I need an incentive. A doctor's warning isn't an incentive and to be honest, if I've left it that long, it's probably too late. I have adjusted my dietary needs but now I have to exercise to reap the benefits? There's always something else.

Now there's a couple loading their bags into the house car. Are they off home or going on holiday? They have a lot of stuff, probably off to the Caribbean. Have a lovely flight and a jolly good time. My time for that must surely come. I'm not whinging, just questioning how long before I can afford to leave the UK and see another part of this world.

Italy. I see enough of it on TV, and even on a postage stamp the three S's – Sorrento, Sardinia and Sicily – look fabulous. Until such time, I must keep on swimming until my life raft comes. Like most of us I'm tired, but I can't stop swimming, because it's paying the bills. The gas or council tax man have no regard where you get your money from, as long as you pay what you owe.

A new one from car insurance companies. If you're paying by instalments and you're a pound short so you don't meet your monthly mandate, they just cut you off! No warning, no compunction. In the old days, if the direct debit failed, they'd try again in seven days, but not now. A few drivers I knew got caught out, and a client did too. Problem is, driving without insurance is six points on your licence plus a big fine.

Thinking music: Christina Aguilera, *Beautiful:*

'There he is!' Looking back at the main entrance, I can see Mr Grumpy standing at the car, waving his arms around.

'Where's my driver, where's my driver?' he's shouting. Always the way, I attend the facilities or stretch my legs and they suddenly appear. I'd best go and make myself available, before he busts his cardiac muscle again.

'Oh, there you are!' he shouts. 'I looked in the car, I looked all over the place.' What a fibber, see how he exaggerates! 'OK, I've had enough and I need to go home, so help me take this flipping jacket off will you?'

I help him into the car while he continues to yap away. 'Do you know, the staff in that place couldn't run a bath! Useless! Oh, your American friend sat at the bar, crossed her legs and the proprietor of this joint scooped her up, sorry! And me, look at the state of me, a flipping junkie!'

'Well you'll feel better once you're in your own bed.' I'm trying to calm him.

'That's it, she can stay here tonight, I need that bed for myself tonight, just me and maybe one of the dogs. The smallest one can sleep and fart all over her pillow. Mind you, he'll probably suffocate from the amount of perfume on her pillow. Do you know she gets up in the night to use the en suite and sprays perfume all over herself?'

Most of the way home he continues cursing. He just can't help himself.

His phone rings. 'Yes, what is it?'

It's his wife's voice, muffled on the phone. The background noise resembles a fish market. 'No, just listen to me, I need you to stay there tonight,' he says. 'No, I'm not sending Paul back, stop shouting and bloody listen. Just book yourself into a suite and enjoy the rest of the night, like I'm going to!' He finishes the call. 'Paul, look, drop me and you are done for the day. I have so had enough today!'

Driving through Swiss Cottage, heading north up the Finchley Road, I start worrying that Mrs Lovely is going to call my phone. I sincerely hope not. Why does the wife put you on the spot when you've chosen to swear allegiance to her spouse, the one that pays your wages? It's conventionally a slow death from there on. Once Mr Grumpy chose a housekeeper while his wife was on holiday. Oh, he told me, she was just what the doctor ordered. When Mrs Lovely returned to be greeted by this attentive new member of staff, a strategy of slow death was deployed. The woman barely escaped with her life. Mrs Lovely told Mr Grumpy that the next bad card would be a red one.

By the time I pull up on his drive, he's snoring. He actually looks like he's beating the crap out of someone in his sleep. The judge, perhaps. I sit for a minute trying to work out the gentlest way to wake him. Or should I leave him in the car? What a racket! OK, let's go for a poke in the rib cage. He jumps. 'Whaaaat…

WHAT IS IT?' he shouts. Once he has gathered himself he realises it's me. 'Oh, we're home. Great!'

I jump out to assist him, as he's staggering badly. I have a headache, but I'm delighted I didn't take what he took. I empty the car and hand him the keys. 'Is there anything else I can do?' I ask.

'Paul, as usual, you've been fantastic. My daughter has texted me and she'll be home within the next half hour, so I'll be fine. Actually would you care for a glass of my favourite single malt? Just one glass?'

'Thank you, but I'd better not. You're still under the influence of your wife's drugs, why don't you just try and sleep? Go and enjoy your bed and spread out like a helicopter!'

'You know, that's doesn't sound like bad advice, thank you. Oh, you know we have another wedding next week? And I'm best man, you know I'm good for some comedy relief.'

Driving away from a job, I always reflect on how the day went, whether I annoyed the client and if so, whether I rectified the situation. Whether they annoyed me, and did they even notice? Whether I scratched the car, or worse, the wheels. Today, I think, went well.

I'm sitting at the lights on the A1/A406 intersection, heading for the M1. Above me is a long telephone wire and there must be fifteen swallows on the line. I wonder where they're conspiring to fly off to... hang on, isn't this an indication that autumn is round the corner?

Well at least I'll get a decent sleep tonight. I'm a very light sleeper, which is so annoying. I have a little Night Nurse in its bottle, and that provides me with a deep sleep. Bliss. What a way to end a day.

To my right I can see a planet, it's not quite dark but dark enough to see it. Am I sure it's a planet? I think so, as stars twinkle and planets don't. This particular one is red, which means it's Mars – it really is. That must mean it's quite close. But even now, at its closest to us, it's still nearly forty million miles away. Travelling at 70mph twenty-four seven and no pit stops, it would take sixty-five years to get there. When it's at its furthest from the sun, it's 250 million miles away from Earth. Two hundred and fifty million miles! How does one comprehend such an immeasurable distance?

I have a clear drive home, just the usual things to contend with, ironing, shower. It's way too late to eat, I can't have food just lying in my tummy all night. But once again, I have made it though another day.

Chapter 9

The road to Monte Carlo

Why am I yawning? I had a lovely sleep. It's 5:45am on Wednesday and in this traffic it will take roughly two hours to get into the 'city with no pity' to collect the car for my drive to Monaco. Window open. Let me smell the mixture of the morning dew and the car fumes. The morning is neither warm nor cool, fresh enough to leave a damp patch on car roofs.

Well I'm all packed up and on my way. I'll probably be driving today for around nineteen hours. I'm not sure when I'll be back, so I've loaded a suitcase. Somewhat intrepid though, as I'm a creature of comfort and there's no Waitrose superstores down there. There are no council estate people like me to catch up with. I'm not sure floating around wealthy people all day will be easy. Like a false sense of reality.

I'm sitting in traffic on the Finchley Road near Swiss Cottage. I still have sleep inertia, as I came this way to leave my car at Golders Green, then realised I won't be back for I don't know how long.

Text messages are coming in, scroll through, yes, one from the King and one from Mr Monaco. Great. I am booked in at the Monte Carlo Bay hotel, on the tenth floor, with an open invitation. I see it as a tip, a really nice tip. OK, he wants me to ring him.

'Hey, all OK?' I ask.

'Yes, all fine. I just require a couple of things prior to your arrival. So what time will you be here, do you estimate?'

'Roughly one in the morning,' I reply.

'Cool, as you know, I seldom sleep. Oh and I have a party tonight on my yacht for a bunch of seriously wealthy international bankers, and I expect this will go on till the following day. Many won't be arriving till midnight anyway, so when you're here just call, because by that time, my yacht won't be in the harbour, as we'll be far too noisy with an American singer and a British band. I'll jump on a speedboat and come back to shore to check you in. Actually, send a text when you're racing past Avignon and then another when you're passing Nice, which will provide me with an understanding of your proximity.'

'OK, fantastic. Which car shall I bring?'

'Well, I have one of my Bentleys down here and I was going to say bring the Maybach, but I really need a diesel, so the S Class. They're all limited to 155mph anyway. I'm sure you won't be far off that.'

'Right, S class it is then. Oh, sorry to bother you, but I'll need to fill up three times, probably a hundred and twenty pounds times three please. And the French barrier/toll things. Roughly fifteen pounds each and there's around twelve of them. Oh and the flipping Eurotunnel. Do you fancy paying that for me?'

'Paul, no need, as I have already pinged seven hundred for expenses, but I need something else. Do you remember the two ladies from the other day, I took them to a shoe shop in Lowndes Square?'

'Right, yes, how could I forget.'

'Well, I have a lady friend who has spotted a pair of shoes from that shop and can't get them in Nice or Monaco, so can you pop over there and pick them up? The shop already have an instruction, my lady friend has spoken to them and the shoes are waiting. I've pinged another three thousand into your account. Please make sure you purchase them in banking hours, as if the bank's closed and you have a problem with your card, you will most definitely spoil my gorgeous lady's buzz.'

'Three thousand pounds, is that the grand total?'

'Well, twenty-eight hundred, to be precise. When they are in your hand, send a picture and wait for a reply. I may need you to go to Asprey, on Bond Street, she has a beautiful dress for tonight, but there's something missing around her neck. Something specific she chose. Look, I'm not sure I could transfer that kind of money into your account without your bank summoning you for a chat. We'll see.'

'OK, just let me know by midday please, as I will want to get going. Wouldn't life be easier if you could just have one woman?'

'Told you before, I am too wealthy for a woman's brain to behave in the normal way. My money would be too much of a distraction for her, it would agitate her, annoy her, provoke her. I don't need that, and a woman doesn't need that distraction or that temptation. I take women out and they have to be gone, out of my life, by morning. Even by that time, I can feel them already planning for me and them, and they become militant in their thoughts and actions. I have to run, fast. I get what I need when I want it. Besides, it's much nicer this way, because once they receive a reward for their efforts, they know where they stand. They hate it, because they develop a taste for the sort of stability they all yearn for, just not with me. So, don't forget, send a picture of the shoes.'

I'm asking myself, is he unhinged? He buys presents for women every other day of the week! I don't mean trinkets, I mean after an evening with him, if she meets the requirements, she could end up with a deposit for a decent buy to let! No wonder they love him. It's for this reason I chose this job, because the right client can really make your life easier. Just that some company directors don't realise a happy workforce produces much better productivity.

As I pull up in Harley Street, two of the wives are reasoning with a clergyman from the church round the corner. I wonder if they've collected enough to fix their roof. I jump out of the car and stand by the steps waiting for one of them to extricate herself from the clergyman's vice-like handshake. He's obviously delighted with his campaign efforts. Finally, the priest accepts that there is no more cash to follow and leaves the two wives with a smile.

'Hi Paul, I have the Phantom key here for you,' says one, while the other hugs me. At that moment, one of the Addison Lee cars pulls up.

'How many have we got?' I ask.

'Oh, I don't know, all we know is the cars are on the way,' she says.

I run off to park my car and acquaint myself with the Phantom again. Standing at the garage door, I look across the news and see that the lady who lives opposite has gone. The windows are bare of the furnishings that adorned them. People move on. Time waits for no one.

By the time I get back to the house, the Addison Lee drivers are already loading up suitcases. I really don't need any exercise today, and they appear to be enjoying their work, so best let them get on with it.

Twenty minutes later we are on our way, heading for the Virgin VIP lounge at Heathrow. I have six taxis following me, but I don't suppose that will last long.

So I have the King and his three wives once again. I feel sad in a way, as this may well be my last time with them. I know they'll be back in two weeks, just not sure I'll be here.

'Paul,' calls the King. 'Thank you for your help this week. Sorry it's short, but you know I'll pay you what we agreed initially.' This basically means any cancellations have to be paid at the minimum cost or whatever one agrees with the client north of the minimum.

'King, it's been my pleasure. I just trust that with all the sudden change, all is OK?'

'Thank you, but my sister has died suddenly. She had cancer and we all thought she was on top of it, but she decided not to share the severity of the situation with us. She's actually in the belief that God gave her cancer for her past sins.'

'King, those are heavy misgivings indeed. But God doesn't bestow cancer upon anyone. I believe those words came from the Apostle James in chapter 1 verse 13: *"When under trial, let no one say he's been tried by God. For evil things God cannot be tried."*'

'Ah but look what happened to Moses's sister Miriam. Because of the spiritual condition of her heart, God struck her with leprosy.'

I think, *Here we go.* 'OK, point taken, but between the three of them – Moses, Aaron and Miriam – they were all commissioned to act upon what they had been taught by God. Their strict instructions weren't like anything God's followers receive today. I suppose God had a point to make in recording events from the past for our understanding. Even Timothy wrote it for us to understand in his second letter chapter 3: *"All scriptures are inspired of God, beneficial for teaching, reproving and setting things straight in righteousness, so that the man of God may prove competent and fully equipped for every good deed."*'

'OK, I appreciate your words and I'm grateful for them. My sister and I haven't really spoken that much due to family disputes, but I wouldn't put a thing past God, he does what he wants.'

His number one wife speaks out. 'Yes, whatever God wants to be he will be, and nothing will diminish the light we so proudly present and represent.' They all collectively vocalise the word 'amen!'

OK, OK, you win. I'm really not in the mood for their righteous disapproval, so I suggested saving my questions for next time. I just say, 'I trust you will have a safe journey, and I'm sure the Three Degrees will look after you.' They all laugh. Although I suppose it could be worse, most discussions I engage in or listen to regard the inherent conflict between science and God.

The journey takes just over half an hour. Heading out to Heathrow at that time of the morning isn't too bad, as most of the traffic is coming into London. Amid the madness of Heathrow, the Virgin VIP lounge is a picture of peace, no one rushing around. The porters peacefully detach the luggage from the clients, who are then offered refreshment after their arduous half-hour journey. Then a representative pops over and checks that everyone who's there should be there, and no one is trying to obtain an advantage by simply wanting to distance themselves from the madding crowd back in the terminals. The representative walks away with a smile and refreshments are offered. This is my queue to scarper.

The King pops out and pulls me to one side. He thanks me once again and digs deep into his jacket pocket. I thank him for the tip and say I'll see him in a couple of weeks. Although the booking goes through the agency, and if it's not me, they'll find another Rolls Royce driver. As I drive off, he reminds me, 'Oh, yes, don't forget, the keys go back to the office and send them your invoice.'

Now my day really begins. Sitting in the bus lane on the M4 I feel an incredible thirst for a cup of peppermint tea with a tablespoon of honey. If you have a dodgy tummy, this concoction works wonders, and it also helps me sleep. I normally have a cup before bed, but occasionally I fancy a cup in the day accompanied by some crackers. I used to love croissants, but like bread, the yeast just bloats my abdominal area.

While I'm in this traffic I'd better check my texts. Nothing is moving, so I may as well switch my engine off and relax. From Harley Street to Heathrow, this engine will stop and start nearly a hundred times. What sort of starter motor finds this appealing?

Irrespective, let me focus on the day in hand. First check my account online. This is a novelty. I conventionally look at my account to check funds before offering my card for a purchase, but now I'm checking to see how much I can spend. Yep, there it is, three thousand seven hundred pounds. Lovely. I often purchase items for clients, especially clients who don't want their wives asking unwanted questions. I am fortunate that clients trust me in this way, they may not thank me or offer grand gestures, but trust for me is paramount.

Right, well, two hours later and I've finished the few miles that were ahead me. Two blinking hours! I've tucked the Phantom up in bed, attached the trickle charger and covered her with a blanket. I genuinely feel sad, as I just love the car. I quickly jump into my own car and drive down the street to Wigmore, where I drop off the key and head towards Victoria. Actually, I really need a drink. I find a Pret à Manger on De Vere Street, pull over and run in. I order a peppermint tea, with two teabags, a separate pot of honey and a flapjack type thing. Lovely. Now I can head off to Victoria.

Driving down Bond Street, window shopping, I incessantly run over things in my head. I nearly forgot the congestion charge, oh man, it's for yesterday and today. Not sure if Hampstead Garden Suburb is in the zone though. When I pull up at the garage to pick up the Benz I quickly go online and pay both days. I could really do without a fine today thanks.

A quick swap over and I remember to lock my car with the key, not the fob. The fob arms the immobiliser, but the key just locks the door. Locking the door with the key means the alarm won't go off and the battery will last a lot longer. With old cars the alarm can suddenly go off and annoy people. I know it's in the garage, but I need the battery to remain alive as long as possible.

Right, off to Lowndes Square, then hit the road. Goodbye England, for however long it will be. Maybe I should come back for the festive season. Nope, nothing to miss there other than watching friends spend what's taken them all year to save for, or spend what they really haven't got. Or maybe I should stay in Monaco for Christmas, at least my ears won't be assaulted by Christmas songs, on the rare occasion I shop at Tesco. All they play is Christmas songs. Then in the aisle you hear a couple of Polish girls singing 'seven geese are singing, six gold rings...' No no, that's the bridge, it's five gold rings, five not six! I won't miss that, or the Salvation Army outside Oxford Street underground station singing.

Pulling up on Motcomb Street, my curiosity is getting the better of me with these shoes. The shop doorway resembles Christmas. It's alive and it's by far the best woman's shoe shop. Right, ring the bell and wait till I'm invited in. A fruit tree greets me curiously, but with a smile. Just remember, shop assistants like credit cards, not people. I mention my situation and she speaks to another assistant, who wanders off into the back. When she brings the box out, it's obvious presentation is paramount. I would have paid for the box on its own.

A lady dripping in diamonds is casting a beady eye on my purchase. Oh my days. Size five, lime green crocodile skin slingbacks with a cleavage. Oh and those inimitable distinctive red soles! Not sure what to think, so I take a photo and send to Monaco. 'Is all satisfactory for you?' the saleswoman asks. Best provide her with a more appropriately elevated title, as I'm sure they feel they warrant one. She removes one of the shoes from the box with a glove on. I honestly feel I need to cover my fingerprints with some form of contraception. It's like looking for scratches on a brand-new supercar.

'Could you please bear with me as I am waiting for a WhatsApp message,' I say. He'd best not be too long, the sales people are looking a trifle concerned, like I'm another shoe kicker.

Text message... OK, apparently she's dribbling over the phone, all is good. 'Check the size,' I'm told. A UK size five, but they are well small. Women's feet are dainty. I know some woman can have size seven or eight. But these are cute. I do often shop for clients, I see the buzz with shopping, especially spending other people's money. Shopping is therapeutic, but some women say taking the stuff back a few days later is the best part. Where is the therapy in taking back items, to swap, change, mess about with and stand for ages in the returns queue?

'Yes, all OK here,' I say to the sales lady. Now the woman dripping with diamonds has just pushed in. She pulls out a black debit card. The sales lady hauls me over to another till and says, 'The card machine is ready, please check you're happy with the total on the screen.' Two thousand eight hundred pounds. I agree and pull out my green Lloyds cash card, and I can see Miss Diamonds eyeballing, so stupid me, I plonk my card on top of the machine, and the sales lady says, 'Sorry sir, we don't have the facilities for contactless.' Well that gave Miss Diamonds some comedy relief.

Finally I have my purchase and I'm holding on to it tight. My destination now is Dover, well actually Folkestone. Best get petrol and start adding up the receipts. I'll get something to eat when I stop off for petrol. Even better, I can get to see the white cliffs of Dover. I haven't seen them in a while. Vera Lynn did that song about the white cliffs. It was a bit like that Doris Day song. Thinking music – *The Black Hills*.

Just a revised version there. Well I'm going to have plenty of time to mess about, it's eighty miles from London to the tunnel, fifty-two miles under water, then from Calais to Monaco it's another nine hundred and fifty. Last time I crossed the Channel by boat. Terrible! It was a rough crossing and I hated it. I hate the feeling of not being in control. The waves were playing with the boat, tossing it about like a lion would a pussycat. There seemed no let up, people being sick everywhere. You know that feeling when you suddenly take a dislike to something and you can't do anything about it but grin and bear it? Travellers went into the toilets to be sick and all the basins were covered, toilets were sprayed with all the colours of the rainbow. No thanks, never again!

An hour and a half later, I'm approaching the tunnel. I did take a pitstop to fill up and managed to find some sustenance for the road ahead. Actually I think I ate too much, as I feel dizzy. Worse still, I could do with a nap.

I've just found out that the train ride is a lot more expensive turning up like this. Well I was told just to buy one when I got here. Hey ho, I'll know next time. I'm sitting waiting for my train, having displayed my identity to passport control. Next train is at 16:09, twenty minutes to sleep. That won't help, not long enough for a dopamine infusion.

The activity around me is mad. I'm sitting in a line of cars and small vans and there must be twenty lines of around thirty cars one behind each other. What a crazy operation, but it works quite well. Although I have seen on the news what happens when it doesn't. Lorries stuck on the motorway for hours, it looks horrendous. How do lorry drivers cope with all that time? They must really like their own company. What a lonely life. At least I'm fortunate enough to have a beautiful car, it really does help. Like now, I just put the TV on. If I was stuck here for eight hours, I have my music, the television, my iPad. The only thing I lack is a toilet, but there are plenty of water bottles.

It's a twenty-eight minute ride through this tunnel. I hate tunnels that travel under water, but here goes. This waiting double-decker train runs to a length of half a mile, or equivalent to seven and a half football pitches. Driving in, you can't see to the other end. There's a constant droning noise that reverberates and sounds not too dissimilar to an MRI machine. Putting my life in the driver's hands, I drive through to the other end. Sitting here, I definitely feel I need sleep.

I think back to last November's drive to Monaco. About eighty miles south of Calais, with roughly an hour to conclude my journey after driving all night, I was so focused I didn't realise the temperature outside was minus three. I was relaxed in the cabin with twenty degrees internal temperature displaying on the screen and I had a T-shirt on. After driving all night, I was pushing it, yet the S Class remained sublime, it didn't compromise its high standards even on the ragged edge. Although a lot of Benz customers are struggling with the seats being too soft, saying they disjoint the lumbar region of the back, and the suspension is too weak and actually feels dangerous! The only other issue with the Benz is that when the car is in reverse and closing in on an object, the park distance assistance only activates two feet away, which is annoying. The 350d and the S600, along with all AMGs, have fantastic suspension, although I haven't the faintest concept what's going on with the rest! Mercedes, please sort it out, clients are seeking alternatives!

A lot of the French roads are so long you could drive at a hundred and fifty and find time to make a cup of tea. There's a never-ending horizon. Most simply wouldn't have the patience for that, even with the dazzling blue sea of the Côte d'Azur waiting for you as a reward.

Then the petrol light appeared on the computer – I hadn't realised it was so low. A petrol sign appeared in the darkness, and at that moment a strange thing happened – I heard my mother shout out my name. Strange, as she died two years ago and I do not believe the dead can just pop up and say hi. I glanced over at the speedo, and good gracious I was pushing it, you just don't realise in this car, it's so well insulated. I took the exit for the petrol station as I knew I wouldn't reach the next one. When I pulled up and got out, my right foot slid straight out in front of me and I fell to the floor. Black ice! That spooked me out.

Driving off, I started to think I'd had a lucky escape. I drove out of the petrol station with caution, because of the black ice. Then, when the car reached around fifty miles an hour, just crossing the line to join the A26, the right rear suspension collapsed and swung the rear of the car anti-clockwise. Trying to keep cool, I forced opposite lock on the steering wheel, only to be thrown clockwise. It was a worrying moment as I was heading towards a solid four-foot high concrete central reservation barrier. I pushed hard on the brakes and came to a stop right in front off the barrier. Horrible!

I moved on to the hard shoulder and got out. Looking at the rear I could see that the body was sitting lopsided, and I just couldn't work out why. I drove on, and at 40mph it felt OK. Got to 50 and the right rear collapsed again. So I limped back to Calais. It was like time was running past me. Weird. When the incident happened, I had forty-two minutes left on the satnav. It finally took me, hobbling along at 50, four blinking hours. By the time I had arrived at Calais, I was battered.

It's 17:01 and we have arrived in Calais. I just roll out of the car train and head out of the terminal. There's a good deal of traffic about, but it's nothing like as congested as the UK. In around an hour, I'll pass the petrol station on the A26 which I've labelled as my grave – well, it could have been. The picture seldom leaves me.

OK, time to settle into this journey. Satnav on for this run, and it's displaying the conventional route with no red line for traffic. It will be late by the time I get to the Champagne region, so I'll miss its beautiful scenery. However, welcome to France, Metropolitan France actually, which is divided into eighteen administrative regions. I've carved out a diametrical line from the Pays de la Loire (Nantes), racing on to Nouvelle Aquitaine (Bordeaux), then through Auvergne and Rhône Alpes (Lyon), then I'll descend on to the Provence Alpes Côte d'Azur (Marseille and southern region). I'm optimistic that I'll be there by 1am. Yes, I can see you trying to do the maths. That's 950 miles in seven hours – go work it out…

One way or another, I'll arrive at a conclusion when I arrive in Monaco as to what I'm going to do with my life. It's imperative to recognise an opportunity when it arrives, and I think this might be one. It's knowing what you want to do with your life. The concept might be in your mind, but executing it is a nightmare. Mr Monaco tells me that in this day and age, you can't make a million without getting someone's back up. Those who have made a fortune would tell you it's hard to find a rich man whose conscience is as clean as a new pillow. Well, I'm not out to make a million, yet my clients discuss the word as if it's a bus fare. But it's weird is how some who appear amiable and kind under normal circumstances seem to undergo a personality change when money is at stake. Surely the more we mature, the more sensitive our spirituality should become.

For me, at this time of my life, it's finding contentment. Finding that way of balancing the heart, rising as high as I can, but keeping my conscience clear. Our consciences are supposed to act as a restraint in protecting us emotionally.

The King whom I just finished working for left me a parting scripture, so I read it. Isaiah 48:17 and here, God is once again imploring the Israelites to listen to him.

> *I am your God,*
> *The One teaching you to benefit yourself,*
> *The One guiding you in the way you should walk.*
> *If only you would pay attention to my commandments!*
> *Then your peace would become just like a river*
> *And your righteousness like the waves of the sea.*
> *Your offspring would be as many as the sand*
> *And your descendants as its grains.*
> *Their name would never be cut off or annihilated from before me.*

In contrast, Proverbs 6:14 states:

> *With a perverted heart, they are always scheming evil and*
> *spreading contentions.*
> *Therefore, his disaster will come suddenly…*
> *In a moment he will be broken beyond healing.*

From what I see daily, no one seems remotely interested in spiritual words. Most seem to find the spirit of the world more favourable.

People love watching magicians perform magic, things associated with the devil, like murder books, violent TV programmes. How many times do we read a murder book before our conscience informs us that the images we allow our eyes to become seduced by are injurious? The more you watch violence or read crime or sexually violent books, the more we become desensitised. Our consciences cannot be working any more. So how can we prevent that? How can we can train the conscience to be more sensitive, so it can serve as a reliable guide? Surely our conscience is a moral compass, an inner sense of right or wrong that can guide us in the right direction. But to be effective, shouldn't it be properly adjusted, or calibrated? When a person's conscience is not properly trained, it does not act as a restraint from wrongdoing. Such a conscience might even convince us that bad is good. How ironic that in committing such evil crimes as murder, religious fanatics violate the very laws of the One whom they claim to worship.

An hour later I'm passing the petrol station where I had my close encounter. I don't think it's healthy to rubberneck for too long. Benz said the problems were to do with the self-levelling Airmatic system failing. The suspension just gave way on me. A missed bullet, so to speak.

Phone ringing… my friend has just landed from Orlando. I answer on loudspeaker. 'I thought you were back days ago from holiday, where've you been?' I ask him.

'Yes, I'm at Heathrow. Sounds like you're driving, I'll call you tomorrow. We just got back, three days late.'

'That good, was it?

'If you can call losing your job a good time.'

'What? How come?'

'First we sat on a Virgin flight on the tarmac ready to go. Me, the wife and the kids. We sat in the heat for two hours with no air conditioning. We all ended up like toast. They thought it was lightning earlier that could have caused it. They eventually moved us onto another plane twenty-two hours later, as they had to fly a plane over from the UK. Then, once we finally got going over the Atlantic, the first-class passengers saw smoke under the pilot's doors. A fire was lurking somewhere and they couldn't find it where it was coming from. The pilots couldn't even see each other. Next the captain declared a mayday. As soon as this was announced, passengers all around me began to vomit. It was like we were watching a movie. Then we were told to assume the crash position. Even the stewardesses were running about visibly crying their eyes out. Then the plane suddenly went into a dive, but the captain dealt with it.'

'I feel sick myself listening to that,' I replied.

'Check the news web pages, I'm sure it will be on there somewhere. Everyone was told to assume a crash position as the plane dropped out of the sky.'

'You're making this up!'

'I wish I was. We eventually landed at Shannon in Ireland and then off to Scotland, then we paid an inordinate amount to fly back to Heathrow. Three blinking days of flying.'

'I am utterly stunned,' I replied. 'Well, you're back now and all safe. I'll call you tomorrow for a chat.'

Three hours after leaving Calais I have whizzed past Reims and I'm a hundred and twenty kilometres north west of Dijon, where I'll meet the A6, which is not an attractive alternative, as it goes through Paris. It's getting dark, so lights on. I think I'll change the internal cabin light setting. It's currently white or ivory. It's very subtle, but I think I'll darken it somewhat. Orange? No. Green? No. Purple – that's more subtle. Like on a plane when you're coming in to land, it calms the cabin atmosphere down. Now all the lights are on it resembles the Starship Enterprise, sunglasses wouldn't go amiss. Oh, and here's my fourth toll. I forgot to get euros. To be honest, a card is proving a quicker alternative, just as long as they calculate it right. This one is even more expensive, nearly thirty euros. Oh look, there's a card in the machine. Well how does the barrier lift if the card is in the machine? Probably rinsing the credit… Ah, there's a woman stopped in front and she's got a Maserati. I pull the card out and it's French, Société Générale. She's coming. She must like white, she's dressed from head to a toe and looks like an angel. Thinking music: Madonna, *Angel*.

You know when the sun makes an appearance after a long winter, or you leave a cold day in the UK, or when you approach Nice down on the Côte d'Azur, the sun suddenly becomes effulgent? You could just turn your back to it and allow the heat to gently stroke it. Well that's what this lady is like as she walks towards me – sunshine! Long brunette hair, burgundy sunglasses, a white suit and jacket like the one Jennifer Lopez wore in that movie *Maid in Manhattan*. But this lady utterly owns the air surrounding her.

'Hi, I believe this is yours,' I ask.

She reaches out with long beautifully-manicure fingers, no nail polish. 'I was distracted on the phone, I'll lose my head if I'm not careful,' she says. She is definitely French, she has that frustrated look about her, but there's a dual heritage, Arabic, or Greek, or something. Her hair is strong, bouncy. The curves on her face, I've known women to pay to look like that with no success. And then when she's gone, there's an invisible hint of whatever the perfume was.

Oh great, I need petrol now. I'm glad this isn't my money. But you can get fed up with spending other people's money, you know. I'm thinking of asking for an overdraft at some point, and I can imagine the bank manager saying, 'Well Paul, last month your spending was way too unstable for me to even consider letting you loose with more cash than you're actually earning!' All right, all right. I can't stand bank people. Actually, it's not even they who decide whether you remain impoverished, it's artificial intelligence.

I'm deeply saddened by my friend's bad luck. I know he saved for three years to take the kids to Orlando and worked even harder than me, so to then come back and lose his job because he was in transit – well, the airline is to blame, so there must be a claim, right? I must make sure he has a good solicitor.

Spooky thing, putting your life in other people's hands. I would struggle sitting in the back seat of someone else's car. Many who you'd think were professionals drive like they've just passed their tests. Even scarier when emotions get involved. They could be on a roundabout and another driver invades their space, and even though they're in the wrong, they refuse to act responsibly by simply giving way. No, they prefer to plough on and crash. Some don't think of the inconvenience it will cause, the time element and probably road rage. Then court, the embarrassment… it goes on.

Five hours after departing Calais, I am heading to Aix-En-Provence on A8, having flown past Valence and Avignon on route A7. I can feel an atmosphere now. It elevates the soul, it's captivating and utterly infectious. I left the sun behind in the UK, but tomorrow it will make an appearance, and it will have a totally different feel to it.

Tiredness is taking hold, but if I pull over and sleep, time will rush by like nobody's business. I just have to get the job done. I can feel a dull ache in my back, but I must hang on in there.

Here's another speed trap. Every so often I come across a section of what we call variable speed limits, measuring your speed between two cameras over a distance of five kilometres. Once I'm through that, it's back on the throttle.

Phone ringing. Ah nice, someone remembered me. It's Colin. 'Hey, are you still alive?' I ask.

'Just touching base, Paul. You OK? Sounds like you're driving.'

'Yeah, on my way to Monaco, and I am not doing too badly. How's the family, and the boy, all OK?'

'Yes, all OK, just thought I hadn't heard from you. Me, the wife and the boy drove down to Brighton earlier to go and see my wife's mother, she's a domineering ninety-three year old. My wife hates pushing her in the wheelchair, so me and my son take it in turns. We took her down to the beach. The old girl didn't want to go, as she would rather moan and whinge and shout obscenities constantly. But off we all went. It was nice and not too busy. I'd been working all week, so my boy reluctantly pushed the wheelchair.'

'Ah, that's nice, a family day out. No problems then?' I ask.

'You're joking. I was getting some ice cream, while my boy and his mother were standing near the pier entrance, at the top of a ramp leading down to the beach. I started walking back towards them and all of a sudden the boy began waving his arms about in the air in front of his face.'

'Why, what happened?' I ask.

'Apparently, a wasp attacked him and while he was protecting his face, he only let the flipping wheelchair go, and the damn thing began rolling down the ramp towards the beach. The scene keeps replaying in my head.'

'Is Granny OK, was she hurt?'

'Well, I dropped the ice cream and ran to help. Once we got her back into the wheelchair, she had a grazed bloody face and a broken wrist, which was the first part of her body to make contact with the ground. Nightmare! So when are you back?'

'I really hope your mother-in-law has a speedy recovery, at least she'll have something valid to have a go at now. I'll call you, not sure right now when I'm back but I'll catch up over the weekend.'

Six hours and fifteen minutes. I've blasted past Nice and heading to Monaco. Battered as I am, the smell of the south of France is drawing me, summoning me to come and indulge in the delights, the sights and the pure unadulterated frivolity. My client only lives here because the UK would kill him for tax. He says he doesn't mind a contribution, but what they want is ridiculous.

What gets me is that he has no siblings and no children, and I suppose not even the tax man, to leave his empire to. I haven't the foggiest what his intentions are, but as he gets older, I know he thinks about it more. On a couple of occasions he's quoted a paragraph from somewhere, I quote:

'This time thing makes one panic occasionally. Although I have all I want, now it's just a matter of surviving and enjoying what one's been given. I have the comfort of knowing that my life has been a life worth living. My friends have gone home, yet I must cease from tears, because when it's my turn, I shall lie right here, till Christ appears.'

It's like the only sure thing for the UK in the coming months is uncertainty. Rich and poor people are also bonded together with that one thread. Back in the UK, for those on the rocks who are fed an incessant diet of gloom and austerity by the government, uncertainty is a constant companion.

Monaco provides a shield for its residents which enables them to remain oblivious to a world that's bleeding. They dwell in a bubble utterly unfamiliar to the majority of us. There's not a council estate for at least a couple of hundred miles, so there's no reminders of poor people as they drive past, unlike in the UK. Council estate one minute and private estate marinated in unbridled wealth the next.

Europe is entering unfamiliar territory trading with the UK, and we're all entering a zone of uncertainty. Back in the UK, my job is a luxury. Chauffeur jobs exist because of the contribution and generosity of these mega-rich people, which allows them to operate somewhat liberally, with the use of their cars, their money, their tailors, their pilots who regularly fly household staff to the four corners of the earth. And many live under the comfort of their employer's roof. When, for whatever reason that protection has been removed, we are back to square one. Reality hits us like a car crash. Uncertainty is never far away. Like when the sun shines or when darkness falls, uncertainty does not discriminate. Anyone can experience it at any time. Down here in Monaco we have a coating of Teflon, or so it seems, so that in a storm everyone down here will shut the tunnel doors, switch off their televisions and radios and wish everyone else the best of luck.

I feel a time is approaching when none of us will be able to hide. For those who think the Bible is just a book of stories, they are all true. But because religion is an unwanted subject for all the pain it has caused, there's very little appetite for it any more. The prophet Habakkuh, like all prophets, was commissioned to pronounce impending doom on the ancient Israelite nations, but with reference to our day, he speaks our common language in chapter one and verse five: '*Look at the nations and pay attention, for something will happen in your days, even if it is told and shown to you, you will still not believe!*'

That's just it. People just don't believe any more and many that do believe they are in a worse position because there are so many variations and avenues to God.

The prophet Isaiah had a unique way of putting difficult things into perspective. In chapter 14 of his book he visualised the trajectory of the people and stated, '*One day, the whole earth will become free from disturbance, the Angels and the people will become cheerful with joyful cries.*'

He continues speaking on behalf of his creator in chapter 14: '*For I am your God and with exception of me, there is NO other God. The creator of the heavens and maker of the earth, who firmly established it and who DID NOT CREATE IT SIMPLY FOR NOTHING. Bring yourselves up close to me and come to me. Those carrying the wood for their carved images, who then create their own inanimate objects and call them Gods in which none can save them... have not come to know me!*'

God reminds us of Jonah. The narrative was a lesson in humility, courage and mercy. The people in Nineveh were not even Jews, but even as Gentiles, they knew of the God of Israel and what he was capable of and they repented, displaying the fact that it's never too late.

Even Moses began crying out to God, when he was leading the Israelites out of captivity and away from the Egyptians. The cloud Moses was following eventually seemed like a satnav gone wrong, as they were led to the Red Sea with no visible means of escape. The Israelites vilified him, saying (Exodus 14), *'What have you done, leading us out of Egypt? It's better for us to serve the Egyptians than die out here in the middle of nowhere.'* Even Moses recognised a dead end and began crying to God, who in his power and wisdom, parted the Red Sea, reminding them, when all seems lost, just have faith in Him.

The good kings of ancient Israel were under attack any number of times, but God invariably told them to stand firm and see Him as their salvation. They seldom fought a battle, as God stood as their shield.

Money has often failed to provide protection for people who have worshipped it or become dependent upon it, like on the *Titanic*. In many countries, money has no value.

Driving through the tunnels, and there are quite a few them, we have street lights. Fantastic! The whole place is lit up like a Christmas tree. I've almost made it, but it was arduous. It's 01:12 and the streets resemble Oxford Street on a Saturday afternoon. Bends and curves everywhere. Oh, another casino. Loads of them. Must be a pastime for when the rich get bored. Don't pay taxes, throw it away at a casino. At least the waitresses will get paid.

What's this road? Boulevard d'Italie. I believe it takes you straight out to Italy and runs along the Côte d'Azur. And there's my abode for the night, the Monte Carlo Bay Hotel on Avenue Princess Grace, right on Monte Carlo Beach. It's straight out of a scene from a James Bond movie. After filling up two and a half times, I have a quarter of a tank of fuel left. Nine tolls at a cost of 223 euros. Distance travelled, 1,175 miles.

So here I am. There a twenty-five foot ramp to drive up, and the wide staircase next to it has lighting on every step. It really is like Saturday afternoon. Oh, I forgot. I was supposed to ring him. Think I will send a text in case he's talking.

Arriving on top of the ramp, my eyes are assaulted by a visual feast of supercars. The lights, people buzzing backwards and forwards. A concierge is running around as by convention. I find a spot, and a few eyes are upon me. Well, I have British number plates, so naturally it will provoke the odd eyeball.

I pull up, waiting for a reply. One of the valets approaches and asks if I am staying. I can't tell him my room number, so I give my name. He runs back to his desk and begins looking on the computer. My phone beeps. That's good, Mr M is climbing aboard a speedboat and coming ashore. Good, because I'm hungry and battered.

People-watching is a funny thing. Immediately behind me, I can hear a loud London accent. A large guy is entertaining. He looks like he's enjoying himself, but the rest of the party seem dazed. There's a white Porsche 959, wow! How old is that? I remember back at school, I had a picture of that on my wall. I think it was the first 200mph production car with just 2.85 litres. Round about the time Jaguar brought out another 200mph car, the XJ220. And Ferrari had the F40. These cars must be worth a million apiece. Hang on, here's the valet coming to inform me I am not booked in. Which wouldn't be a problem, as I would just swap cars and go back home. Seriously, one has to be ready for these short-tempered employers.

'All OK?' I ask.

'Ah oui monsieur. You are staying on floor dix,' he stutters.

'So that's the tenth floor then,' I confirm. The floor I was on last time.

After around twenty-five minutes, Mr M arrives and we have a brief chat. I deliver the shoes safely and he says I can keep the change. I give the keys to the concierge and we both head to the reception. All the madness around me resembles a multi-coloured blur.

'So, you've no energy to come and help out on the yacht then, Paul?' he asks.

'Not a chance, if you've no objection,' I reply. 'I trust all is going well then?'

'Yes, it's all gone OK. I'm doing a bit of networking so to speak, a lot of them are friends and business colleagues I've known for years. You couldn't comprehend the wealth if I accumulated all the money on that boat. But they're on the yacht, stuffing their faces, only fools and horsemeat really. They're relentless social climbers. A handful in there know what it's like to climb and exactly what it's like to reach the top, and they know that road is paved with nothing but hypocrisy. But as most of them have found out, the higher you climb, the rarer the atmosphere. Their heads are so deep in the clouds that if the world came to an end they wouldn't even notice. Most are from privileged backgrounds, but those who aren't certainly don't snivel at how arduous life has been. It's a shame you're not up to it, I could have introduced you to some people.'

'I really hope you don't mind.'

'No, not at all. Please, wander up to your room. Do what you have to. The kitchen is open twenty-four hours. Order a bottle of Chablis on me, just make sure it's the Grand Cru. Relax. Take the load off and I'll see you in the morning. I expect that will be midday, which isn't a problem as late breakfast is an extra provision!'

He thanks me for bringing his car, and looking like James Bond in his tux, he walks off back into the night. Phew. Time to chill. Oh I'm so looking forward to this.

Once I have checked in, I walk off towards the lift. The bar's there, but I ask the receptionist to send up a bottle of Chablis

Grand Cru, cold. On the way to the lift, I notice that the bar has about nine or ten cocktails lined up, with all the colours of the rainbow. Hotel guest are enjoying the delights of their surroundings. Some of the women resemble fruit trees, while others remind me of the Côte d'Azur itself when the sun is shining on it.

The closer I get to the bar, the more I'm being pushed back by the weight of the diamonds the women are wearing. I can barely see. If I had epilepsy, I'd be laser beamed to the floor. Never mind photography lights, diamond light is far more dangerous. Women wear them freely here without fear of confiscation by local reprobates. Their teeth shine as brightly as their diamonds. Best keep walking, I wouldn't want to delude myself by dreaming I am worthy of sitting in the same room as these women, let alone of offering them a cup of peppermint tea. I am not remotely jealous, no unattractive emotions here. Besides, envy induces depression. I am delighted for them.

I have to force the key card into the door a few times because of my eagerness to chill. Walking through the door, I switch the lights and the TV on. My name comes up all over the fifty-inch screen. It actually says, 'Welcome back.' Not sure this is the room I had before, but it's on the same floor.

I walk straight out on to the balcony with the room phone in my ear. 'Yes, room service?'

'Splendid. Can I order dinner please?' There's a gentle breeze up this high. The breeze and the moonlight begin to refresh me. I walk back in and grab a wine glass from the table, then walk straight back out to greet the breeze. Its a huge balcony. There's a three-piece suite out there, with enough room for twenty people. Pouring a glass of the Chablis, I can see it has a strong colour. It's crisp and delectable.

'Hi, yes, can I order the gravadlax to start please and the turbot for main, with a large portion of vegetables of the season. Possibly some mashed potatoes and actually, I'll have a portion of French fries too, please. No, nothing else for now, thank you.'

Leaning on the balcony wall, glass in hand, I can faintly hear people down below. I can definitely hear supercars racing around. Not too dissimilar to Knightsbridge, except you don't hear the residents moaning. For a moment I close my eyes and imagine I have just won the lottery, and I'm here on my own merit, not at the mercy and generosity of an unscrupulous businessman. As my client says, no one makes this kind of money without ruffling a few feathers.

I shall just make the best of what I have and take each day as it arrives. Now, let me go and immerse myself in the massive double shower heads that are waiting for me in the en suite. They actually work – no dryness on the head from hard water. No trickling. They are extremely powerful, and I feel blasted clean and revitalised.

Roughly seventeen minutes later there's a knock at the door. As it's not a night nurse I've summoned, it must be my food. A French waiter rolls the trolley in and my food is simmering under a silver cover. He looks at me and I thank him. He is still looking at me. 'Oh,' I say, 'forgive me, I'm not familiar with being on this side of the fence. How could I miss that one. Sorry, I only have a credit card.' I take my card out of my phone and apologise. I feel bad, because at two-fifteen in the morning, I would have expected a tip as well.

Lifting the lid reveals a delightful sight. I may not be rich myself, but if you can't beat them, you can jolly well join them.

I look at the TV but think, it's French, no point. The French doors to the balcony are ajar and I think, they must be shut tonight. The last time I came, room service brought me up some breakfast and I left the trays out on the balcony. Yes two trays, I had to try the full French breakfast and the continental! I ran back in to use the en suite, and when I came back out, six or seven fat seagulls were helping themselves to my breakfast. I nearly ordered again, but couldn't think of any excuse. The fat birds made a right mess. They had doggy eyes. They saw me coming and carried on eating. When I saw how brazen they were, I stopped and looked round to see if I could break off one of the chair legs for defence. A couple of them looked at me standing in the doorway and one of them was licking the beans off the plate and another had a whole fried egg in its mouth. One of them looked at me and said, 'You best go and sit your skinny ass back down on the en suite toilet!'

I replied, 'No, I demand you give back my breakfast!' The seagull licking the beans said, 'You'd better come over here and get it then, hadn't you?' As those seagulls appeared more than capable of pecking my eyes out, I think I will close that door tonight. There's a really nice breeze but think I'm safer with the air conditioning on.

Well it's true with French food, there isn't much of it, but it looks lovely and tastes divine, washed down with three glasses of Chablis. That was just what the doctor ordered. Imagine eating like this every day... No, I don't need to imagine. That's just temptation trying to confuse what I want with what I need. Right now, I feel the need to walk off this food and probably bring back a peppermint tea to help me unwind and sleep.

I get dressed and go for a walk, as I have to take stock of my prospects. I need to find my future. The lift doors open, and it's busy. Nocturnal life in Monte Carlo is effervescent. The bar is full of inebriated people, and the foyer is busy with people talking. Outside, the supercars are really buzzing around. Walking down the steps, I want to find somewhere I can think, so I decide to walk round to the back of the hotel on to Princess Grace Avenue and down to Monte Carlo beach. There's a wine bar across the road and it's rammed full of people, falling out onto the street.

There's the beach. To my left I walk past a couple who are talking about something serious, and in the dark the diamonds on her neck and hands light up my path. She must have been hiding from the sun, as her face is white with dark makeup. She has clearly had a force five facelift, because you can see the lines of sacrifice.

Out on the soft sand, I look around and there's no one, just me. I can hear pockets of people in the background, and I can see that people in the apartments are still up, as the lights are on. The casino across the road seems calm and civilised on the outside, but I bet it's intense downstairs. The moonlight illuminates a long line across the Côte de Noir.

I listen to the waves gently ascending and descending the shoreline. About a quarter of a mile out, I can see a large yacht with a couple of small boats around it and it's lit up like a Christmas tree. My employer must be on that boat, as it's the only one out there, although the harbour's full of boats and I expect a few parties are in play. Diametrically across the sea are Tunisia and Libya. How come immigrants don't end up on this beach? They are just over the water.

A rock to my side invites me to rest upon it. I check my pockets for my iPod, but it's in my bag in the room. It's been a long time and many years I have been driving, constantly seeking a position that sticks, one that will provide me with a little stability. Times are getting worse, for all. The rich man now jumps in his Starship Enterprise, switches on his satnav and drives himself. They won't think twice about reminding you, when you've been unfortunate and made a mistake, that for all the money they pay us, they could simply drive themselves, they don't need us. First the tips stopped, and now the work is becoming more fragmented. Uncertainty rules, everywhere. Worrying times. I must continue treading the streets for food. This is me, a chauffeur, I don't have the skills for anything else, or the appetite to learn anything new.

Thinking music. Adele again, *Chasing Pavements.*

You know what? Tomorrow is another day. Let's continue as usual, and you never know. Another job, and the same ethics apply. But then, when I least expect it, who knows, who really knows, what might happen?